Deliver Us
From Evil

THE NORTON ESSAYS IN AMERICAN HISTORY

Under the general editorship of

HAROLD M. HYMAN

William P. Hobby Professor of American History
Rice University

Deliver Us
From Evil

An Interpretation of
American Prohibition

Norman H. Clark

New York W · W · NORTON & COMPANY · INC ·

FIRST EDITION

Library of Congress Cataloging in Publication Data
Clark, Norman H
  Deliver us from evil.
  (The Norton essays in American history)
  Includes index.
  1. Prohibition—United States. 2. United States—
Social conditions—1918–1932. I. Title.
HV5089.C48 1976   322.4′4′0973   76–26035
ISBN 0 393 05584 1 (Cloth Edition)
ISBN 0 393 09170 8 (Paper Edition)

1 2 3 4 5 6 7 8 9 0

Contents

Deliver Us
From Evil

1
Indulgences
and Disciplines

FOR MOST PEOPLE today it is difficult to imagine the aura of debauchery and degradation which for a century Americans associated with the old-time saloon. Even to suggest this association is to offer unseemly irreverence to a mystique now rooted deeply in national legend. And to question the legend is to challenge the veracity of honorable men who yet warm themselves with these soft and fleeting images: the free flow of fellowship, the easily creative euphoria, the refreshing restoration of confidence in human dignity which true individuals found at an altar shaped in dark mahogany, gleaming crystal, and polished brass.

Old men sometimes remember that in the saloon they were granted refuge from the tedium and humiliation which inevitably overtake the human spirit, or that in the very character of the saloon they were sheltered from the afflictions of loneliness, disorder, and ancient sorrows. Even as the images were fading, the young Jack London would write of the finely masculine satisfactions he had found in a favorite saloon "where men come together to exchange ideas, to laugh and boast and dare, to relax, to forget the dull toil of tiresome nights and days." In the images of legend, the saloon was a dignified and decent place to drink, and drinking was perfectly consistent with the dignified and decent comportment of honorable men.

Yet Jack London, like many other robust drinkers of heroic capacities, poured himself still another glass while musing over his dedicated support of Prohibition. He did not find this support either awkward or dishonest. In his book *John Bar-*

leycorn, which is in many ways keenly introspective, he concluded that alcohol was the "soul poison," and that he must help "drive the nails" into Barleycorn's coffin. This was, he insisted, not because he had become a compulsive drunk—"I am not stupid, I am not a swine"—but because the universal accessibility of alcohol in his society, the omnipresence of it, had finally brought him to the fatal taste. In time, he hoped, a nation of sober men would know of the saloon "only in the pages of history" and would come to regard saloon drinking as a "quaint old custom similar to bull-baiting and the burning of witches."

He could write this because he knew how the saloon had baited and burned Jack London. He knew also the openly sordid face of the "poison shops" which he urged his fellow drinkers to prohibit. What is difficult for the unburned to remember is that the saloon was more than an altar of fellowship. It was also a place where dirty old men spat on the floor and conspired toward the subversion of public and private moralities, where the fathers of young children floated away a week's wages that could have gone to food, clothing, and education. It was a place where addiction enslaved many a man, insulating him from the lifestyle of decency and responsibility by sinking him into a blurred phantasmagoria of whores, drug fiends, pimps, thieves, and gamblers. Such phrases are in part an exercise in literary license, but they evoke images essential to understanding a reality as it was understood by Prohibitionists. To approach that reality is to fix the mind's eye, as Jack London's contemporaries did, upon a sort of metaphorical slave ship in middle passage, upon the images of sodden drunks, of hideously fat men sucking stale cigars, of toilets fouled with vomit and urine in the haze of alcoholic narcosis, of the blind idiocy of drunken violence. But the license is not mere local color. To dismiss these images as high camp would be to dismiss the absolute seriousness of millions of men who voted as Jack London did, and it would be to ignore a crucial issue in two hundred years of American life.

It is no less difficult an imagination—in an age when

alcoholism can be a relatively sophisticated affliction of well-to-do and perfectly respectable men and women—to evoke the terror of the old-time drunkard. But there is a significant reality locked in his sorry image: Improvident to the brink of madness, he threw his wages to booze and gamblers; seduced by toothless whores, he was induced to lure small girls into back alleys; having brawled with honest citizens on the sidewalk and having insulted their honest wives and daughters, he was dragged off to jail, at a considerable expense to the taxpayer, or he was simply left to retch in the gutter. At home, finally, the deeper terror began. He scoffed at a cold hearth and empty larder; he befouled the furniture; he spewed out the dregs of his violence or lechery or remorse upon his wife and helpless children. Himself enslaved, he had power only to enslave others to a grim progression of violence, poverty, disease, crime, and ignorance.

This image—with a reality as stark as the image of Simon Legree flogging the black slave—was seared across the American conscience for generations, and it would be wrong, again, to depreciate it. For a century it ignited the energies of a thousand sermons, songs, and verses, all of them as absolutely serious as this verse written for a Sunday School lesson in 1840 by Charles Jewett to raise a striking specter of personal anguish and family distress:

> Shoeless, over frozen ground
> His wretched children go
> And away he staggers to where the sound
> Of drunken revel is ringing round
> To taste his cup of woe.

The saloon business, in this vision, was the slave business. Called the "liquor traffic" by three generations of reformers who demanded liberation, it was a commerce not only in beverages but in flesh, in corruption. It was not without reason called variously the "drunkard-making business," the "whore-making, criminal-making, madman-making business" that drew a fat and filthy profit from the predictable failures of personal morality. The saloon business could degenerate into a competitive frenzy which might infect even a town of only a few hundred citizens with dozens of dingy saloons. The competition was to lure customers into drinking as much as they could possibly hold. After the famous—and notoriously salty—"free" lunch, the thrust toward competitive advantage often lay through prostitution, gambling, and, later, narcotics. In a broader and more insidious fashion, the liquor traffic presented a protective facade for organized criminal activity, which was often organically linked to the saloon.

And when they were pressed to defend themselves, the liquor interests for decades herded blocks of semiliterate voters, tyrannized political party conventions, bought elected officials, then diligently frustrated the forces of law, order, and reform. As the traffic became national and industrial, the big breweries, which owned about 70 percent of the saloons, needed the local business licenses that only political influence could provide, and they had the kind of fluid cash incomes that corrupt politicians could not resist. At every level of municipal or state responsibility, the liquor interests polluted politics and fought viciously against efforts to restrict their adjunctive relationships to prostitution and gambling. They repeatedly financed campaigns in opposition to women's suffrage, and they did their best—they performed at their worst—in perverting democratic practice in the many state and local referenda on the question of licensing saloons.

The public wrath they brought upon themselves was vividly measured in 1912 by the Reverend Mark Matthews, then moderator of the Presbyterian General Assembly and pastor for the largest Presbyterian congregation in the world, when he called the liquor traffic "the most fiendish, corrupt and hell-soaked institution that ever crawled out of the slime of the eternal pit." It was, he claimed, "the open sore of this land." Even the Congress of the United States, Matthews accused, "has been dominated by the liquor interests for the last forty-two years, and the two great political parties are rum-soaked, saloon-cursed, and without conscience on the question of the abolition of this great enemy.''

Such images, colored even by the racy rhetoric, are an integral part of American social history, as substantial as the images of black slavery, of wage slavery, of stunted children in the coal mines and haggard women in the textile mills, of street beggars and hooded lynchers, of families robbed of dignity by a railroad or a dust storm, of breadlines, chain gangs, welfare moochers, and drug fiends, of individuals cowering in cities where there are no shelters of charity, justice, or human grace. Taken singly, these images are open to an easy and lurid inflation, yet they signal coordinates, as it were, with which we can chart an American conscience. Taken collectively, they help define the American reform tradition, for they illuminate the historic reality of disorder and abuse and injustice against which American reform energies have always been directed.

For many readers today it is difficult to suppose that during the first century of this reform activity, the relationship of the American Temperance-Prohibition Movement to the reform tradition was usually quite clear and obvious to those men and women who gave the movement its significant direction. At many times in American history, Prohibition was to many people the *most* important reform, indeed, the *most* important question in American life. It is curious, then, that since the "dry decade" of the 1920s, the essentially liberal—or liberating— motives of the movement have not been so obvious. One purpose of this study is to explain how, during the 1930s and thereafter, historians as well as reformers came to separate the movement from the motive and the tradition and to see liquor legislation as the very antithesis of reform, as a sort of extended experiment in repression that was conducted in three episodes: temperance, Prohibition, and repeal.

The three-part division is a clean and neat one, and it can yield solid esthetic satisfactions to students thoughtful enough to suppose that social movements always have an organic unity and coherence and who are especially pleased when what appear to be antilibertarian movements have an easily identifiable beginning, middle, and end. To such students, the value judgments of history are not often complex, especially as they rise from the history of Prohibition. According to the conventional wisdom, the Temperance Movement was probably a good thing inasmuch as it promoted the domestic tranquility by encouraging the common people to be sober, frugal, and industrious. Its many positive achievements, however, do not excuse the fanaticism embedded in the allegorical saga of sex-starved women who were inspired by demented creatures like Carry Nation to embrace a sinister Puritan bigotry; they do not excuse such women threatening the right of decent citizens to their cocktails and storming around the United States with hatchets, chopping up saloons.

The emotional violence of this "hatchetry" gave issue, in this view, to the Prohibition Movement, which was something quite different and quite distressing: a stern and repressive paranoia, a driving intolerance of individual differences and sacred personal freedoms. In the sudden success of the 18th Amendment, the movement was a pathological fluke or an accident—certainly not an accurate expression of the American tradition of progress and reform. Fortunately, the aberration was only temporary, as all social aberrations must be; and the healthy response of liberals in the Repeal Movement restored the social stability based on a mutual respect for civil liberties and on American common sense.

The charm of such distortions is both compelling and enduring, but they are distortions nonetheless. They are, first of all, the distortions of popular art forms, of which they are perhaps a natural extension. The conventional interpretations of Prohibition reflect the stereotyped rhythms of human behavior—the lineal continuity of social action, the symmetry of the triad—which in their simplicity must deny the complexity and often the sadness which a less predictable history would suggest. A popular view of repeal, for example, supposes that the basically liberal and generous American spirit won out over Puritan tyranny—a striking structural and thematic resemblance to the movies of the 1920s. The good and the bad have clear identities, their conflict is dramatic, the resolution

allows the righteous person to feel at ease. What is wrong is that
the view is shaped in ignorance of Puritan morality, in ignorance
of the terrors of nineteenth century drunkenness and debauchery, and in ignorance of the progress in solidly scientific
revelations—many of them discretely concealed since
repeal—about the impact of alcohol on the human organism and
on the modern American. It also ignores the many emotions
Americans brought to the Temperance-Prohibition Movement
through at least a century of anxiety. It was a century during
which they came with good reason to fear that the security of
their families, of their lifestyles—even of their assumptions of
what their "American" identity should be—was threatened by
the drunkard, the liquor traffic, the saloon.

At this point an explanation of some fundamentally re-
visionist assumptions is in order. The first is that a careful
history can show why some societies (like the United States in
the early 1800s) were drunken societies which generated
Prohibition Movements and why others (most notably, Latin
and Hebrew cultures) were not. Indeed, without this historical
key, any interpretations of Prohibition will be colorful combinations of bias and legend. A corollary here is that drunken
comportment is determined by the culture in which the drunkenness occurs. Though alcohol may have a predictable
physiological impact upon the human nervous system, the
patterns of drunken comportment are nevertheless culturally
learned and of rich variety. A drunk may be predisposed to
slobbery, violence, sentimentality, and sexual aggression (as is
often the case in the United States) or to passivity, tenderness,
or religious transcendence (as is the case, for example, among
some Andean Indians) by the cultural circumstances of his
drinking. Thus the old-time American saloon and the old-time
American drunkard reflect the cultural value system of the
old-time America. What the historian must ask is why at a
certain period many Americans became compulsive drinkers,
why they often drank to morbidity, and why, to many of the
drinkers themselves, this drinking became an urgent social
problem.

The second base line is that the word *temperance*, when it has referred to drinking, has usually meant avoiding drunkenness, a problem which in most societies and in all but the most recent centuries has not been very urgent. Although almost every society in human history has known fermented beverages, only a few of these have ever been deeply troubled by intemperance. The origins of this particular social urgency lie in the technology of distillation, which became generally popular and functional in the Western world after it was successfully applied to grain and then to molasses in the late seventeenth century. Not long thereafter, drunkenness became so common in parts of the Western world that it generated a profound cultural crisis. William Hogarth's famous engraving "Gin Lane" shows in London of the early 1700s a scene of appalling moral wreckage: gin-soaked and rag-covered adults, trembling young people, abandoned orphans, a suicide, a child falling to its death from the arms of a grotesquely drunken mother. It records an endemic drunkenness so menacing that the magistrates of Middlesex felt compelled to petition Parliament for the Gin Act of 1736, their resolution asserting that gin had already destroyed "thousands of His Majesty's subjects" and that the survivors had been rendered "unfit for useful labor, debauched in morals and drawn into all kinds of wickedness." The act they sought established license regulations so stringent as to be prohibitive. People of several Western nations, in fact, were beginning to call for the *prohibition* of the traffic in debauchery, which was the commerce in distilled liquor.

Here both the past and the definitions grow murky. Most people in the United States at one time hoped to abolish entirely the use of "intoxicating" drinks, which they then usually thought of as the products of distillation but not of fermentation. One of the first "temperance" organizations in the country drew together a group of men who met regularly to plan their opposition to "intemperance"—and drank wine while they talked and had their dinner. Many Americans of the new Republic simply did not regard beers and wines as "intoxicating" and had no thought of ever denying their use to anyone.

This was not a case of general stupidity and surely not of

ignorance about the nature of intoxication, but rather of how the word *intoxicating* was then generally used. If pressed on the matter, most people would probably have admitted that they could indeed get drunk on beer or wine, as surely the children of Moses had done, but to do so, they would have to work hard at it. They believed that in normal, sensible use, fermented drinks were not *in fact* intoxicating. This was a folk wisdom fixed as early in the American conscience as when Increase Mather had preached to the Puritans that "the wine is from God" but had warned them sternly that "the drunkard is from the Devil." Thomas Jefferson had hoped to develop in his countrymen a taste for the "temperance" beverages of wine and beer so that they might be cured of drunkenness. Thus "the wine of life" endured as a rich metaphor and "Demon Rum" became a terrifying personification.

This was carried into the twentieth century. By 1916, a majority of the states had what were without hypocrisy called Prohibition laws, and these laws had come about because the case against the saloon, the drunkard, and the liquor traffic then rested on the social statistics of crime, delinquency, poverty, prostitution, disease, and corruption that careful students of these problems had accumulated for three generations. But hardly any of these laws prohibited the personal use of wine and beer outside the saloon.

When Congress and then the states approved the 18th Amendment, they did so after a century's experience in local regulation and at a time when a majority of the people in a majority of the states wanted this truly national effort to influence national morality. Many people who rejoiced in the triumph of the 18th Amendment did not regard beer and wine as thereby prohibited. Others, to be sure, hoped that all such beverages would in fact be prohibited; and even some of them, were still dedicated and determined drinkers. Their case did not rest on foolishness or prejudice alone. Prominent psychologists and neurologists—more ominous even than Increase Mather— had declared that alcohol in any form was in fact a poison. Physicians were everywhere condemning its use, even as a therapeutic agent. Scientists, businessmen, and generals were taking the pledge of abstinence. It was then, as a matter of national health and personal well-being, more difficult to defend the personal use of alcohol than it is today to defend cigarette smoking.

To the generous mind, if the 18th Amendment could cover a law that might possibly abolish the personal use of all alcohol— and the National Prohibition Act was an attempt to do just that—such a law would surely promote the cause of human progress. In this regard the 18th Amendment was close in spirit to those amendments which gave citizenship to former slaves (and covered laws that might abolish racism), allowed a tax on incomes (and might help abolish poverty), provided for the direct election of United States Senators (and might help restore statesmanship), and extended the franchise to women (and might help toward the realization of true democracy). Whatever the ambivalence of their passage, these were expressions of a lofty idealism. They were reforms, not experiments. They were based in a broadening perspective—clarified by a sometimes desperate urgency—on the quality of American life.

It is unfortunate, then, that some historians have denied that Prohibition was in any way consistent with this perspective. Among these historians, the influence of the late Richard Hofstadter has been especially pervasive. Hofstadter called the Prohibition Movement "a ludicrous caricature of the reforming impulse," a "reaction against the Progressive temper"; and he turned the record upside down by labeling it a "pinched, parochial substitute for reform." It was, he said in a casually devastating phrase, "carried about America by the rural-evangelical virus," which infected the nation with an aversion "to the pleasures and amenities of city life, and to the well-to-do classes and cultivated men." The Hofstadter view, or that extension of it by Andrew Sinclair in *Prohibition: The Era of Excess* (1962), is prominent today in many textbooks of American history. A view of recent history expressed so vividly will not be put down easily nor easily seen for what it really is—a pinched and parochial interpretation.

If Hofstadter had been referring to the most glaringly awkward compromises of the National Prohibition Act, or to the exhortations of the several fanatics who flocked around Prohibition, then one could accept his interpretation of them as "caricature" or "reaction." But he meant the Prohibition Movement of the nineteenth and twentieth centuries, and he was 180 degrees wrong. He was perhaps turned that way because as an urbane and generous-minded liberal he was so offended by the "Americanism" of the movement, which was indeed, as we shall see, an essential part of it. Yet whatever else the "Progressive temper" might have been, we know now that among almost any representative group of social activists who worked for child labor laws, for the regulation of industrial working conditions, for tax reform, for direct legislation, for women's suffrage, or even for honest government, most worked also for state dry laws and for the prohibition of the liquor traffic and the saloon.

We know now, as Hofstadter did not, that studies of several states present a new level of regional detail which challenges the definition of Prohibition as a "rural-evangelical" contagion. There were, for example, many millions of young and well-educated city people who supported prohibition, among them most members of the Women's Christian Temperance Union (WCTU) and the Anti-Saloon League. And behind them in solid support were the deep ranks of urban business leaders, labor leaders, attorneys, physicians, teachers—both Catholic and Protestant—to mention only parts of the movement. These people, furthermore, regarded liquor as a serious national problem, not as a uniquely urban problem. Hofstadter simply did not, in this analysis, ask significant questions about the people who ignited and then guided the social movement that he so strongly felt was offensive to "cultivated men." He did not look beyond his own parish of New York (or even deeply enough into it) to see the rank-and-file activists and supporters who gave their talent and energy and money to secure the passage of the 18th Amendment.

It is even more unfortunate that on this occasion he ignored the many levels of cultural complexity which he at other times had so brilliantly woven into his interpretations. Had he given thought to the Temperance-Prohibition Movement in Canada and in modern Europe, even in Russia, he would not, with this particular oversight, have inspired other historians to propound a dreary list of Freudian prejudices about the collective sexual and racial fears which in the United States supposedly lay at the roots of rural superstition. Had he given closer thought to the continuities of the Temperance-Prohibition Movement in Europe and America from the Age of Jefferson to the Age of Wilson, he might have seen it as an expression of a new lifestyle then rising with such remarkable vigor throughout Western civilization.

This seems especially important today. Since Hofstadter wrote about Prohibition, several studies have described how this lifestyle gained strength as the Protestant faiths gained strength, how it was validated by Martin Luther and John Calvin, how it became an essential if painful phase in the reorganization of interpersonal relationships encouraged by the Reformation. It slowly crystalized in a new configuration of morality, at the center of which were values such as domesticity and conjugality, that gave vitality to the nuclear family and demanded of individuals a new sense of nuclear responsibility. In contrast to the polymorphous patterns of family life before Columbus, these fresh perceptions shaped a new consciousness evident in the emergence of words which appeared in their modern usage only two or three hundred years ago—words such as *self-confidence, character,* and *conscience.* This developing consciousness of individual, rather than communal, dignity, this turning inward for new sources of individual direction, destiny, and discipline, is what John Lukacs has called the "bourgeois interior" that was coming to dominate American and European life during the nineteenth century.

Except as we can see the Temperance-Prohibition Movement as an expression of this bourgeois interior, the movement will always appear either irrational or repressive. And it is here that we must begin. A thesis of this study is that whatever *temperance-prohibition* has meant to the American people—rural-urban, Catholic-Protestant, immigrant-nativist—the movement became a significant social and political force during the time when these people were developing a bourgeois interior. And Prohibition (in the United States and in Europe) became a social movement when public drunkenness became a social problem. The revealing slogans are those remarkably consistent phrases that echo from Lyman Beecher's famous sermons in the 1820s through Elizabeth Cady Stanton's pronouncements in the 1850s to Herbert Hoover's conviction in the 1920s: The purpose of Prohibition was to protect the values sheltered by the American nuclear family. The origins lay in the slow articulation of deep anxieties: that the new world of industrialism, opportunity, and social turmoil (new in Europe as well as in America) was a moral frontier, that it demanded new patterns of interpersonal relationships, and that these new relationships were threatened by the unrestricted use of distilled spirits. The movement gained power in American society as that society rejected the older, more open, even public style of life and began the internalization of its loyalties, energies, sentiments, and disciplines. What we are after is the intricate relationship of liquor reform to a system of values which could sometimes adapt to a new environment but could at other times force the new conditions of life to evolve in ways consistent with an older morality.

2

The Cup
of Woe

IN COLONIAL AMERICA, alcohol was vital to the myriad social and cultural expectations which colonists had brought with them from England and the Western world. It was universally honored as a medicine for almost every physiological malfunction, whether temporary or permanent, real or imagined. But even more, it was *aqua vitae*, the water of life, and "the good creature of God"—in St. Paul's and then Increase Mather's cheerful phrases—a mystical integration of blessing and necessity. And so it had been for as long as men had recorded their fears or their satisfactions. "Give strong drink unto him that is ready to perish," reads the *Book of Proverbs*, "and wine unto those that be of heavy hearts. Let him drink, and forget his poverty, and remember his misery no more."

The "wine" which could so soothe the heavy heart was most likely the "mingled" wine (probably one part wine to two of water) of *Proverbs*. The "strong drink" for those in extraordinary distress was probably the unmingled or undiluted wine of Biblical times, not the "ardent spirits" of the later Christian era. The Indo-European equivalent of this Proverbial wine was, with similar probability, *mead* or fermented honey, for etymologists can trace the Middle English *mede* all the way back to the Sanskrit *madhu*. Besides the honey, Europeans had since Neolithic times been using grain, which they probably learned to ferment as soon as they learned to eat it. The art and craft of brewing in England was certainly as old as any identifiable Anglo-Saxon culture.

Distilled spirits, however—as distinct from fermented wines or beers—are of comparatively recent origin, and it is the impact of their innovation that altered the cultural function of alcoholic beverages during the Christian era. The word *alcohol* is of Arabic derivation, and it was an Arabian alchemist known as Gerber who about 800 A.D. produced the first recorded distillates. But for hundreds of years Gerber's liquid remained an alien and esoteric substance, a curious and interesting transformation in alchemy but of no conceivable social or scientific value. Then, near the end of the thirteenth century, a French chemist named Arnauld de Villeneuve refined Gerber's methods and applied them to fermented wine, developing a technique which he said yielded the essence of the wine or the *aqua vitae*. But to Arnauld, it was even more than an essence. Because he sincerely believed that alcohol could prolong his life, he was also pleased to call it "the water of immortality."

This confidence fixed alcohol fast in the mysteries of Western medicine, where it remained for several more centuries. Europeans who used it regarded five or six drops a day as an adequate dosage. Not until the middle of the sixteenth century were there records of Europeans using the *aqua vitae* for purposes at once more casual and more profound than the purposes of medicine. This was during the French Wars of Religion and the Revolt of the Netherlands, when Europe was for years in a vast turmoil of massacre and riot, of religious refugees and political murders, of English, Spanish, Dutch, and French armies. Then apparently millions of distressed people were learning that *aqua vitae*, even more than wine, could offer a warm if momentary comfort for misery or grief or despair. Only then did Western culture begin to accommodate "ardent spirits," or the "strong drink" of modern times.

But it was not until the seventeenth century that distilled spirits came into fairly general social use, and not until the middle of that century that the English were distilling from grain and flavoring the liquor with the juniper herb called in French *genièvre*, a word which soon became the English *gin*. English distillers produced four million gallons in 1694, then eleven

million by 1733, and over twenty million by 1750, when whiskey
began to come in from Scotland. Within the relatively short
period from 1585, when British troops brought gin back from
Holland, to 1690, when the British government first encouraged
distillers to use corn, the English had assimilated distilled spirits
into the cultural patterns worn smooth by the prehistoric
beverages of brewing and fermentation.

The period can be marked by the alarming rise of public
drunkenness in English life. James I found it necessary to
punish drunkards with fines and jail sentences. Gentlemen of
the London Company became distressed by the "infamy"
which was known "to all that have heard the name of Virginia"
and caused the governor of that colony to issue a proclamation
against drunkenness in 1622. The governor of the Colony of
Georgia prohibited the importation of "ardent spirits" into his
colony in 1735—but without success. Rumrunners usually were
tried before juries of their peers; few of them ever voted for
conviction. Thereafter few people tried to prohibit rum in any
way, for the conceptual achievement embodied in the phrase
"good creature of God" would not easily be compromised.
Even in the Puritan colonies, where the governors were stern in
their determination to root out personal temptation and public
indecorum—drunkards might be publicly whipped—none condemned the beneficialness of alcohol when it was used as God
had intended. Until well after the American Revolution, to
refuse a drink in New England was to deny God, reject
fellowship, and stand as a fool before custom and medicine.

In colonial Maryland, the laws defined drunkenness as
"drinking with excess to the notable perturbation of any organ
of sense or motion," and courts might deny the suffrage to any
freeholder convicted for a third offense. In Virginia, where
public officials avoided such scrutiny, the laws implied that
intoxication was a legally recognized form of "low recreation"
and was probably a necessity for the many "low" fellows of
whom—one might conclude from reading the diaries of William
Byrd—Virginia had more than its natural allotment. The
government of the colony made an honest Anglican attempt to

regulate drunkenness at least upon the Sabbath, when the law imposed restrictions against drinking "more than necessary." The law also prohibited the sale of liquor to slaves—a restriction passed on to the state of Virginia and not widely respected until after the Nat Turner insurrection of 1831.

Thus the principal consideration here is that the colonial period in American history was precisely the period during which English-speaking peoples were integrating the use of distilled spirits into their way of life, the period during which the *aqua vitae* was actually replacing fermentations in the routines and ceremonies of daily existence. Like wine and beer—but more profoundly—it warmed the gestures of hospitality, tightened the gravity of oaths and contracts, enriched the mysteries of birth, marriage, and death. It softened the edges of sorrow and fatigue, eased the burden of poverty, glorified king or republic. And it did all this to the pace of an accelerating social phenomenon, that of private and public drunkenness.

Yet the alcoholic haze in the colonial experience, at least until about the time of the American Revolution, seems to have presented no endemic personal or social problems. Though Puritan magistrates might fix the letter "D" to the drunkard and expose him to public scorn—certainly a serious matter to the individual drunkard and his family—this was no more serious a problem to society than theft or adultery, which society could very well contain. While Hogarth was engraving his "Gin Lane" in England, the sophisticated elite of colonial society could still find humor in drunkenness. A satire published in Boston in 1724 and reprinted in 1750 was called *The Indictment and Tryal of Sir Richard Rum, a person of noble birth and extraction, well known to both rich and poor throughout all America.*

This lack of any urgent and general social concern suggests that among the truly benign luxuries of the agrarian, preindustrial world, at least beyond New England, were alcohol, and an established church, and a traditional technology. A liturgical religion relieved the individual of at least a few of the more burdensome cosmic uncertainties and allowed him to drink until

he could "forget his poverty and remember his misery no
more." The traditional, preindustrial arts of medicine did not
doom a man to worry about the color of his liver, and the
techniques of work and play specified no more than a very few
chores or pleasures which required an icy sobriety. In a world
not yet oppressed by the god of objectivity and mechanical
precision—when a man could spell his own name differently
every day of the week if he wanted to, and when no one
measured the length of a harness or the trueness of a furrow in
millimeters—a soft alcoholic cloud to filter the harsher reflec-
tions of reality was both a prudent and a providential comfort.

For the American family even in the early 1800s, the morning
routine might well begin with a generous dram for young and old
alike; it prepared one to meet the inexorable demands of a raw
world, and it warded off attacks of the "bad humors."
Thereafter the rhythm of the day could be marked in drams—
"grog time" at about 11:00, then beer or wine with the noon
dinner, then grog time again about 4:00—until early evening
when families repaired to the tavern, thirsty for social contacts,
for the opportunity to share their day and to reassure themselves of their essential humanity. More effectively than the
beer or wine, the *aqua vitae* was a balm for their emotional and
physical tension, the barrier between soul and reality which was
ever proof of God's word and of His enduring mercy.

In the early 1800s, the United States was an alcohol-soaked
culture, and it became markedly more so because of changes
that occurred during the times of George Washington and
Thomas Jefferson. When New England distillers had refined a
technology which would allow them to produce much more rum
than the slave trade or even England could absorb, the domestic
consumption of rum began to rise sharply. This, however, was
but the beginning of excessive production and consumption. In
London, Dr. Samuel Johnson first tasted whiskey in 1773,
which was about the time when Scotch and Irish farmers of
western Pennsylvania were finding it more profitable to distill
their grain than to transport it by the bushel. The annual per
capita consumption of distilled spirits from commercial distil-

leries in the United States in 1790—when almost every town and village had one or more stills—seems to have been about 2.5 gallons.

The statistics of American consumption from this period, however, are not the kind in which historians can take much comfort. We can get a rough idea of how many commercial distilleries there were and how much they produced. But this is indeed a rough guess, and it will not include the thousands of home cookers that were dripping out thousands of gallons each month. United States government statistics are not very helpful until after 1862, when liquor was taxed by the barrel to bring in revenue during the Civil War. For the earlier period, the estimates of temperance societies themselves are the most reliable indicators. They were loaded with prejudice, perhaps, but probably not badly, for most temperance leaders were responsible men whose success depended upon the integrity of their information. When Herbert Asbury wrote *The Great Illusion: An Informal History of Prohibition* (1950) and made one of the first serious efforts to work with these estimates, he found that his best sources were the *Permanent Temperance Documents of the American Temperance Society*, published in 1835. They are still the best sources. For the year 1810, for example, they indicate that 25,499,382 gallons of ardent spirits were produced by Americans in commercial distilleries. The country exported 133,823 gallons, but it imported 8,000,000 gallons more, bringing domestic consumption to 33,365,559 gallons. The authority for this estimate was Samuel Dexter, a former Secretary of the United States Treasury, who himself found the figures almost incredible when he rounded them out to a per capita consumption of 4.7 gallons.

Dexter's figures, however, actually conceal more than they reveal. In the first place, we should add about 8,000,000 gallons—a rough (and probably low) guess at the capacity of home stills; the total is then about 41,365,559 gallons. The equivalent of this in terms of absolute alcohol—which is the more modern and precise calculation for comparative purposes and is to be distinguished from the gallons of "distilled" or "ardent spirits" used in the nineteenth century—is about 45 percent of the ardent figure, or, for 1810, about 18,614,502 gallons. But this is not yet all, for most historical statistics suggest that Americans were at the time also drinking quantities of beer and wine, which, in terms of absolute alcohol, added about 10 percent to their annual consumption. Thus, with this addition, we have 20,475,952 gallons of absolute alcohol consumed in the United States in 1810.

The next question, and the one that Samuel Dexter did not ask, is: Who got it? A fair guess is that blacks did not get very much at all and that people under fifteen years of age did not, relatively speaking, drink very heavily. In 1810 there were in the United States about three million male and female whites over fifteen years of age, and if these people drank the approximately 21 million gallons of absolute alcohol, their per capita consumption was about 7 gallons. The comparable figure for 1850, after a generation of temperance agitation, is 2.10, and in the difference we see the impact of the early Temperance Movement. (The figure for 1970 is 2.61.) And things would get worse before they got better. The Temperance Society in Albany, New York, after a careful accounting, estimated that the 20,000 residents of that city consumed 200,000 gallons of ardent spirits in 1829—a per capita consumption of 10 gallons. If we make the conversion described above (figure about half the population in 1830— according to census figures—was over fifteen years of age, convert 200,000 gallons of distilled spirits into 90,000 gallons of absolute alcohol, add 10 percent for wine and beer, and ignore home pots), we have about 10,000 people drinking 99,000 gallons of absolute alcohol, an annual per capita consumption of absolute alcohol—not "ardent spirits"—of about 10 gallons. This is a figure which would probably have stunned Samuel Dexter's imagination.

These statistics are credible for another very good reason; they demonstrate a phenomenon which was not uniquely American. They are roughly similar to those we have for the same period in Sweden, where drunkenness was endemic and presented a grave threat to the very survival of the nation. Even while there were widespread food shortages and malnutrition throughout the country in the 1820s, a third of the Swedish potato crop was distilled into *aqua vitae*. The annual overall per capita consumption there in 1830 reached about 50 liters, or about 13 gallons, of ardent spirits—higher even than consumption in Albany.

Given this truly staggering amount of hard drinking, we look naturally for a cause. But the statistics for the United States and for Sweden do not correlate with any national crisis or social malaise which the two countries might have shared or which might be regarded as causes for national drunkenness. In contrast to the apparently healthy, secure, expanding, affluent, and optimisitic American society, Sweden after the Napoleonic wars was defeated, poor, sullen, and cynical. In an hour of national desperation, Peter Wieselgren, then a professor at the University of Lund, began a national crusade for sobriety. Wieselgren organized temperance societies in the 1830s, spoke throughout the country in their favor during the 1840s, and finally in 1855 successfully placed before the king a law to restrict the sale of liquor. As we shall see, his work as a reformer during this period closely paralleled the career of the American author of the Maine Liquor Law, Neal Dow. Thus in two quite different countries, drunkenness and reform ran together during the first half of the nineteenth century, though the statistics of alcohol consumption correlate only with the increasing availability of distilled liquor in both areas. When we suppose again that all women and young people did not usually get their annual per capita share, the figures of 10 to 13 gallons are by any measure the statistics of drunken societies.

Beyond the statistics, furthermore, we have a wealth of literary evidence that points to the same conclusion. A history of South Carolina, published in 1808, noted that "Drunkenness may be called an endemic vice of Carolina." President James Madison, whose problems are not usually associated with liquor, commonly drank a pint of whiskey a day, most of it before breakfast. In his last years he joined with other living Presidents in urging young men to abstain, as he had not, so that they might promote "their own benefit" and "the good of the country and the world." In 1812, the Presbyterian General Assembly appointed a committee "to devise ways of restricting the use of intoxicants." The Reverend Lyman Beecher, a clergyman in Connecticut whose sensitivities and powerful exhortations would soon inspire the nation's most significant revival of moral energies, was then brooding at length about Americans, their lack of social discipline, and their liquor, and concluding that drunkenness was a national curse. Abraham Lincoln, in his temperance address of 1842, recalled his own childhood in a society locked in an alcoholic mystique:

> . . . we found intoxicating liquor . . . used by everybody, repudiated by nobody. It commonly entered into the first drought of the infant, and the last drought of the dying man. From the sideboard of the parson, down to the ragged pocket of the homeless loafer, it was constantly found . . . To have a rolling or raising, a husking or hoe-down, anywhere without it, was *positively insufferable*.

Though one cannot quantify this kind of evidence—and should not want to—it lies heavily upon the records of nineteenth century American culture. When the historian Henry Adams looked across this period, he noted sadly that "almost every American family, however respectable, could show some victim of intemperance." Family disaster came as drunken accident, as alcoholic poverty, as crime, as mental distress. The booze-brained relative in the attic was the grim price of universal excess. Lincoln said that in his youth, liquor—which he personified as devastator—came forth in society "like the Egyptian angel of death, commissioned to slay if not the first, the fairest born of every family."

That insight had not come easily or quickly into public consciousness. In 1774, a Quaker intellectual named Anthony Benezet published an antidrink pamphlet he called "The Mighty Destroyer Displayed," in which he tried to convince his readers that alcohol was the cause of most afflictions of the body, the soul, and human society. The publication had no notable public impact, except that it impressed Dr. Benjamin Rush, who was later the surgeon-general of the Revolutionary Army and the first American of any high medical prestige to raise serious questions about the basic medical assumptions of his generation. Inspired by Benezet to gather some of the first really scientific medical data, he began to examine the relationship of drinking milk and water to "health, wealth, serenity of mind, reputation, long life, and happiness." He began to correlate the drinking of liquor to "vices, diseases . . . suicide, death, the gallows." Dr. Rush was so disturbed by his findings that after the Revolution he called for ministers of every church to help him in an effort "to save our fellowmen from being destroyed by the great destroyer of their lives and souls."

This first of the scientific warnings drew only slightly more public attention than had Benezet's tract. This may have been in part because Dr. Rush's research into what was or was not intoxicating was woefully incomplete. He did not understand, for example, that the terrors of whiskey or rum could be evoked as forcefully by plain wine if the drinker were adequately motivated. Nor did he understand very much about other narcotics or the problems of compulsive behavior; his prescription for alcoholics was that they should abstain from ardent spirits and instead take in regular dosages his compound of wine and opium.

Nevertheless, Dr. Rush's radical view of the physiological effects of distilled spirits deeply influenced Thomas Jefferson, who had already found in France, where the use of wine was then universal but not compulsive, a quality of moderation or temperance which was far more to his liking than the brash, omnipresent drunkenness of his native Virginia. Like Rush, Jefferson came to see alcohol not as a blessing but as a curse, and to regard liquor as the national disease of Americans. For the rest of his life he cultivated a keen scientific interest in vines and yeasts that might thrive in the New World, hoping that he might encourage the use of temperate wines and beers in the place of gins, whiskeys, and rums.

James Madison, John Quincy Adams, and Andrew Jackson all signed the testimonial which began with the statement that "ardent spirit as a drink, is not only needless, but harmful; and the entire disuse of it would tend to promote the health, the virtue and happiness of the community . . ." This sentiment had spread widely among most educated people before Lincoln's temperance address in 1842, in which he claimed that the social and personal disasters brought by liquor came not "from the *abuse* of a *very good* thing" but from "the *use* of a *bad thing*." The general acceptance of this truth, Lincoln believed, marked a great moment in American consciousness. He saw a beautifully historical coherence: the political freedom won in the 1780s, the moral freedom to be won, he hoped, in the reform crusades of the 1840s. This was progress, he said, toward a time when "there shall be neither a slave nor a drunkard on the earth."

3

Moral Stewardship and Social Disorder

LINCOLN'S AUDIENCES in the 1840s could anticipate in their public speakers an enthusiastic personal testimony of belief in progress toward individual and social perfection. On the Illinois frontier, seated in a new building in a new country, they expected a pledge of allegiance to America's freedom to reform itself of all the deep-rooted institutional evils which their forefathers had imported from the Old World. To this first generation of native-born Americans, God's hand was then obvious; after years of conflict, of revolutionary war, of constitutional crisis, of conspiracy and intrigue, they, the chosen, were at last free to work God's purpose, which was their individual perfection, and in which, through the exhilarating sweep of American energy and innocence, the world itself might find salvation.

Surely the most abundant of their prospects were the apparently endless opportunities of the western frontier than open to those whom God in His wisdom had chosen to lead the world toward freedom. To most Americans of the first generation, *freedom*, in its larger meanings, was measured in economic and social and spiritual opportunities: the freedom to move, to respond to new wealth and new ideas, the opportunity to acquire land and status and also to advance and to create, to test and to enrich human life. Fulfillment would begin in the rejection of Old World geographic, political, religious, and economic restrictions and in the circumvention of Old World corruptions. The new American would not be bound by the place or the circumstances of his father's birth, by the dogmas of his father's king or priest, or by their presumptuous efforts to restrict a freeman's response to the natural and holy laws of enterprise and ambition. Fulfillment was in God's progressive liberations of the human spirit: to free every man from poverty, to free illiterates from ignorance, to free women from oppression, to free both blacks and whites from slavery, to free families from drunkenness.

Ralph Waldo Emerson had described these energies when he called for "the sluggard intellect of this continent" to rise up and "fill the postponed expectation of the world." And he had meant that Americans could and should do so immediately. To suppose that his contemporaries could perform so magnificent a service required a conceit and a faith which transcended mere nationalism—a conceit rejecting belief in the depravity of man (a doctrine, it must be noted, which allowed a man at least a few indulgences), a faith in each individual's essential strength, purity, and temporal perfectibility. In Emerson's lyric optimism, the "expectation of the world" was freedom from want and drudgery, from traditions of oppression and tyranny, from institutions of greed and exploitation—from all threats to man's divinity. Nor would the expectation be long postponed, for he saw people everywhere seeking the truth in individual reform and self-reliance. Men *could* and *should* and *would* divest themselves of ancient evils. "What is man born for," he asked, "but to be a Reformer, a Re-maker . . . a restorer of truth and good . . . ?" In his "Lecture on The Times" he rejoiced that "the Temperance-question" was dominating "the conversation of ten thousand circles" and was under discussion "at every public and at every private table," a development which expressed the quickening "conscience of the time." From the millennial perspective—which Emerson gave great dignity— the temperance question was an inevitable expression of national character then rising to the moral opportunities of a new and progressive age.

This millennial view, however, is at best a narrow and oblique perspective on American history. It never faces squarely the more persistent and tumultuous realities of American life and character before or since Lincoln and Emerson. The angle of vision obscures dimensions of those darker streams in American social life which threatened at any time to rush unchecked toward retrogression and disorder. It ignores the possibility that the bonds of parish, priest, king, and organic community may have been the fabric of common trust, common decency, and shared existence. The traditions of the Old World, as Emerson saw them, may indeed have been disposable; self-reliance may have been possible; and individual freedom may have been very real. But progress was not thereby inevitable. The disposable traditions may have been those which served to protect other societies from licentious indulgences—the restraints implicit in a sense of organic relationships, interdependencies, expectations. The self-reliance may have easily become a brutal arrogance. The freedom may have been a freedom to murder Indians, enslave Negroes, rape Mexicans, and then glorify the passions of self-destruction and Civil War. While Emerson contemplated the collective soul of the universe, the "conscience of the time" had every reason for agitation. In a society of accelerating drunkenness, where were the shelters against family disruption or exploitation, against interpersonal violence, or social disorder? In a society of conventional brutality and racism, where were the restraints upon greed or slavery? What were the barriers to civil war?

The millenial view, furthermore, ignores inescapable historical realities which are essential to any working conceptualization of American problems. It ignores, for example, the reality that both drunkenness and slavery were *solutions* before they were *problems*. It ignores, moreover, the reality that social *reform* is not so much a progressive realization of divine destiny as it is a desperately conservative effort to *regain* a lost security or stability, to protect a threatened opportunity, to guard a cherished freedom.

More to the point, the romantic idealism of Emerson made it almost impossible to see the now classic configurations of social turmoil, alcohol, and personal anxiety. It could not approach the question of why individuals, or large numbers of them, would at any time become compulsive drinkers. We know today from recent research and insights that one essential condition for this morbidity is that the use of alcohol must be integrated into the ceremonies, the rituals, the daily expectations, the very fabric of cultural values of the society in which the drinking occurs. This is surely the case in Western civilization. Another essential is that alcohol be readily available in quantity throughout the society; and this, after the technology of distillation was no longer a secret, was surely the case in Europe and in America. Still another condition is that regular and excessive drinking, even to drunkenness, be culturally acceptable—as it is not, for example, in some non-Christian cultures in which the public response to drunkenness makes it virtually taboo. In the mainstream values of the United States and northern Europe, drunkenness, if not universally acceptable behavior, has been at least a matter of often poignant ambivalence. To many Americans getting drunk might be pitiful or humorous or contemptible behavior, but to many others it is an almost ceremonial validation of masculinity or individuality or social class identity.

Given these conditions, there is yet another requisite for morbidity, and this is a pervasive and relentless sense of personal anxiety. The sources of this anxiety are clear enough in Europe, for war and social disorder have usually been primary causes of personal anguish. But what then of the United States in the early 1800s? To explain why the United States produced so many drunkards—and a Temperance-Prohibition Movement of great impact for at least a hundred years—is to explain why and how, from its earliest republican beginnings, there has been something terribly wrong in American life.

In the colonial past, what was wrong was usually not so wrong as to be intolerable. The drift toward disorder was implicit in a tentative community facing the infinity of an unknown frontier. But this drift was checked by the stability of custom and convention, by the structure of Anglican and Anglo traditions, by the irreducible minimum of expectations in interpersonal relationships shaped by these traditions and upon which, in the colonial world, individuals and families could depend. However uncomfortable the rigidities of the Colonial-Yankee-Federalist nexus may have been, they did not provoke social hysterias over drunkenness, or adultery, or murder, or the mistreatment of women and children, or slavery. In these regards, the real problems—the problems for which these disorders are *solutions*—had been successfully defined and contained.

But in the nineteenth century these securities were perilously undermined by the fall of the established church, by the rush for cheap land, by the complex impact of the cotton gin and the textile factories, the canals, and the commerce. They were shaken by the windfalls of economic and geographic mobility and of unlimited moral freedom. The migrations of thousands of people westward after 1814—and the continual surges of migration and immigration, of settlement and dispersion—began a period of social turmoil and sustained disorder which Rowland Berthoff, in *An Unsettled People: Social Order and Disorder in American History* (1971), has called "unparalleled in the world." The history of American society since the opening of the frontier has been a reaction to disorder and near chaos. In the years after 1814, Americans knew few of the certainties which are secured by an established religion, a sense of organic community, and a strong government. They faced a world in which children worked in mines and women in factories, in which, shortly, those who remembered the established order would hear the cadences of foreign tongues and see the symbols of an alien religion. These people would learn the new fears and hatreds of class and ethnic conflicts. They would learn that interpersonal relationships were no longer predictable. They would know a society in which children grew up to leave home and disappear forever.

As Douglas T. Miller shows in *The Birth of Modern America, 1820-1850* (1970), the children themselves expressed in their popular songs a sort of guilt-ridden but sentimental reverence for the old Yankee order: "Home Sweet Home" (1823), "The Old Oaken Bucket" (1825), and "Old Folks at Home" (1853). Miller also explains how the art, poems, novels, and histories of

the "American School of Catastrophe" in the 1830s—with its
fascination with cataclysm and destruction—could also be a
sensitive response to American anxieties. It was a society, says
Berthoff, in which "the functional design of reciprocal rights
and duties, the nuts and bolts which put together a stable social
order" had been wiped out, a society in which the everyday
expectations of sex and race, church and family, work and
money had rapidly come undone.

In a stable society such as Emerson's grandfather had known,
there would have been a sense of traditions, a sense of religious
and ethnic identities and loyalties, a sense of community which
would define the scope of interdependencies, expectations, and
individual comportments. It may be that such societies in-
stitutionalize the use of alcohol just as they do the most vital
interpersonal relationships, including sexual comportment, in
such a way that the society itself is never internally threatened.
They may then be able, without crisis, to absorb the stress and
strain which would accompany such cultural innovations as the
introduction of distilled spirits and even of quantitative changes
in the incidence of drunkenness. On the other hand, in an
unstable society—such as the one Emerson himself knew in the
1820s—even the uncommon drunkard, unless predisposed by
whatever cultural background lingered within him to avoid
irresponsibility and violence, would have been a potential social
catastrophe. He was a mobile disaster looking for victims. And
if drunkenness were quite common, in the absence of institutional protections, some social movement toward promoting
temperance would become an absolutely necessary social
function.

Thus the temperance "reform" was a deep and often frenzied
social adjustment. It erupted from the necessity for security and
rationality in a society that had been shaken by perhaps the most
grievous gaps between generations.

From this perspective a reform is a profoundly conservative
change. It is not to reject the past because the past may seem
crusty, inhibiting, or irrelevant. It is the attempt of a

dominant—and probably newly dominant—social class to force a disturbingly pliable and volatile society to conform to a fleeting image of order, purity, or stability. It is to *re-form*, to *form again*, in the most literal sense.

No one sensed this more keenly than Lyman Beecher, who by all accounts was the most vigorous and persuasive young preacher in the young Republic. Born in 1775, Beecher reached his maturity with the conviction that his generation had fallen away from truth and discipline and morality during and immediately after the American Revolution and would have to be re-formed again in the spirit of the old orthodoxies. When he entered Princeton in 1792, he could number only two professed Christians among an "enlightened" and cynical student body. He was disturbed by the casual and relaxed sexual discipline which, some statistics suggest, allowed as many as 50 percent of the new brides to approach the altar already pregnant. He worried that women were threatening family stabilities by coming too much into business, commerce, and public affairs, and that parental authority had diminished as the frontier became more attractive. Like many other young preachers who felt the same anxieties, he feared that Americans were moving west in greater numbers than they were joining the Church. It seemed to Beecher that the West, the immigration of non-Protestant foreigners, and the softness of Jeffersonian philosophy were sources of disorder which threatened to collapse the old securities and to disestablish the churches entirely.

And he was right. In 1826, at the age of fifty, Beecher came to the Hanover Street Church in Boston to commit his great energy to the reformation. He began a fearsome attack upon modern morality, especially upon liquor and intemperance, which he called "the sin of our land." Praised and emulated by other ministers in every state, he led this first generation of Americans in a revival of orthodoxies so successful that it had, within fifteen or twenty years, shaped an evangelical and Protestant nation. Thus Lincoln's temperance audience in 1842 could well remember the stable world of Puritan times—Beecher and his fellow preachers never let them forget it. And to this audience the word *reform*—be it in reference to temperance or women's rights or the restriction of slavery—meant the revival of order and security and social discipline in American life.

Following the exhortations of Lyman Beecher, New England Christians organized the American Society for the Promotion of Temperance in 1826. It was during this decade that temperance work was aimed clearly at individual reform and became a clearly evangelical movement, for the pledge-signing, the songs, the verse, the temperance revival meetings spread across the country in a remarkably spontaneous fashion. When, for example, the Reverend Abner Clopton began to organize temperance work in Virginia in 1826, he was not aware of Lyman Beecher or of the American Temperance Society. Though this group was sometimes disrupted by doctrinal disputes among those who believed in total abstinence and those who believed in abstinence from "ardent spirits" only, it increased its membership by 500 percent between 1831 and 1834 to a total of over one million persons, and it counted local organizations in every state and territory.

Thus probably no American anywhere could avoid either the movement or the message. In 1840, a group of six drunks sitting in a tavern in Baltimore caused one of their fellows to present himself before a temperance lecturer—this may have been a great joke—after which he was to explain to the drinkers what all the public excitement was about. He did so in a report so sobering that to a man the group signed "teetotal" pledges in which they vowed to "safeguard against a pernicious practice which is injurious to our health, standing, and families." Each agreed to bring a friend to the next meeting. Out of their enthusiasm came the Washington Temperance Society, usually called the Washingtonian Movement—which they named after the great man's character, not his drinking habits. The movement spread as a subrevival to New York City, then to every major city in every state. While they urged others to renounce the use of all alcoholic drinks, the Washingtonians spoke candidly, drawing freely from their own unhappy case histories, their own degradations. By 1847, they claimed over 600,000 members, all of them formerly "intemperate" drinkers or reformed drunkards. An interesting and distinctive feature of their work was their formal indifference to religion; many of the men were atheists, simply not at all concerned with the churchly implications of personal or social reform.

It is very significant that Washingtonians felt impelled to stress their obligations to their families, and that they did so illuminates another unhappy dimension of American social disorder. In this regard we can raise still another corollary: In a corporate, stable community, with its intricate interdependencies and subtle disciplines, society would have institutionalized a high degree of physical and emotional security for women and children long before the emergence of what we call the Victorian family. We know that before the seventeenth century—because of the tenacity and legitimacy of family loyalties and because of a pervasive linkage of family to parish to village to nation— European societies could accommodate a variety of family patterns. Children could be, and often were, raised and trained outside the home by the extended family or the corporate community with little or no anxiety to their natural parents or to society. An absence of these institutionalized physical and emotional securities, however, would be an agonizing anxiety. It was all the more so to the American family as it moved toward the frontier and away from communal protections. A signal fact of social history is that American families, in accepting geographic freedom, were accepting the loneliness as well as the terror of nuclear isolation. Boredom, loneliness, and feelings of impotence are, we know now, common qualities in the lifestyles of people who tend to use alcohol or other narcotics compulsively. For many American families the realities of isolation in a wilderness were often these: The loneliness eroded emotional securities; the freedom encouraged the strong to be exploitative, brutal, and sadistic; the economic opportunity cut cruelly into the spiritual core of family loyalty.

An equally important consideration in this regard is the cultural inducement to drunkenness which seems to rise naturally in an individualistic society. A recent cross-cultural study

of drinking shows that drinking to drunkenness tends to become
a social morbidity in societies where individuals suffer a high
degree of conflict about their own qualities of dependence and
independence. To put it more specifically, morbid drunkenness
is common in those societies which do not tolerate very much
dependence in adult males—where every man is expected to
make it on his own, to resist complaining if he doesn't make it, to
be achievement-oriented and splendidly self-reliant. (This
would be a nearly perfect Emersonian society.) In contrast, in
societies where males can acknowledge their dependencies,
complain of their inadequacies, or develop a sense of community rather than a drive to compete, drunkenness is seldom a
solution or a problem. In early nineteenth century America, the
reformation urged by Beecher and his brethren provoked a
critical transformation in social sex role differentiation. We are
in this historical matter much aware of the suffering of women
and largely indifferent to the anguish of men: Induced to project
images of extraordinary strength, courage, and self-reliance (a
new "masculinity"), they soon were bending to the new
convention which made the measure of a man's character a
measure of gender. Thus the new social values of a nation of
sturdy freeholders were tension-producing values which generated individual anxieties. And of all the things which alcohol
does for individuals, what it does best is to relieve tension and
anxiety.

  A society of potentially drunken male adults and nuclear
families—this situation of potential terror must have accelerated the processes by which families of all Western societies
were creating "the bourgeois interior," the internalization of
life and of the vital human conditions. The bourgeois interior of
privacy, of personal dignity, of highly sensitive conscience, and
of strict parental responsibility for children—these values were
solidifying as middle-class, Western values. Especially in the
United States, they were becoming the absolutely necessary
shields against social turmoil and individual freedom. Thus from
Jacksonian America the mind's eye can fix in tableau the
symbolic essence: the farm family at Sunday dinner and prayer,

the father presiding over matters of collective decorum and individual obligation; the family circle at Christmas Eve, the father spreading Christian virtue and equalizing family abundance; the family kitchen or sewing room, the mother finding her domestic fulfillment; the church groups in session, the mother doing her part to protect the purity of the home; the bedside of the sick child, the mother applying her particularly feminine virtues; the family fireplace, the boy lying on a bearskin rug reading by the light of burning logs, the younger children secure against fear and cold and ignorance.

Yet this internalization and these new relationships could too soon be perverted. Laced with alcohol, they could—precisely because of their vital importance and inevitable rigidity—extend intolerable threats of psychological and physical violence. Lincoln's temperance speech carried just such a message when he pictured the drunkard with his "naked and starving children" and his wife "long weighed down with woe, weeping, and a broken heart." This echoes one of Lyman Beecher's early temperance sermons, in which the preacher contrasted the sober village of "temperate, thrifty farmers and mechanics" with his vision of alcoholic wreckage in the "village of riot and drunkenness, made up of tipplers, widows and degraded children, of old houses, broken windows and dilapidated fences."

These phrases so impressed the young Neal Dow that many years later, as a very old man, he quoted them in his reminiscences. When he first heard them, Dow had already thought long about the "wretchedness and squalor" of a drunken neighbor's home in Portland, Maine. There, in a population of 12,000 in 1840, he numbered 500 "common drunkards." He saw also at least 1,000 "addicts to excessive use"—men who, when under the influence, Dow noted somberly, would lose more money, wreck more ships, derail more locomotives, explode more boilers, and cause more physical disasters and moral delinquencies than the sodden drunks who could not stagger beyond their taverns. Dow thought that the state of Maine was particularly depraved in this regard because of its many rum distilleries and because of its visible working class: the lumbermen, fishermen, and seamen—many of them unattached to families—who led lives of idleness and loneliness which left them uncommonly exposed to the temptations of drunken indulgence.

Dow was born in 1804, and he came into the Temperance Movement as an advocate of what he called "moderation," which meant that he was opposed only to drunkenness. But at the age of twenty-five, after considerable thought, he decided to become what he called a "teetotaler" and to instruct his friends in the doctrine of total abstinence. He was soon opposed to the use of *any* intoxicating drinks, and as a wealthy young businessman he went about his daily affairs urging everyone to react as he consistently reacted to the havoc spread in Portland by the many grogshops. "I saw health impaired," he wrote, "capacity undermined, employment lost. I saw wives and children suffering. . . . I found helpless victims of a controlling appetite that was dragging them down to ruin." In these experiences he found what was to be the central theme of his life for over half a century, "that the traffic in intoxicating drinks tends more to degradation and impoverishment of the people than all other causes of evil combined."

The most important question to ask about Neal Dow is why—after having determined for perfectly good reasons to leave booze alone and to encourage others to do so—he later wrote laws which *required* others to do so. We should next ask why apparently most of his fellow citizens at least for a while wanted him to write these laws. For Dow became the driving force of Prohibition, bringing the first real Prohibition law in American history to his state of Maine in 1851. As the personification of a social movement, he would lead people throughout the English-speaking world to demand laws modeled after his achievement in Maine. The Prohibition Movement before the Civil War was "Maine Law" Prohibition. Dow was called both the "Napoleon" and the "prophet" of Prohibition because he made his crusade a principal issue in

American political and religious life.

One can ask first of his background. Dow's family had been in Maine for generations. A great-great grandfather with the wonderfully Yankee-Puritan name of Hate-Evil Hall had done his best to populate western Maine; when Hall died in 1797 at the age of ninety, he had 12 children, most of whom also had 12 children, so that he left a total of 495 descendants. Dow remembered the old man with his large house, his deep-rooted sense of time and place in New England, and his New England sternness. By temperament, Hate-Evil Hall, so much closer to the Puritans than Neal Dow, should have been the prohibitor, but he was not. In his day, the regulation of drinking was structured and traditional and never regarded as a matter of urgent social concern.

Dow's father was a devout Quaker and a devout moralist. From the strong traditions of the Yankee-Federalist-Quaker community, Dow in his early youth learned the principles and the attitudes of moral stewardship which flowed so strong and so deep among the progeny of Hate-Evil Hall and among all the leading families—from the Mathers to the Adamses—in New England. A man should set an example; he should protect public morality; he should know that indifference to the welfare of others, even if they are his inferiors, is a serious sin. It was in this sense of trusteeship, of communal responsibility, that Neal Dow was first impressed by the conditions of the town's poor during the depression years that followed the War of 1812. He was equally disturbed by the presence of lower-class elements—the drifters, the seamen, the unemployable or the unemployed. And he was appalled by what seemed to him an obvious relationship between drunkenness, poverty, depravity, and family disintegration.

This relationship became an obsession. After the War of 1812, the social order in New England, which for almost two centuries had been stabilized by the established churches and the mercantile aristocracy, was fast coming apart at its seams. The disruptions of trade had ruined the merchant elite; the politics of war had shattered the Federalist dominance; the new freedom

had eroded church-state relationships. Out of the collapse of the
old order, a new business elite, of which Dow himself was a
leader (he had a tannery, lumber interests, and real estate), was
asserting itself; and it was this new leadership which was so
much impressed by Lyman Beecher's cry for a reformation, for
a return to the moral certainties of the Puritan past.

In the years of reformation, Dow himself became a Con-
gregationalist. In the 1820s he joined the American Temperance
Society. In the 1830s he was a spokesman for those employers
who were growing bold enough to question the social utility of
the traditional "grog-time" tolled by the town bell at 11:00 and
again at 4:00, when workmen everywhere dropped their tools to
relax over a ration of rum, which, also by tradition, the
employer was expected to provide. Neal Dow and his friends
resented the cost of the rum as well as the consequent
inefficiency of the labor. And Dow, who was perhaps more
concerned than most with the plight of drunken laborers who
could not support their families, was soon widely known as an
outspoken and sometimes merciless crusader. As a representative of the family culture, he was never troubled by the
questions of individual liberty which his arguments seem to
present. "No one," he could say in utter self-righteousnes,
"has rights which are inconsistent with the general welfare."
And in a town where almost everyone knew everyone else, he
never hesitated to make his arguments direct and personal. The
former Quaker, raised in abhorrence to violence and "carnal
weapons," was soon taking boxing lessons and carrying pistols
in his coat pocket.

Among the events which carried him into political life, as
Dow later told it, was an occurrence one day in the early 1840s
when he found a job for an impoverished relative who was also
an ex-drunkard. He then forthwith marched into the nearby
grogshop and explained the situation to the owner, requesting
that, in the interests of his relative's wife and children, the
reformed man not be served if he should ever weaken and come
into the shop for rum. According to Dow, the barkeep curtly
refused, saying that he was licensed by the city to serve rum to

anyone he pleased and would do so for the welfare of his own wife and children. Dow determined then to fix that—''With God's help, I will change all this''—and began at that moment his long work to achieve a law which would prohibit both the manufacture and the sale of intoxicating drinks in the state of Maine.

By then Neal Dow had also become an abolitionist, which is but one indication of his moral fervor. As he campaigned across his state and later across the country in the Temperance Movement, he found a natural affinity among those who opposed liquor, slavery, and—not unexpectedly—the immigration of Roman Catholics. The recent Irish immigrants (who were coming, particularly to New England, at the rate of about 30,000 a year in the 1830s), seemed to Dow to present real obstacles to any antidrink movement. They seemed to him excessively given to lower-class indulgences and disgracefully lax in family disciplines. The more his movement grew, and the more immigration increased, the more hostile he became to foreigners. In the disruption of American political life to which he himself was contributing, Dow found loose coalitions of ''Maine Law'' Whigs, Free Soilers, ''Anti-Nebraska'' Democrats, and the nativist groups then called the Know-Nothings—most of the people who were moving toward the Republican Party in the 1850s—usually sympathetic to Prohibition.

The passage of his Maine Law in 1851 gave confidence to temperance workers everywhere. Dow spoke widely in Canada and in England, where the United Kingdom Alliance was formed to bring the ''Maine Law'' prohibitions to Great Britain. As he came more and more to be the ''prophet'' and the ''Napoleon'' of Prohibition, Dow became also more and more the fanatic. He spoke recklessly of those who ''gratify their body-destroying and soul-damning thirst'' by enslaving themselves to ''that deadly desire.'' He saw no legitimate use at all for any alcoholic drink, and he soon assumed that anyone who did was either twisted in greed or lost to personal depravity. Yet in his own eyes, he was the modestly aristocratic liberator—

liberating families from the tyranny of drink.

The phrases of militancy which to Neal Dow came so easily—"crusade," "temperance soldiers," "battle," "fight," "victory"—were no casual figures of speech. During the Civil War, he carried through with the logic of his image as a liberator and volunteered for service. Though he had no experience whatsoever in military matters, he raised a regiment. He was soon a general, and a fairly good one, for his military virtues were of a high order: discipline, courage, dignity, integrity, and willingness to die if ordered to do so, even for a foolish objective—which was the case when he tried to take Port Hudson on the Mississippi in 1863. During the attack which he personally led upon that fortress, Dow was nearly killed, then was captured. In Libby Prison, he became even more of a national hero—the imprisoned "temperance general" who stood liable to a death sentence from a Confederate military court because while serving in the South he had continued his abolitionist activities. The hero's fame would serve him well in the temperance campaigns yet to come.

Like the moral stewards who followed him in great number, Neal Dow never worried himself about *why* men drink. There is in this regard no psychological or philosophical reflection of any significance in his rich reminiscences. He worried only about what drinking did to drunkards, and this was no abstraction; he saw inefficiency, irresponsibility, violence. To Neal Dow, the drunkard was improvident, brawling, wife-beating—a man who terrorized his family.

This family morbidity—the drunken rejection of bourgeois values—was the principal theme of the books of Timothy Shay Arthur, the extremely successful novelist, editor, and women's rights worker who became the foremost writer of temperance fiction. His *Ten Nights in a Barroom, and What I Saw There* was probably inspired by Neal Dow. It clearly resembles in significant ways the book that was concurrently a best seller in the United States, *Uncle Tom's Cabin*. Just as *Uncle Tom* was a literary response to the Fugitive Slave Law of 1850, *Ten Nights* followed the controversy over the Maine Law of 1851. Both were taken quickly to the stage, and as plays or novels boldly dramatizing bourgeois values, both had a profound appeal to many Americans.

Ten Nights (allegedly drawn from a situation in Allentown, Pennsylvania) marks the progressive degradation of Joe Morgan, a young man who in the beginning of the melodrama is blessed with a wholesome, happy family, steady employment, and every opportunity for success as a citizen in a free country. But Joe is seduced by the grogshop owned by Simon Slade. As he staggers toward his certain grief, he loses his job and mistreats his wife—the perfect "guardian angel" of the Victorian sex role for middle-class women, who never considers her own fulfillment, only the moral uplift of Joe and the children. He reduces her and the children to poverty and malnutrition. And he is hooked; he cannot stop. Though he is essentially a good man, even the most piteous pleas fail to move him. When his older child, the angelic Mary, comes personally to lead him away from the barroom because there is illness and terror at home (in the stage version she sings "Father, Dear Father, Come Home with Me Now"), the scene explodes in violence. The drunken Simon Slade throws a tumbler at the drunk and maudlin Joe Morgan, but it misses its target and hits and kills poor Mary. This, finally, is enough to sober Joe Morgan.

Climactic though the killing of Mary is, Arthur continued with scenes of "nature outraged" until his readers could not escape the truth: It was the sacred structure of the family in Joe Morgan's town which was coming unraveled. In "shocking exhibitions of depraved human nature," a wife of one drunk is taken to the madhouse, a son to prison; a well-to-do father goes to the almshouse. Simon Slade, the barkeeper, "half-intoxicated" and "nearly blind with passion," falls into "bloody strife" with his own son. A few nights later, the younger Slade, "infuriated by drink and evil passions," commits the ultimate crime of murdering his own father. Though it is a fate which, as the corruptor of unnumbered Joe Morgans, old

Slade richly deserves, the crime to family culture is more profoundly awesome than the lurid poetic justice.

The unspeakable furies of these "drink storms" finally sober Joe Morgan, who miraculously escapes his slavery, takes the pledge, and joins the movement. "The accursed traffic must cease among us," Joe says at the end. "You must cut off the fountain, if you dry up the stream. If you would save the young, the weak, the innocent. . . . Let us resolve, this night, that from henceforth, the traffic shall cease in Cedarville."

We should take *Ten Nights* seriously as social history, as Arthur's readers did, or we will slip smugly into the error attributed earlier to Richard Hofstadter. Men and women in the 1850s, and for several decades thereafter, took *Ten Nights* seriously precisely because of its Victorian sentiment, its breathtaking portrayal of Victorian paternal tyranny, martyred innocence, and family disaster. The action is based upon Neal Dow's theme that alcohol could disintegrate social and family loyalties and that this disintegration would be followed by poverty and crime and a frightful depth of conjugal squalor. This in turn could breed children who would grow to become emotional and physical cripples and who would inflict chaos upon an unsettled society.

A number of things are clear here. First of all, the functional design of the social order in Cedarville was not much of a design at all and not much of a security. The structural posts were unseasoned, warped, and crooked; the supporting beams were miscut; the nuts and bolts were mismatched, or simply missing. It was a society without cultural cohesion, without any hope of withstanding the drink storms in Slade's tavern which struck directly at the family. During such a storm in Cedarville, women and children had few protections, and this situation was the focus of the cultural crisis that produced *Ten Nights*. The story shows how delicate and how fragile Victorian family security was in America; it also shows how very necessary it was to any acceptable design for social order. It shows, finally, how in an otherwise chaotic society the values of self-discipline, family loyalty, and responsibility for children—as well as of personal ambition, self-reliance, and accomplishment—were at the heart of the Prohibition Movement.

This essentially conservative view of American reform reveals several paths of social history which might otherwise go unnoticed. If social reform was the effort to protect the bourgeois interior of American life, our view shifts away from the conventional historical concern with the individual and toward the bourgeois family, which, during the nineteenth century, was the most vital shelter for emerging values. This view has caused Gilman Ostrander to write in *The Rights of Man in America, 1606-1861* (1969) that before and since the American Revolution, the advocation of liberty has been "not so much of the individual as of the family," that Jeffersonian republicanism was "familial rather than . . . individualistic," and that "the humanitarian era of the mid-nineteenth century was most fundamentally a reflection of the changing character of the family in American life."

Because the disorders of a frontier country made protecting the family a matter of compelling urgency, we can begin to see how the suasion of "temperance" became the repression of "prohibition." When moral suasion failed, as it did with the Washingtonians and the early temperance societies, the persuaders moved smoothly to place the law on their side. All societies have legislated or dictated for their own protection, and the conditions under which the bourgeois family emerged in the United States encouraged not only the temperance-prohibition laws against barrooms but a host of other mandates for the same purpose: laws against slavery, adultery, gambling, seduction, prostitution, and traffic in narcotics.

There is, in fact, a congruence of energies here which illuminates the transition from a stable society of polymorphic lifestyles to one of bourgeois anxieties; no one in either society could long believe that a law itself could forever solve the personal problems that propel an individual to excess and destruction. Yet it is inconceivable that a republican society dependent upon newly defined and delicate values would not protect itself by legislating against the threats and challenges.

Thus the movements toward antiliquor and antislavery laws ran parallel during the 1830s and 1840s. After the Civil War, antisaloon achievements were concurrent with "white slave" panics; the Mann Act, aimed at prohibiting prostitution, and the Volstead Act, aimed at prohibiting the liquor traffic, are chronologically not far apart. It seems clear that these issues were raised to the level of national legislation because most people regarded the Victorian family as an institution essential to national survival. Thus Herbert Hoover, who had written a book called *American Individualism*, became the engineer of strict Prohibition. It was, he said, his "sacred obligation." And this was the language that most good progressives used when they acknowledged their determination, in Hoover's words again, "to protect the American home."

4

Counterculture

"AN ACT FOR THE Suppression of Drinking Houses and Tippling Shops"—it was Neal Dow's phrase and the climax of his work across a decade—came before the legislature of Maine in May 1851. Representation that year in Maine was strongly Democratic, and a leading opponent of the act attacked it as one of the "inquisitorial edicts of the temperance fanatics of Portland, headed by its popinjay Major, a Whig abolitionist of the most ultra stripe." The issue, however, was above simple partisanship. Dow appealed personally to House and Senate leaders, who pushed the bill through with two-thirds majorities in each chamber. Within two days after his appearance in the capital, Dow was able to lay the law before the governor and obtain his immediate signature. This triumph inspired temperance workers in every state of the union to organize, petition, and rally. With Dow himself leading the crusade, there followed a remarkable series of victories: Minnesota, Rhode Island, Massachusetts, Vermont, Michigan, Connecticut, Indiana, Delaware, Iowa, Nebraska, New York, and New Hampshire. A total of thirteen states had Maine Laws by 1855.

These laws prohibited the manufacture and sale of "spiritous or intoxicating liquors," which in Maine meant almost anything alcoholic that was not intended for medical or mechanical purposes. In other states amendments would soon permit wine and beer. The laws did not prohibit the personal use of whatever beverage an individual might import or brew up for himself or have stored away before the laws were signed. The goal was to abolish public drunkenness—usually, as in colonial Virginia,

associated with "low fellows"—not personal or private drinking, and only a few dissidents regarded the laws as in any way
repressive. Indeed, it was the public character of life during the
Federalist generation which the Victorian society was rejecting.
The older lifestyle—in its insensitivity to the values of privacy
and internal dignity, in the exuberant, open, and even shameless
character of its delinquencies and its fellowship—was utterly
inconsistent with the bourgeois values then fastening upon the
middle-class American conscience. (It would be difficult to
imagine the wonderful lithographs of the open, public society
sketched during the Jacksonian period—or even the great street
scenes painted by George Caleb Bingham in the 1850s—as being
done after the Civil War, when most serious American art had
become deeply personal and introspective.) In the 1850s, laws
to abolish the public grogshop could be seen as laws to protect
the family from the kind of lower-class public drunkenness
which the grogshops themselves generated. When, for example,
drunks in DuQuain, Illinois, protested the Reverend William
Bird's support of a Prohibition law by demonstrating in front of
his house and, according to Bird, exposing themselves "in the
most *shameful manner possible*," they brought credit to Bird's
cause. It is also significant that in *Ten Nights*, Joe Morgan was a
public, not a solitary, drinker, and that it was the grogshop, not
his personal problems, which reduced him to irresponsibility.

It is also significant that when Neal Dow campaigned for his
law, he faced no really effective opposition of organized vested
interests. In those days, before beer was pasteurized or even
effectively bottled, the service areas of breweries were entirely
urban, and temperance workers could confront them locally.
Americans were not drinking much beer anyway, and there was
no "brewery power" that could be politically threatening. In
those days, too, distilleries had at best a regional influence, and
attacking them was of local rather than national concern. Thus
in New York state in 1846, voters—all of them male and few of
them of the "low-fellow" class—determined in 728 of the 856
towns and cities to stop the licensing of taverns and grogshops.
To this extent the state was "dry" of the traffic before the Maine

Law was debated in the state assembly. As he moved from state to state, Neal Dow found that it was the Temperance Movement, not the liquor traffic, that had a national dimension.

Within the context of state traditions, within the mainstream of state reform movements and a changing lifestyle, the Maine Laws found hardly more opposition than did the various laws against adultery, dueling, and lotteries which were then passing through most state legislatures. With the ceremonial judgment of ballots and roll-call votes, Americans of the 1850s were rejecting what they regarded as the excesses of the Federalist generation, of the old Yankee morality. They were validating a set of values which seemed more appropriate to their own times. And it was, in the most part, largely ritualistic, for there is little evidence to suggest that the Maine Laws had an immediate impact upon the lives of most Americans. The middle-class Joe Morgans of the country had, in an impressive measure, gone far toward liberating themselves from the grogshops even before the laws overtook them. The measure is again statistical; the annual per capita consumption of absolute alcohol had fallen from the 10 gallons of 1830 to the 2.10 gallons of 1850. Apparently the Temperance Movement had been a part of the broad revision of public attitudes through which many Americans were deciding that they did not want—and should not allow others—to gamble or commit adultery or get drunk in public or fight duels.

It seems that Americans of that generation accepted such laws as an inevitable phase of social adjustment, and, in the case of Prohibition, were not greatly concerned about the enforcement of the laws after they had been signed and coded. State governors were expected to articulate the proper sentiments of law and order, but no state legislature supposed that it should appropriate substantial funds for state policing or for a police state. City governments were only slightly more inclined to insist that the law, if not honored everywhere, should at least not everywhere be indecently disobeyed. One exception, however, was the government of Portland, Maine, where Mayor Dow was the object of international attention and as such felt some obligation to prove that the law could in fact prohibit. His opponents were equally determined to prove that in fact it could not, and they inspired some of the first and now classic episodes of subterfuge and wily evasion. Some storekeepers in Portland stopped selling grog, but they charged five cents for a soda cracker, which they served with a free drink. Others charged admission to see a "blind pig," the viewing of which entitled one to a free tumbler of rum. Thus *blind pig* became the nineteenth century equivalent of *speakeasy*. There were similar evasions everywhere, of course, but a general assumption seems to have been that sooner or later almost everyone would quite naturally want to obey the laws, and that this revision of attitudes would occur without the need for any unseemly coercion.

The Maine Laws were, accordingly, quite easy to get rid of before the Civil War. In eight of the thirteen states they were, in part or in their entirety, found to be inconsistent with the several state constitutions. And after the court rulings in each case, temperance organizations made no concerted efforts to repair or to revise them. This dissipation of a significant social and political movement was not a matter of public indifference or hostility toward the temperance cause. It occurred as the Kansas-Nebraska Act of 1854 presented the prospect of slavery spreading into the new territories—an issue which plunged the nation into political turmoil and absorbed almost every other concern. When the Prohibition Party leader D. Leigh Colvin, in his book *Prohibition in the United States* (1926), did a careful study of each state to determine what actually happened to the Prohibition Movement after 1855, he found that in each instance a political situation developed which left the issue of Prohibition potentially too dangerous for a major political party to handle. The Whig leaders, through whom the temperance reformers had usually attained their Maine Laws, were finding it impossible to hold northern and southern states together in the same organization. As their party disintegrated, they held desperately to any friend, be he wet or dry.

In a typical legislative situation of 1856, Whigs were abandoning their loyalties to the old organization and leadership, while the new Republican Party, eager to build the largest possible majorities, could afford no more than polite sympathy to those groups who thought it important to debate the dry laws. In New York, which again is a good example, the Republican Party in 1855 had seemed happy to build on the natural affinity that was obvious between antislave and antiliquor reformers. But in 1856 the state platform committee politely ignored the temperance petitioners. That year even Neal Dow, who had helped organize the Republicans in Maine, yielded to his friends who insisted that Prohibition be excluded from the state platform so that the campaign might be conducted on national issues alone.

Thus, as the nation moved through upheaval and toward new political alignments, the Prohibition laws fell away. During the war there were few if any legal restrictions on manufacturing, selling, or giving away anything that humans wanted to drink. This is not to say that the United States again became a drunken society, for the cohesion of the Victorian family and the vitality of the bourgeois lifestyle were probably enhanced by the anxieties of war. In many regiments, boys from temperance families gathered in heroic groups for spiritual self-defense. When Neal Dow accepted a commission as commanding officer of the 13th Maine, he did so with a demand, granted by the governor of the state, that he be able to choose his officers from among "temperate and upright men." In his training camp he allowed no alcohol, no profanity, no brutality. Dow and his officers received letters from fathers and mothers all over the north begging that their boys be allowed to serve under him in a "temperance regiment." There were, in fact, several temperance regiments. But on the other hand, the German and Irish regiments did develop frightful reputations for hard drinking. One would suppose that the disorders of war would encourage more people to drink more freely, but one could also suppose that the war itself would have rigidly limited the comportment of such drinking. During these years the United States was a regimented society. Drinking would occur within both the license and the discipline of a truly national crisis.

On the day of his death, Abraham Lincoln remarked—according to a temperance advocate who had spoken with him briefly—that "After reconstruction the next great question will be the overthrow and suppression of the legalized liquor traffic." It was a statement widely quoted in temperance circles. If Lincoln actually did make such a prediction, he was indeed perceptive, for to many people during the next thirty years the liquor question was a question which obscured, or at the very least confused, all others. We can see the force of it in a simple chronology.

N.B.

The National Prohibition Party was organized in 1869. Then, in 1873—when there were about 100,000 saloons in the country, or about 1 for every 400 men, women, and children—the extraordinary "Women's War" broke out across the United States with a dramatic, if transitory, impact upon hundreds of towns and cities, closing thousands of saloons. The more enduring achievement of the "war," however, was to bring together in 1874 the women who would call the first convention of the WCTU and begin the complex and broad influence which that organization would have upon the social history of the next generation. Concurrently there was widespread agitation in a majority of the states when temperance workers began the bitterly disruptive process of amending constitutions to make them consistent with the dry laws overruled in the 1850's. Kansas was the first to amend and the first to elect a Republican governor in full sympathy with the amendment.

By 1880, the annual per capita consumption of brewery beer (which had been 2.7 gallons in 1850) rose to 17.9 gallons. This increase was not so much a measure of drunkenness as it was of the immigration of beer drinkers and of the growing number of saloons; there were probably 150,000 saloons in 1880, but this figure would almost double by 1900. Many of these represented the worst features of the urban industrial culture; they were working-class, often obviously lower-class and ethnically oriented, blatantly and aggressively masculine to the mood of a sneering *machismo*, linked sordidly to organized crime, organized prostitution, and the organized herding of mercenary voters. This development was so distressing to many people that in the 1880s thousands of men and women were demanding that the saloon question become a political question. Their vigorous intrusion into Republican politics drew many states into a tide of social and political turmoil that did not subside until the voters of these states had suffered at least one and perhaps two divisive referenda on the issue of the state's licensing these saloons or forever prohibiting them.

At the same time, the "social question," which was a cluster of fears about the alarming urban change whose symptoms were saloons, slums, poverty, and prostitution, was raised urgently by middle-class writers, speakers, editors, preachers, and political leaders in every state. Out of it came the "social purity" crusade which swept many national leaders and perhaps millions of followers into a highly emotional campaign against prostitution—then a particularly ugly reality of urban life—and against the saloons where it was nourished. Then, too, the "Women's Movement" was making significant gains, especially in the states where the social purity cause was becoming most intense. In the late 1880s the Republican Party was being torn ragged by a profound conflict between the power of antisaloon, "purity," women's rights crusaders on the one hand and the growing power of immigrant-urban conservatives on the other. It was a conflict between two lifestyles, two views of the nation's future, and it wrenched the party into a reluctant and ambiguous but nevertheless positive endorsement of "temperance and morality." In the 1890s there were severe losses in that crusade, but at the same time the Anti-Saloon League was quietly organizing and testing the kind of pressure it would use to lead triumphantly, after 1900, toward national Prohibition.

Each of these developments needs explanation, for around each lies some of the most important aspects of social history in nineteenth century America. Here we must turn again to some of the original premises of this study—that the Prohibition Movement was to protect the home and family at a time when their security was far more urgent to society than were the rights of an individual. The movement was stronger in the United

States than in western Europe because the American family stood deprived of the institutional securities extended in other countries by strong and centralized governments, by traditions which bound church to state, and by the social texture of rich ethnic and community cohesions. The American family became increasingly vulnerable to disorder when, following the peace brought in 1814 by the Treaty of Ghent, the westward movement really began and the churches were permanently disestablished. Social disorder generated a kind of personal anxiety which—occurring as it did within a system of cultural values particularly hospitable to alcohol—inclined individuals to drink in excess and in a comportment of excessive drinking which to Americans presented even more terrible threats to home and family. While we have no entirely satisfactory measures of spiritual distress among a whole people, the extent of excessive drinking—or of drinking to morbidity—is one useful measure, and what we know of this reveals in the United States before the Civil War a society for which it might be difficult to underestimate the extent of disorder.

After the war there were the inevitable and immeasurable dislocations of death and physical destruction which many American families had to sustain through the trauma of Reconstruction. There was also the concurrent collapse of public morality at every governmental level—federal, state, territorial, and municipal. Political corruption became a steady source of fear and suspicion. The deepest anxieties, however, may have come from the complex and disturbing acceleration of the urban-industrial processes and conversions: the vast commercialization of almost every aspect of life; the proliferation of mills, factories, machinery, railroads, industrialized mines, steam-driven saws, smelters, rolling mills; the immigration of millions of Catholics who did not speak English; the growth of slums, wage slavery, prostitution, saloons; the unparalleled opportunities for mobility, anonymity, violence, progress, and poverty.

To the native American of the 1870s, the values that defined his identity seemed gravely threatened on every hand. More, perhaps, than ever, the home was to him a vital fortress for his progeny and for the moral values so recently articulated as the bourgeois tradition: self-confidence, conscience, sexual discipline, ambition, measurable accomplishment, loyalty, reverence, responsibility, respect. So disorderly was the world outside the home that the home itself became almost a sacred symbol; again we see the family hearth, the Christmas tree, the generous, benevolent, but deeply principled father, the mother of warmth and tenderness, the family table, the Bible, the Sabbath. Outside the home there was likewise an increasingly ominous counter-symbol of filth, permissiveness, and irreverence—the urban-industrial saloon.

Before the 1830s, temperance workers condemned the "grog-shops," "barrooms," and "taverns" which were then traditionally integrated by law and custom to the wayside hotel or inn. In most of the older, more stable towns and cities the "host" could not sell liquor by the drink without also offering food and lodging. In this regard, the barrooms of wayside inns were qualitatively distinct from the whiskey tents and booze barns which, along the frontier settlements from Kentucky to California, openly encouraged drunkenness. (The word *booze* was coined in the vernacular during the presidential campaign of 1840, when an imaginative entrepreneur named Edmund C. Booze obtained whiskey bottles shaped like log cabins and the "booze bottle" became inordinately popular.) This relationship of food, shelter, and drink did not necessarily guarantee society that the barroom would always be a benign institution, but it did tend to shape the public drinking parlor as a pleasant retreat for the sort of fellowship and relaxation which was not inconsistent with moderation and public safety.

But this relationship changed radically when the railroads began to bypass the more rural hotels and inns, leaving the "host" of early American public hospitality a rarity by the 1860s and almost extinct after the Civil War. Thereafter, state laws began to recognize and to license the separate existence of the barroom, which became a place where drinking was not an adjunct to relaxation but rather the central indulgence to which all else—be it fellowship, rest, commerce, or politics—was subordinate. In the changing social function and structure, the newer name gained currency—the drinking "saloon."

To be sure—as we noted at the very beginning of this study—there were in every city some saloons which offered a haven of grace and dignity. They were places where a man could unburden himself of caste and status and social inhibition and breathe for a moment without anxiety, humiliation, or shame. They could provide a momentary but essential refuge from worry or from the deep abrasions of daily life. They could offer to a grateful clientele an honest and felicitous distinction between relief and abandon. Because such saloons did become centers of urban social life for many wage earners who were not yet bound to the mandates of Victorian family life, they clearly served a variety of human needs. They were informal employment offices, and they were shelters for the unemployed— warm, relaxed, hospitable. To explore this function, a committee of clergymen and educators in the 1890s examined a number of urban saloons and concluded that the good ones were "meeting the thirst for fellowship, for amusement, and for recreation" that no other institution of the urban-industrial society could provide. A good saloon could be a "poor man's club" and even a center of charity. This is to say that the saloon they saw was not so much a *problem* as a *solution* to problems which the urban-industrial society had created.

In our own time, memories of the good ones have become inexhaustible inspirations for a glowing nostalgia through which the saloon seems to have been perhaps the most humane institution in a harshly industrial age. Thus a newspaper reporter named Jim Marshall, who gained a detailed and intimate knowledge of saloons during the 1890s, later defended them as places of refuge, the only public places where men could congregate in working clothes, "with grimy hands and faces, and where they could think and talk uninhibitedly." The saloon, he said, "was a place where all men were equal and where every man was a king." In a saloon, a man informed himself about the social and political matters of the day. And because a journalist could mingle there with mill workers, mechanics, politicians, drifters, and businessmen, an afternoon in a saloon kept him close to the texture of American industrial life. "We learned our social and political fundamentals bellied up to the bar," he wrote, and it seemed to him that drunkenness was not a serious problem. "I cannot recall that we ever got drunk, but upon occasion we were moderately stimulated and inspired to create and announce immprovements in government, or denounce social inequities." And surely within such nostalgia there was a wide core of reality.

But there were also saloons which increased poverty, crime, and degradation. Born of the urban-industrial culture, the saloon could reflect its ugliness. The moral dynamics of this unhappy development—given the character of the competitive capitalism within which it occurred—now seem as inevitable and as inexorable as the iron law of wages. The mandates of industrial competition emerged from a rapidly progressive technology, from heavily capitalized brewing and distilling, from refrigeration cars, from the process for pasteurizing beer, and from the crown bottle cap. With the completion of transcontinental railroads, these innovations released the breweries and the distilleries from their regional confinement and opened the entire country to saloon farming. Again our statistics are vivid: The total annual consumption of beer in the United States was 36 million gallons in 1850; 204 million in 1870; 414 million in 1880; 855 million in 1890. During the same period the population increased from 23 million to 63 million—about 300 percent.

The principal feature of growth in the brewing industry was a fierce and relentless competition among large producers. In order to lock in exclusive franchises for their beer, breweries would advance money for fees and rentals to get a new saloon started, then provide the internal fixtures and initial inventories, all at alluring terms. There was an almost frenzied rush down each new mile of railroad track to stake out new territory or to clutter up the old. As we have already noted, some communities with only a few hundred citizens were infested with dozens of saloons. In 1888 in California it was estimated that there were over 12,000 saloons, or 1 to every 91 residents. Soon almost every urban neighborhood of wage earners and every small town along a railroad track had its saloons—and its orgy of competitive excess.

The Anti-Saloon League's version of saloon history, as seen in the *Standard Encyclopedia of the Alcohol Problem* (6 volumes, 1930), focuses upon this excess, then uses the details to evoke an insidious bigotry:

> With the change in the character of the retail liquor business there was also a change in the character of the proprietors of the saloon, and the traditional "mine host" gave way to the foreign-born saloon keeper, who was without standing in respectable society and commonly ranked with the lowest and criminal classes. The dealer who desired to conduct his business in a decent way was forced out by competition with one whose only aim was to make money as fast as possible. Almost without exception, saloon-keepers were ignorant and brutal individuals, and their trade policy resembled that pursued by criminal bands.

Even in this distortion, there is a strong element of truth. Many saloonkeepers were foreign-born, and their antecedents had a high visibility. And when almost anyone could become a saloonkeeper, many of those who did were less than respectable. Furthermore, he who took the job became a debt-slave to brewers, who proved to be harsh taskmasters. The new saloonkeeper, pressed by his obligations, was soon competing for customers.

The common protest against the saloon was that it encouraged a defiantly anti–middle-class indulgence and produced drunkenness. More than any other offense, this seemed to unite saloon critics from all regions. At worst, there were the notorious price-cutting saloons where hundreds of men were crowded together, not for warmth or fellowship, but for hard and fast drinking; those too drunk to buy more were pushed out the back door to retch in the alley or street. And even the best saloonkeepers seldom refused a man's impulse, no matter how many drinks he may have already taken; the customer's freedom was to gratify his impulses as far as he could pay for them. The consequent loss of physical and moral control was in itself threatening enough to bourgeois values, but it was the *public* character of saloon drunkenness—the foul-mouthed, blasphemous drunk, reeling and staggering from saloon to street—that so deeply offended the disciplines and values of the Victorian home. All across the country after 1870, men who in no way opposed the personal or private or home-use of alcohol were protesting the licensing of saloons near the public markets, stores, post offices, and schools, where members of their families might have to confront the public drunkard.

In this regard, a common complaint was that saloons stayed open for business twenty-four hours a day, seven days a week. The competition dictated that they do so, and the saloon power in municipal politics usually meant that the Sunday closure laws of most states would be openly ignored and that Sunday debauchery could be defiantly exhibited to outrage the bourgeois values and Sabbatarian sympathies of most native-born Americans. With equally open defiance, some saloon-keepers served not only minors but even young children. And it was predictable that saloons would be hangouts for prostitutes, who in the competitive spiral were often necessary, as were, progressively, gamblers, pimps, and petty criminals. In 1901 in Spokane, forty saloons had "wineroom" attachments which left rather little to the imagination: Private "boxes" with couches, according to a group of Protestant and Catholic leaders who investigated them, permitted "immorality in its most depraved form." Jim Marshall, the newspaperman who in later years reflected so romantically on his favorite saloons, remembered also that the hustling for a quick dollar led some saloonkeepers to traffic in morphine and "Spanish fly." This was no uniquely urban phenomenon, for it was, if possible, even worse in the rural West, where competing saloons in a small town might cater to the depravities of hundreds of migrant miners or railroad workers.

Implicit in every objection to the saloon was the conviction that the very nature of the saloon and of saloon drunkenness seemed to encourage sexuality, brutality, and violence. A cultural enigma of American drinking—in contrast, say, to Jewish or to South American Indian drinking—is that it has usually been disinhibiting. It seems to incline the frustrated toward the argument, the brawling, and the bald-faced sexuality which have never been flattering aspects of American life. It has always cast a sinister aura across the tippling house, before, during, or after the days of the saloon. Until the most recent past, the phrases *drunken violence, drunken murder,* and *drunken lust* could easily evoke the saloon image. This image was each year constantly refreshed by newsworthy incidents, for the chronicles of Prohibitionist history are linked by the martyrs who were beaten or even killed by saloonkeepers or saloon thugs. It was not, for example, difficult for newspaper readers to believe that in 1909 a saloonkeeper in the lumber town of Aberdeen, Washington, sold out his business and devoted himself to the antisaloon movement because, he said, the sixty-nine men murdered in his town that year had been the victims of saloonkeepers and prostitutes.

Drunken comportment, as we have earlier noted, is ultimately determined by the culture in which the drinking takes place. In some cultures it is the dread comportment of murder and mayhem, and in others it is that of quiet introspection, of religious devotion, or of a loosely structured and maudlin sentimentality. What is abundantly clear is that within the cultural context of Judeo-Christian societies, both drinking and drunkenness have long been associated with a loss of sexual discipline. When in *Genesis* old Noah first fermented wine, he so enjoyed his vintage that he fell into a drunken stupor and lay exposed in his nakedness—and felt so guilty during his massive hangover that he cursed into slavery the unwitting Canaan. And as the world knows from the same record, it was obvious what the daughters of Lot had learned about Noah's fermentations when they said to each other, "come, let us make our father drunk with wine, and then lie with him, and so preserve our race."

In London during the late 1700s, when the streets were figuratively awash with drink, James Boswell casually recorded the progress of rather typical evenings when he became "so intoxicated that instead of going home, I went to a low house" where "I lay all night. . . ." In the coming age of bourgeois family values, Boswell, Lot, and Noah would become examples of an apprehension so fearful that it was almost inarticulate.

But these episodes may tell us less about drunkenness than they do about the societies so hospitable to these drunks, for intoxicated men do not universally expose their nakedness, lie with their daughters, or spend the night in a brothel. Furthermore, the extent to which drinking obscures a person's sexual values in Judeo-Christian culture is determined also by the specific circumstances, the environmental and institutional circumstances, of the drinking. Sophisticated cocktail-party drinking, for example, is not the disinhibitor that barroom drinking is or was. And of course not all drinkers become sexually aroused or aggressive, and not all aroused or promiscuous persons drink.

The images of depraved sexuality evoked by the saloon raise at least two questions. First, to what degree in American society does the drug alcohol, in and of itself, stimulate sexual passion or aggression—that is, is it actually a Judeo-Christian aphrodisiac? And second, if it is, did the circumstances of drinking in an American saloon excite sexual passions which would not have been aroused by drinking under other conditions? No two questions could be closer to the heart of the American Prohibition Movement.

The answer to the first question is unfortunately incomplete. Like many other drugs, alcohol can affect different individuals in different ways at different times and under different circumstances; and the results have few reliably predictable norms. But research does make it reasonably certain—see, for example, *Alcohol and Health* (1971)—that one effect on most organisms is in some measure to relieve the organism of the burdens, and the securities, of learned fears, including those that concern sexual and religious experience, violence, and pain. Thus a cat that has learned from electric shock stimulation to avoid a source of food will, when given enough alcohol, approach that source without fear. Or a human bus driver, after several drinks, will be less reluctant to take what he has learned to be uncommon risks of the road. With alcohol in the brain, according to Berton Roueche, "there is an almost instantaneous slackening of the neural tension essential to full cerebration. The governing grip of the mind on judgment then begins to loosen, emotions normally held in check drift into consciousness, and inhibitions lift." This may not be a universal reaction, but when it occurs within the context of Western cultural traditions, the "grip of the mind on judgment" is the grip of the anxieties—self-criticism, fear of embarrassment, and fear of guilt—which are the substance of restraints so essential to bourgeois family security.

In the nineteenth century these restraints were deemed absolutely necessary for the protection of children, for a private individuality and dignity, and for the continuity of the family itself; they were the barriers against naked abandon, incest, and orgiastic indulgence. And this neural slackening releases also a widening glow of self-confidence that, like sexual experience itself, is essentially mystical. William James wrote that alcohol was "the great exciter of the Yes function in man," that it brought men "from the chill periphery of things to the radiant core," that it made them "for the moment one with the truth." It was not "through mere perversity," he added, that men pursue it. This, then, has usually been the character of the alcoholic elation in some Western societies where that elation has also been a root terror in bourgeois life: a spreading euphoria of relaxed anxieties, a rising self-confidence warm enough to melt through the cold walls of inhibition, not the least of which are those of sexual discipline.

But the pluralisms of Judeo-Christian culture have shaped sexual mores and inhibitions of striking variety and inconsistency, from the lofty regard for chastity, even male chastity, in pietist America during the nineteenth century, to the permissiveness of some Latin cultures during the same period, in which it was not uncommon for a middle-class father to lead his son to initial rites in a brothel. It was in the abrasions of these pluralisms that the American movement to restrict the use of alcohol found an urgent sexual dimension.

Though the relationship of drink to sexual indulgence was integrated in the conventional wisdom, there were apparently few overt currents of sexuality in the typical American barroom before the Civil War. Indeed, as we have seen, many of the barrooms were islands of peace and conviviality, where travelers rested, where circumspect men paused for a leisurely refreshment under conditions which rendered any strong overtone of illicit sexuality utterly inappropriate. And if in the course of drinking, the cup did raise the level of sexual appetite, this appetite was seldom given any direction by the barkeep. It seems unlikely that in any but the most debauched areas of a few large urban centers—the waterfront dives of New York, Boston, and San Francisco were the most notorious—were there enduring linkages of barrooms to prostitutes or brothels. Between the stimulation of the cup and the fulfillment, a man was usually on his own. Only by the most tentative implication could one see the troubles of Joe Morgan in *Ten Nights in a Barroom* as sexual troubles, and even then the implication could only be that Joe had so completely drowned his energies in Slade's booze that he had become mentally, morally, and sexually incompetent.

But in the upward swirl of competition after the Civil War, the atmosphere of many urban saloons drifted toward a libidinous haze. It became one of raw masculinity, of muted or blunt sexuality. In the wall murals of consistent nudity and of lascivious intent, in the language, and in the relaxed attitudes toward sex, saloonkeepers found a perfectly natural attraction for lonely male customers. As Roy Lubove has shown in his article "The Progressives and the Prostitute" (1962), reformers of the period regularly emphasized their discovery of an organic relationship between the competitive saloon and urban prostitution.

The proximity of a saloon to a public dance hall, for example, could be a real competitive advantage; men in search of self-confidence could drop in for a few rounds before beginning the search for a partner on the dance floor—a common and inexpensive but anxiety-ridden recreation for the urban poor. Vice investigators were later to note the almost invariable presence of liquor in the dance halls, where, according to one report, young girls under the influence were often carried "half fainting to dark corners of the hall and there . . . subjected to the most indecent advances." And why indeed should the enterprising saloonkeeper provide only the preliminaries? Some saloonkeepers encouraged prostitutes to solicit on the premises. Others had regular arrangements with full-time procurers. Still others became pimps: the room in the back of the saloon for agreements, the understanding with nearby hotels. Others institutionalized their association with a few prostitutes or with a fully functional brothel. As the competition increased, the associations became more and more blatant. A major difference, then, between Simon Slade's prewar barroom and the urban-industrial saloon was an atmosphere heavy with ubiquitous sexual stimulation.

It is clear also that many saloonkeepers saw their own roles in this stimulation as only slightly compromising. Many came from cultural circumstances in which prostitution was accepted as a normal if unseemly part of life, and they saw no reason not to use the competitive advantage, not to link a natural demand with a natural supply. This was for them a fatal linkage, and here was the crux. In the American pietist tradition, colonial prostitution commonly had been condemned from the pulpits and the townhouses—more so in Puritan New England, less so in Revolutionary Boston or New York—but it was often tolerated, especially in seaports. At least people did not organize movements to exterminate it.

However, as the new country struggled for stability in the 1820s and 1830s, it was clear that the practice of prostitution was totally at odds with the moral necessities of a bourgeois society in which there was no church or state or organic community to sustain public or private virtues, and in which individual pride, decency, dignity, and conscience were sheltered by the overriding values of family cohesion and family loyalty. Though they had not yet associated it with the liquor traffic, members of the bourgeois culture would come to view prostitution with disgust and increasing horror. Parallel to the rising temperance agitation in the 1830s, for example, the American Female Reform Society organized women to work for the suppression of "vice." Its members were encouraged to spy out brothels and through the society to report what they discovered to the local police.

But the growth of prostitution in the United States paralleled the growth of the saloon. In the industrializing society, brothels became more numerous and more competitive, and they soon needed the saloons as much as the saloons needed them. Thus they multiplied as the saloons multiplied, for the impressive increase of organized prostitution throughout urban American life was based on progress and poverty; on urbanization, for only populations of the larger cities could maintain the more elaborate brothels and their competitive excesses; on immigration, for brothels thrived not only on young recruits from the rural areas of the nation but also on those from the countries of Europe, and on the lifestyles of Europe which gave public prostitution a certain legitimacy; and on industrial poverty, for prostitution needed the image of an existence more glamorous and more rewarding for young girls than life in the urban slums.

In this increasingly pluralistic nation, the duty of governments to condone or to attack prostitution was not at all clear. The traditions of Lyman Beecher's pietist republic were to oppose what was an obvious abomination. That young republic, however, had referred such matters to city governments. And Beecher did not live to see Chicago. But other traditions in currency after the 1830s were indifferent to what was regarded as the oldest profession; like the saloon, however unlovely it might be, the brothel served a social purpose. If the nonpietist traditions took note at all, it was to urge the regulation and control of prostitution in the interest of public health and convenience.

Lying beneath the superficially political question, moreover, were two opposing theologies in juxtaposition. The pietist view was that the whore had a soul that might be receptive to redemption and salvation when the institutional circumstances of her iniquity (the brothel, slavery, the saloon) were abolished. One's duty to God was to strike at the institution and save the soul. The opposing tradition expressed the assumption that whores were "fallen from grace" and doomed anyway—that maybe society needed them as safety valves for the pressures of sexual energies which, without relief, would surely corrupt the essential virtue of young women who had not fallen from grace but who at any moment might be so tempted and lost, and that in any event such matters may concern the church but not the state, and it would be quite improper to conceal their existence. Thus a poignant conflict between the "abolitionists" and the "regulationists" was in the making.

The "abolitionists" had assumed since the founding of the Republic that their own attitudes and assumptions were preeminent. They were profoundly shocked in 1870 when the political leaders of the city of St. Louis imposed upon their red-light district the "Paris" model of regulation (later repudiated by the state legislature): licensing prostitutes and requiring of them weekly certificates of venereal health and—by obvious implication—condoning their presence. This shock sent a great charge of moral energy into the Social Purity Movement, for it seemed to pietist groups thereafter that the populations of urban centers were determined to recognize whoredom, legitimize (even stimulate) evil, and serve the Devil.

The pietist conscience might tolerate a low incidence of underground illicit sexual activity, assuming, as it did, that the lower classes were naturally the morally weaker classes, and assuming, further, that individuals from the better classes who might in perversity yield to an impulse had surely in their homes and churches been properly admonished and that surely God would punish their deliberate provocation. But it could not tolerate the public stimulation of appetites for illicit sex, which was the wildly nonpietist nature of brothel competition. When illicit sex became not only legitimate but elegantly public, the pietist conscience was electrified. As David Pivar shows in *Purity Crusade: Sexual Morality and Social Control, 1868-1900* (1972), pietist women after 1870 rushed toward political and social protest with "almost an involuntary cultural response" to save the bourgeois family.

We shall see this response in the Women's War against the saloon in the early 1870s and in the organization of the WCTU. These developments, however, will be clear only after we have looked more closely at the increasing intensity of the response, and this brings us to a most somber current of the social purity anxiety: Prostitution was obviously responsible for the vicious spread of venereal disease in American life.

As the fear rose toward the end of the century, we see it in the broodings of Scandinavian drama which so deeply impressed both European and American audiences. In Ibsen's *A Doll's House,* the liberation of Nora from family loyalty and sexual obligation had inspired a general anxiety about feelings which were nearly as potent with danger to the established social order as had been the emotional turmoils of the Reformation. Then Ibsen's *Ghosts* used the affliction of syphilis—never mentioned on the stage, though every audience knew what the playwright had in mind—as a striking symbol of the hideous indemnities which the past could impose upon the present and the future. The tragedy is focused as much upon the mother as upon the son.

There soon developed throughout the country what might be accurately called a syphilis hysteria. Around 1900, leaders of a social hygiene movement, most of them physicians, made the first really public and candid revelations about the nature and the enduring devastations of the disease, particularly and most shockingly its impact upon innocent victims—the wives and children of infected men. In 1913, a stage play called *Damaged Goods* dramatized this impact for New York and Chicago, inspiring a wave of "white slavery" dramas that reached a wide audience. As the revelations spread, "syphilis of the innocent" impressed reformers as an appalling menace to society and a desperate matter for social control. (It was a substantive matter: Wassermann tests during World War I indicated positive evidence of syphilis among about 10 percent of the men inducted by the army; among prostitutes who favored army training camps the incidence was as much as 74 percent.)

Thus it was saloon-based or saloon-linked prostitution, in the judgment of the Chicago Vice Commission, which was spreading the disease and working a terrible devastation upon the "innocent wife and child in the home." It was to be feared "with as great horror as a leprous plague"; it scattered misery across the entire society, "leaving in its wake sterility, insanity, paralysis, the blinded eyes of little babes, the twisted limbs of deformed children, degradation, physical rot and mental decay." Nothing could have galvanized the bourgeois family into a greater sense of militant class consciousness and determined class aggression. It may well be that in that image of diseased depravity we can see the principal force which would ultimately bring about the destruction of the American saloon.

The illustrated posters of the Anti-Saloon League, bold and lurid and very public, grasped the spirit of this terror in italics that exclaimed *"Alcohol inflames the passions. . . . Alcohol decreases the power of control. . . . Avoid all alcoholic drinks absolutely . . .* and disease, dishonor, disgrace, and degradation will be avoided." Recently Kate Millet has suggested that women of that era developed several defenses, among which frigidity and chastity were perhaps the least satisfying, against the tyrannies of the Victorian head of household, against sexual slavery, against their forced submission to disease and humiliation through drunken lust. One does not wonder, then, that women came in great numbers to swell the reform movement against the saloon, which they could see as the dark passage between a frail virtue and an utter depravity; nor should one wonder that thereafter it was almost impossible to distinguish the antisaloon movement from the social protest against organized prostitution.

As this movement of protest grew in the United States, reformers came to realize that their municipal governments, which controlled saloon licensing, could be adamant in their refusal to do anything about it. There was, on the one hand, the obvious money power of the breweries and brothels, which converted easily into votes. But far more dispiriting to reformers was the discovery that in most larger cities the saloon interests were almost inextricably entwined with the structure of working-class and ethnic ward politics. The saloon was often central to the political machine that glued together an aggregate of social, economic, religious, and political life. They learned too that in the saloon wards, saloons were often refuge camps for the unemployed—or for tramps, moochers, and bums—and that voter registration might increase by as much as 50 percent when the word went out to round up the vote.

So integrated, in fact, were the saloons with the political-urban-industrial establishment that the traditional avenues of democratic protest and social change used successfully by reformers before the Civil War were effectively closed. A reformer could no more approach the saloon nexus than he could the Pullman Company or United States Steel. And to more and more reformers, the saloon—like a riot, a plague, or a social insurrection—demanded immediate and direct social control.

5

Protest and Reform

～～～～～～～～～～～～～～～～～～～～～～～～～～～～～～～～

DESCRIBING THE transition toward urban complexities, Robert H. Wiebe, in *The Search For Order, 1877-1920* (1967) called the United States of the nineteenth century "a society of island communities," each one secure in the confidence that it could "manage the lives of its members." Each was also confident in "the belief among its members that the community had such power ." This confidence rose from the values and expectations which followed easily from the intimate, face-to-face relationships among groups and individuals, and it failed during the 1880s and 1890s. In a society of tightly connected industries and cities, according to Wiebe, the very processes of industrialization and urbanization so altered the circumstances of work, family, and community that the vital relationships became alarmingly distant and impersonal. The old cohesions began to slip. And with the increasingly blatant challenges to pietist values, the slippage became vastly threatening to the middle class. These people, then, in their enduring "search for order," shaped a new basis for functional stability in what Wiebe calls "bureaucratization"—the linkage of groups and individuals into associations, agencies, and voluntary organizations for social action, which, through a centralization of impersonal authority, might impose what they regarded as the absolutely essential expectations of social discipline.

Looking closer, Wiebe distinguished between at least two articulate responses to disorder in the half century after Reconstruction. The first, *protest*, he sees as the reaction of confused and often frightened people who felt an impending chaos and cried out for a return to the older bonds of intimate community. Their efforts, of course, often ended in bitter frustration. The second, *reform*, was in his view the equally anxious but more creative response of the new middle class—the new professionals, specialists, and technologists who were in fact building the new physical and spiritual environment. They began deliberately to reshape old institutions, especially those of democracy, the family, and laissez-faire capitalism, in ways appropriate to the new industrial age. This distinction—which is quite consistent with our earlier view of reform as a conservative response to disorder—provides a coherent conceptualization for the social movements toward Prohibition after the Civil War.

On the face of it, the national upheaval had wrecked the Temperance Movement, for only five states still had Maine Law Prohibition in 1865. However, in the months following Appomattox, several state temperance conventions were called to order. In August, these conventions came together at Saratoga Springs, New York, as the National Temperance Society, an organization strong enough to assure its members that the agitation would almost everywhere be resumed. The rising social concern—and the "bureaucratization"—can be seen in the vigor of the Independent Order of Good Templars, who were "total abstinence" men, admirers of General Neal Dow, militantly committed to prohibiting by law the "manufacture and sale." The Templars increased their American membership from 50,000 in 1859 to 400,000 in 1869, and most of this growth was in the northern states, where the entrenched Republican Party organizations were steadfastly indifferent to the Templar's repeated petitions for state Prohibition. Late in 1869, leaders of the Right Worthy Grand Lodge of Good Templars at Oswego, New York, asked for a political solution to what they regarded as a political problem. Disenchanted with Republicans and without any hope for Democrats, they called for delegates from churches, Sunday schools, and from all the state temperance alliances to meet in Chicago and form the National Prohibition Party. The first National Prohibition Party Convention convened there during the winter of 1872.

A remarkable feature of this convention was the number of men notably distinguished in national affairs whose names were placed in nomination. For their presidential candidate, delegates nominated Salmon P. Chase, Chief Justice of the United States; Gerrit Smith, the wealthy landowner and famous abolitionist from New York; Wendell Phillips, known to delegates as the "foremost orator of the anti-slavery movement"; General Neal Dow of Maine; and General Benjamin F. Butler of Massachusetts. Following a period of friendly discussion, the convention accepted the candidacy of a former member of the Washingtonian Society, James Black of Pennsylvania, who had built a national reputation as a Maine Law campaigner, a Templar, an organizer for the Republican Party in the 1850s.

Black's platform called for a Prohibition amendment to the federal Constitution and for other amendments to achieve a federal income tax, the direct election of United States Senators, and the right of suffrage for women. In 1876 and consistently thereafter, the party also stood against the "foul enormities" of polygamy and "the social evil," which meant, of course, urban prostitution. This was a perceptive if symbolic inventory of national anxieties, taken by men and women of considerable prestige who were convinced that these would be the major issues of their generation. This conviction was no less an illusion than were most political projections of the time, for who could say, after a tragic and turbulent decade, what critical questions would follow Reconstruction.

To the delegates at Chicago in 1872, their new configuration of personalities and issues seemed to have a potential at least equal to that of the new and uneasy Republican alliances. "Slavery is gone," their keynoter told them, "but drunkenness stays . . ." Across the country, they sensed a deep restlessness about disjointed times. Reconstruction in the South was ending in corruption and cynicism. The federal government, having under Lincoln won a sacred victory, seemed under President Grant to have lost its very integrity. And the Panic of 1873 spread gloom, uncertainty, and confusion. For the next few years, numbers of intelligent people supposed that the Prohibition Party might indeed be triumphant.

These suppositions became expectations when, during the winter of 1873-74, anxieties about liquor and society became electrically dramatic. First, in Hillsboro, Ohio, on Christmas Eve, a group of seventy women led by the daughter of a former governor marched from a church meeting to a nearby saloon, where with song and prayer they demanded that the saloon-keeper give up his business and that his patrons give up their drink. Thereafter, from December through June, Committees of Visitation appeared daily to sustain the harassment. At the nearby town of Washington Court House, praying women actually convinced one liquor dealer to surrender his liquid stock, which flowed into the street gutter before a crowd of astonished citizens. Shortly thereafter several more saloons closed, the news spread rapidly, and the Women's Crusade ⋎ against the saloon broke across the eastern and western states in a sort of civil and social insurrection. With almost incredible spontaneity and concurrence, women of the prosperous and well-education classed went into the streets to become demonstrators and protestors, offering themselves to the indignities of passive resistance, singing, praying, kneeling on sidewalks to suffer the sneers, curses, and often the manhandling of sometimes violently outraged men.

The initial uprisings in Ohio had occurred shortly after the appearance there of Dr. Diocletian Lewis, who was then on tour through several states lecturing on temperance and hygiene. Lewis had been educated at Harvard, had practiced homeopathic medicine, had founded the Boston Normal Physical Training School for girls, and had written the books *Chastity* and *Our Digestion*. An ardent advocate of sex education and of physical exercise, he was also known as the inventor of the beanbag, which he had fashioned to encourage females into activities of some physical vigor. Lewis had publicly urged total abstinence but not, curiously, legal prohibition. Though his wide reputation is difficult to assess, except that he was a spokesman of protest against the infirmities of modern life, he

was an emotionally impressive speaker and either an impassioned health evangelist or an impassioned fraud. In Ohio
that season he had told women's groups how his own mother,
forty-three years before, had saved his drunken father by
closing a saloon with prayer. Having illuminated the thought
and the dynamics, Dr. Lewis himself left the field and was never
a part of the agitation. He later wrote another book, *Prohibition
a Failure*. Without his blessings, then, the crusade spread west
and east, far from any circuit he had ever ridden.

Women attempted saloon visitations in San Francisco, and
the antisaloon excitement that spring brought women into the
streets throughtout the state of California. In Portland, Oregon,
where the historian Frances Fuller Victor joined a visitation, the
women were rudely seized during the praying by Walter
Moffett, the proprietor of the Webfoot Saloon, who thrust them
into the street, shouting that he ran a respectable house and
didn't want any "damn whores" hanging around. But Frances
Fuller Victor and her companions—all of them wives of attorneys, physicians, and prominent businessmen—held their
ground tenaciously, singing on the sidewalk and blocking the
entrance. As Moffett became progressively more distraught, he
hosed them down with cold water, then had them arrested.
Since the wives of Portland's elite were unlikely to remain long
in the city jail, the visitations continued. Moffett soon closed the
Webfoot, quit the saloon business, and went to sea. In
Cleveland, the mayor quickly issued an anti–street-meeting
ordinance to protect the domestic tranquility. Women there
obeyed the laws, but 10,000 of them signed pledges never again
to touch liquor in any form. In Chicago, 65,000 women
petitioned for a law to close saloons on Sundays. There were
mass meetings in Philadelphia. In Boston, women closed the
saloons for one day on the centennial of the Battle of Bunker
Hill.

The historian Gilman Ostrander writes that this first mass
movement of women in American history was especially
meaningful because women were not agitating for the franchise
or for equality of any kind. Most of them had never thought to

challenge, and never would challenge, the conventional wisdom of woman's place being in the home. But in responding to the emotional magnetism of the crusade—and to the exciting possibilities of an organized Women's Movement—they were in fact responding to the view later articulated by Frances Willard of the WCTU that defenders of the home and its purity had the right and the obligation to enter the streets. The enduring result of the crusade, in fact, was that from it Frances Willard had learned how the antisaloon movement could dramatically raise the level of women's social consciousness, which, when expertly organized, could generate the powerful social pressure she applied through her "Home Protection" Movement.

This was first clear in Kansas, where "home protectors" entered the divisive public debate over a proposed amendment to the state constitution which would prohibit the "manufacture and sale." It was an appropriate time and place. Nowhere in the nation was there a more disorderly society than Kansas—disorder from the bloody turmoil before the war, from the war itself, the coming of railroads, the migration of tens of thousands, the dislocations following the Panic of 1873, and disorder inflamed by raiders, jayhawkers, bank robbers, cow town revelries, farm failure, and farmers' protests. In this environment, the competition of saloons was vicious and sustained, a daily outrage to those who were trying to shape the structure of a bourgeois society. The outrage provoked a dismal pathology; as early as March 1874, at the height of the Women's Crusade, two women in Burlingame had demolished part of a saloon with hatchets, thereby raising an ominous symbol and extending the state's somber traditions of violence.

In 1876, a young lawyer and Civil War veteran named John St. John, then a Republican state senator, made known the fact that Republican leaders of the state had offered him the party's nomination for governor. St. John publicly refused the offer because, he said, these same leaders had advised him to suppress his antisaloon convictions. In rejecting the nomination, he announced that unless the Republican organization in Kansas chose to endorse the proposed Prohibition amendment, he would go over to the Prohibition Party. This caused political leaders in all states to think for a while about saloons. In an even more striking development, the Republican Party of Kansas soon did precisely what St. John had asked. With a Prohibition plank in its platform, the party nominated St. John in 1878. He easily won the governorship. Supported with broad enthusiasm by the state chapters of the WCTU, he then personally led a campaign which carried the Prohibition amendment through the legislature and to ratification by the voters in 1880. St. John himself was that year reelected.

By 1882, however, the distressed "liquor Republicans" of Kansas were working hard to keep the party's nomination from going to St. John for a third time. Failing this—for St. John's delegate support at the state convention was invulnerable—they combined and conspired with the state's Democratic leaders to cause St. John's defeat by a Democrat in the November election. This Republican loss in Kansas, and the injection of Prohibition and anti-Prohibition into state politics with such power and bitterness, threw other state Republican organizations into confusion. The revolt of "liquor Republicans" shattered the party in Iowa, where St. John had been helping the dry Republicans then working for a Prohibition amendment.

The same situation brought serious problems to the Republican Party in Maine, Indiana, Oregon, Pennsylvania, New Jersey, Michigan, Connecticut, Illinois, West Virginia, Arkansas, Texas, Wisconsin, Nebraska, New York, Vermont, Minnesota, Ohio, Washington, and the Dakotas. As the movement continued through the decade, Prohibition amendments carried only in Kansas, Maine, Rhode Island, and in the sparsely populated new states of North Dakota and South Dakota. But in other states the margin of defeat was so narrow, and the Republican split over the issue so wide, that many people anticipated a great sweep of Prohibition sentiment—similar to that of the 1850s—throughout the entire nation.

By then Frances Willard had decided that she must herself be a political leader. In an 1880 address, she predicted that

American women would "lift the banner of the party that declares for home protection and saloon destruction." She was not then asking for assistance or for shelter—she was raising a threat and a challenge around which she organized the Home Protection Party in 1881. This was more than enough to cause the Prohibitionists to emphasize their endorsement of women's suffrage and to give it the prominence that France Willard demanded. Hoping to attract the dispirited admirers of John St. John in every state who felt betrayed by the Republican bosses, she joined with the Prohibitionists and formed the Prohibition Home Protection Party in 1882.

This was an organization of many reform goals and energies: prohibition, women's suffrage, direct legislation through initiative and referendum, a federal income tax, civil service reform, government regulation of monopolies. It added a new and entirely unpredictable potential to Prohibition politics. From this new base, St. John himself renounced the national Republican Party for its refusal to respond to petitions from the WCTU; and with the full support of Willard and her unions, he accepted the nomination of the National Prohibition Party (the same fusion with the name changed again) for President in 1884. The party was then militant and aggressive, stronger than it had ever been, or ever would be. It may have been the decisive factor in a critical election. St. John, to be sure, did not rise up to shatter American political alliances as the first Republican candidate, Frémont had done in 1856. But 1884 was the year when, after a long tenure, Republicans did lose the presidency. In the crucial state of New York, Republicans lost the election to Democrats by only 1,047 votes. The Prohibition Party in New York took 24,000 votes, many of which, in the absence of St. John and Willard, would surely have gone to the Republicans.

In some histories of the election, the "Burchard Alliteration" is marked as the critical factor in the defeat of the Republican candidate, James G. Blaine. This incident plagued Republicans after the Reverend Dr. Burchard, speaking for a number of Protestant ministers in New York City, had haplessly remarked before an Irish-Catholic audience, "We are Republicans and don't propose to leave our party and identify ourselves with the party whose antecedents have been Rum, Romanism, and Rebellion." The phrase was so well publicized that it undoubtedly turned numbers of voters, especially in New York, against Burchard, his ministerial friends, and their Republican candidates. But as St. John's campaign manager later boasted, the Prohibitionists had set out deliberately in 1884 not only to win votes but to derail the Republican Party by throwing antisaloon sentiment across its tracks at carefully selected corners.

In the state of New York, Republicans depended heavily upon the votes from the solidly middle-class counties of Allegheny, Monroe, and Orleans, and it was in these areas that the Prohibitionists did their best work. Though their national total was only 150,000, in New York they cut away thousands of votes which, if cast for Blaine, would have won him the state and thus the nation. The Prohibitionist press release in New York City claimed a signal victory: "The Republican Party having been removed from the path to the graveyard, the Prohibitionists will at once organize to bury the whiskey Democrats four years ahead." Nor were the Republicans disposed to minimize in any way the treachery of the Prohibitionists; in Kansas, the Republican-controlled state legislature voted shortly thereafter to give the name "Logan" to the county it had previously named "St. John."

The national Republican leaders knew very well that St. John and Frances Willard presented serious and complex problems. In state after state, bosses were finding it awkward and often difficult to restrain the antisaloon Republicans who threatened to leave the party if they could not have Prohibitionist platforms. Furthermore, rising sentiment against the urban brothels was a matter of urgent public discussion, and the Prohibitionists seemed to dominate it. The "abolitionists" had in the early 1880s—notably in New York—beaten back the "regulationists" and were openly attacking the "white slave traffic" and proposing state laws to ban prostitution. Wet Republicans, on the other hand, especially in the urban centers, were rising in an insurrection of their own, threatening to go Democratic. Republicans who had supposed that the issues of civil service, or tariff, or corruption in government would endure through the 1880s were forced to consider the "bureaucratization" of American life and to revise their estimations.

They did so quickly. In 1886, the Republican platforms in ten wet states favored legislative action which would allow the people to vote on Prohibition. In five dry states, the platforms favored sustaining the dry laws. Two years later, party leaders, with great tenderness and caution, raised the issue to the national level by accepting into the national platform some careful phrases which would touch the loyalty of dry voters and win back the admirers of Frances Willard without offending too many wets; the party stood for "the purity of the home" and for "temperance and morality."

It was apparent thereafter to all but the most fanatical that the Prohibitionists were not destined to break the loyalties of most Americans to the major parties. There had been no substantial growth in their ranks during the 1880s. While antisaloon sentiment grew, the party did not. In the states where the question had been submitted to the people between 1880 and 1890, about 46 percent of those who voted on the issue favored state constitutional amendments for Prohibition, but hardly anywhere was there any evidence of health in the Prohibition Party. Americans would vote for Prohibition but not for the Prohibitionists. And by the end of the decade it was also clear that the issues raised by agrarian unrest—free silver, tariff, immigration, the regulation of banks and industrial monopolies—would soon be preeminent. As the country moved toward the brink of the Panic of 1893, these symbols of disorder became more and more ominous. Within the Prohibition Party, they generated internal strains so severe that its members were soon moving in more than one direction.

There were those who, like St. John of Kansas, kept the faith with the original program for state constitutional amendments. But in twelve of the fourteen states where people voted on such amendments between 1887 and 1890, the voters rejected them. Party zealots, many of them men and women whose careers and personal identities had been bound up in the cause for twenty years, nevertheless attended state and national conventions, served on the committees, and contributed their money to keep evangelists in the field. St. John himself went out into the South as a lecturer, delivering 3,500 speeches before 1896 and taking an active part in every aspect of the party's existence.

St. John was an uncommon evangelist, a protestor-reformer who was trained as a lawyer, had been a practicing and successful Republican politician, and was twice governor of the state of Kansas. Year by year in the 1890s, his speeches began to reflect assessments of national issues other than Prohibition—especially questions of tariff and monetary reform—which were becoming increasingly urgent. At the party convention of 1892 he found that Prohibitionists could easily be encouraged to ventilate criticisms of the urban-industrial society which had in so many ways dealt harshly with their values and aspirations. He then argued for and achieved the most "broad gauge" platform in the history of the party. The platform predictably condemned the liquor traffic as the "arch enemy of popular government," a phrase which gained currency as more and more Prohibitionists were convinced, not without cause, that the "saloon-slum element" in American urban politics actually determined the course of congressional and presidential elections.

But the "broad gauge" in 1892 meant broad protest: that a tariff should be levied "only as a defense against foreign governments which levy tariff" on American goods; that railroads "should be controlled by the Government"; that "foreign immigration had become a burden . . ." St. John, however, insisted that the Prohibition Party, if it were to survive at all, must embrace the reform of free silver. This insistence shattered the 1896 convention into "broad gauge" reformers behind St. John and "narrow gauge" drys behind General John Bidwell of California. In the political farce which followed, St. John, then a man of pure principle and utterly no politics, led his free-silver drys out to form the National Party, which polled a sorry 15,000 votes that November.

Thereafter, the single-minded Prohibitionist protestors almost disappeared into the deserted ruins of American political history. They felt that they had been cheated and victimized, that their defeats and failures resulted from a conspiracy of money-mad powers in the United States—the aggregate of migrant–party-boss capitalism which financed the corrupt elections and controlled the press. Without hope, they became increasingly impatient with political processes and suspicious of the political procedures from which they had indeed suffered, increasingly convinced that the American public was locked in a closed circuit of an industrial-saloon establishment and would never vote as it should. A depressing record supported this conclusion: Prohibitionists occasionally elected a state legislator or minor municipal official, but they never came close to the assumption of serious political power in any state. One sees their fate represented in an obscure Prohibitionist coroner of Gibson County, Indiana, who in rendering a verdict of death for a man killed by a railroad train in the 1890s recorded that if the man "had not been drunk, he would not have been killed," and that "if there had been no saloons to tempt him, he would not have been drunk." He concluded officially that in the matter of this death the voters of the state and the state legislature were equally guilty.

Before they disappeared, some of them, to be sure, reached the stern-minded conclusion that the public should be *forced* into Prohibition, though none ever devised a coherent plan for bringing about such coercion. A case study in this set of mind (because we have an autobiography) is Edward B. Sutton, the lecturer sent by party leaders into the West in the late 1880s, when they thought there was a good chance of voting Prohibition into the constitutions of the new states of North Dakota, South Dakota, Montana, and Washington. Sutton's father was from England, his mother from Vermont. Both, he said, were antislavery "fanatics" who had worked the Underground Railroad in Michigan. Sutton fought in the Civil War and marched with Sherman to the sea. He was "converted to God in his twentieth year" and ordained in his thirtieth. He often compared himself to William Lloyd Garrison, whose single-minded and passionate fanaticism he greatly admired. Sutton's burning ambition after the war was to "annihilate the drunkard-making business."

He was the kind of articulate and often fascinating speaker who could tell a thousand jokes, mimic a drunkard's incoherence, then burst into a highly emotional condemnation of drink, saloonkeepers, and saloons. He delivered 400 speeches a year in the early 1890s. He had been viciously beaten by a saloonkeeper, a critical event in his life which distinguished him as a martyr and inflamed his militancy. "The question," he would call to street crowds in the small towns than springing up along the tracks of the Great Northern Railroad, "the question is not, Is public sentiment ready for prohibition, but Is prohibition right? Public sentiment was not ready for the Ten Commandments when they were first given." Or he would consider the matter of personal liberty: "If your liberty to take a glass of beer when you want it means the subjugation of a nation to the worst enemy man ever had, I would dash your beer glass into a thousand pieces."

For a few of the darkest years of the 1890s, Sutton was seized, as were many of his friends, by the kind of class-conscious hostility to non-Protestant foreigners which, since the time of Lyman Beecher and Neal Dow, had occasionally gripped Prohibitionists when they observed the drinking habits of recent immigrants—"the ignorant horde," a Prohibitionist newspaper reported, "that Europe sends over here to rule America" with the ballot box "via the rum hole." Sutton joined the American Protective Association, an anti-Catholic group of men and women, most of whom could believe that the pope in Rome was commanding Catholic immigration into the western states so that priests could there begin to control American schools and governments. With fellow Protective Association conspirators in the 1890s, he worked secretly through several political organizations to keep known Catholics from being hired by the public schools or elected to political office. From abolitionist to

Prohibitionist, from victim to conspirator, he always believed that the end justified the means—a belief shared by many of the Prohibitionists who stayed with him into the twentieth century. The means to the end, however, were never available, and in the next decades they came together more to share their common rejection than to explore any political reality.

Such people were openly cheering Carry Nation's "hatchetation" when it erupted in 1900. Carry Nation had been a jail evangelist, a member of the WCTU, and a protestor close to Prohibition politics since 1888. When she began destroying saloons with rocks, iron bars, and then hatchets in the town of Kiowa, Kansas, the saloons were flagrantly open and illegal. Saloon interests were making a concerted effort to change the constitution of the state, which, since the governorship of St. John, had prohibited the manufacture and sale. In the dozens of raw, new towns, saloons had become omnipresent, but many state and city officials refused to close them. Because they were illegal and thus free from any regulatory standards whatsoever, they were also an open mockery of bourgeois values, as debauched and corrupt as any saloons in the country. As such they were an invitation to violent expressions of frustration which might be consistent with the state's background in bloody mayhem.

Carry Nation's own background was one of disease, misfortune, and madness. She saw herself in the image of John Brown, as a self-annointed martyr who from the deep well of fanaticism had drawn the courage to strike against evil when nonviolent methods failed. She found an antisaloon, abolitionist following, and the more she chopped and smashed, the more she was praised and cheered by her followers. She did go to jail, but never for long, for city officials found it awkward to prosecute her if they had to admit the existence of illegal saloons. Ministers and businessmen paid her fines. Crowds followed her from town to town. Encouraged by the Prohibitionist press, she soon saw herself not only as a protestor but as a divinely ordained liberator.

During her greatest notoriety, writers found it easy—as they still do today—to humor themselves with distortions of her possible significance to the saloon business, to the Women's Movement, and to the state of Kansas. They saw her as a comic figure, a sort of bizarre clown riding on what was quite literally the lunatic fringe of the Prohibition Movement. And Carry Nation did say and do things that were not in good taste or even in good sense; she was quite capable of stripping herself of her essential dignity. In a recent biography called *Vessel of Wrath*, Robert Lewis Taylor describes a raid in which

> Mrs. Nation smashed one saloon's Venetian mirror with brickbats, flung stones through a second saloon's windows, leveled a half-brick at the head of a boy attempting to sweep up . . . ripped some candid and stimulating prints from the walls, powdered the bric-a-brac and glasses, separated the rungs from all chairs, drop-kicked a cuspidor over a pot-bellied stove and threw a billiard ball at what she mistakenly took to be Satan lounging behind the bar. . . . Before leaving, she begged to be arrested and then sang a number of hymns, only to express herself as insulted when a saloon-keeper said it was the worst atrocity she had committed yet.

And she did play to the crowds. She passed out miniature hatchets. She made absurd claims and predictions and fell easily into the conceit of presumed authority and leadership. And few events of the day could have been more newsworthy than a wildly determined middle-aged woman who smashed huge mirrors, destroyed expensive paintings of nudes, knocked drinks from the hands of respected citizens, and slashed the polished mahogany, all to the high chant of her communications with the Holy Ghost.

At the time of her death in 1911 she had become something of a carnival freak. As a sideshow for a series of county fairs, armed with hatchets and her Bible, she cried out to the amused crowds that gathered for her fantastic appearances. Some historians have since found it easy to analyze the frustrations and inhibitions and repressions that drove her into God-ridden fears and fantasies. To most people who know her name today she probably evokes an image of sensual and sexual distortion—the blue-nosed Puritan, the personification of stern, life-hating denial and negation.

To understand Carry Nation, however, it may be more significant to analyze the frustrations, inhibitions, and repressions of bourgeois aspirations in Kansas. The saloons were illegal; they were blatantly defiant; they were both symbol and reality of social disorder. It is easy to overlook the startling fact that Carry Nation could impress thousands of people with an urgent emotional logic which caused men—college students, merchants, ministers, lawyers, mechanics—to join mobs. In Winfield, Kansas, for example, in 1901 the "war" was no comic figure of speech. When Carry Nation aroused 2,000 men to move with her against the illegal saloons, these men brought out 500 rifles and hauled two cannons to protect their churches, which had become fortifications for antisaloon families. Churches were stoned, homes were burned, and wells were poisoned. Though there were no deaths in Winfield, the antisaloon mob issued an ultimatum in which they promised to hang the first man who harmed one of their members. The saloons did close.

The image of blue-nosed morbidity can also obscure the terrible and terrifying spirituality of Carry Nation's energy. She had suffered as few have suffered, even in Kansas. With a family history of sometimes grotesque insanity (her mother thought herself to be Queen Victoria. and Carry Nation was in childhood already afflicted with visions), with a personal history of disease and convulsion, she was throughout her life humiliated, insulted, cursed, physically abused, and threatened with death. In Enterprise, Kansas, a dingy cow town in 1901, she marshaled the temperance families against the saloons and started by swinging an ax at the head of the town marshal. But she was set upon by hired thugs and prostitutes, pelted and drenched with rotten eggs. whipped with rawhide, beaten with clubs, clawed until some of her hair was torn out, kicked in the gutter. Blood streamed from her face, and she was in that episode very nearly murdered.

The middle-class respectability which Carry Nation sought always eluded her. Trying desperately to be a decent wife and mother, she was stricken by marriage and then divorce from an alcoholic—who staggered drunk to the wedding altar, drunk to the nuptial bed, and drunk to an early grave—then marriage to a self-styled minister of the gospel who was a weak and self-deluded fraud. Her daughter was enfeebled and diseased and was sometimes regarded as insane. Her life was a crooked line of poverty, disorder, sorrow, disaster, madness. Herbert Asbury's fine study, *Carry Nation,* (1929), shows that she had a "shattered nervous sytem" and was, during some seizures, darkly demented. Rather than as the comic, she should stand in social history as the kind of character Dostoevski might have imagined on the plains of Kansas—dedicated, suffering, and possessed.

To see Carry Nation as more saint than clown, more a symbol of social disorder than of Victorian sexual distortions, is not to dismiss her destructive fanaticism as casually as earlier critics dismissed the objects of her grief and determination. As Clarence Darrow wrote in pointed reference to many of the Prohibitionists he had known, "the number of people on the borderline of insanity in a big country is simply appalling, and these seem especially addicted to believing themselves saviors and prophets. It takes only a slight stimulus to throw them entirely off balance." Carry Nation was among those so unbalanced, though her stimulus was by no means slight.

We may return now to the conceptualizations which began this chapter—of a society responding to disorder through the process of "bureaucratization," by which sensitive citizens were learning the techniques of organization, centralization, and impersonal authority, and were applying these techniques to the purposes of social discipline. If we stress again the different responses of protest and reform, our most dramatic examples emerge in the contrast between Frances Willard and Carry Nation.

In her remarkable career, Frances Willard had been first
attracted to the cause of women's rights, and then to temperance, but she was soon deeply concerned with the campaigns
against the many perils to bourgeois values which seemed to
grow more distressing each year: wage slavery, prostitution and
venereal disease, slums, political corruption, public ignorance.
Formerly the dean of the Women's College and professor of
esthetics at Northwestern University, she was admirably prepared for leadership in the "bureaucratization" of American
life. When she accepted the presidency of the WCTU in 1879,
she began her sustained effort to shape a new consciousness in
the United States—woman consciousness. She was all the while
a profoundly conservative defender of duty, individuality,
dignity, and self-respect. To secure these vlaues, she twisted
the phrase *home protection* into a sort of rhetorical armor for
temperance, equal suffrage, and other reform activities which
women of the late nineteenth century would join to shape
instruments of social control.

From the beginning of her association with the movement,
Frances Willard held views essentially at odds with the views of
fanatics like E. B. Sutton and Carry Nation. She was always
more inclined to organize the social agencies through which
decent citizens might persuade a saloon regular to join the sober
and respectable middle-class America than she was ever
inclined to confront him personally and terrorize him into giving
up his antibourgeois ways. Or, if the drunkard were beyond
help, she wanted an impersonal but effective social agency to
save his children. For example, in the 1880s the WCTU began a
campaign for state laws which would make "scientific temperance instruction" mandatory in the public schools. Women
organized to endorse candidates for public office who favored
such laws, and they learned to pressure legislatures with letters,
with attendance at open meetings, and with impressive petitions. Applications of these techniques were notably successful
in New York in 1884 and in Pennsylvania in 1885, where the law
was a model of its kind—and of control—because it denied
funds to school districts which failed to provide temperance
instruction.

What the WCTU wanted, though, was hygiene education advocating total abstinence and stressing the conviction that alcohol was a poison. At first, legislators were reluctant. More seriously, textbook publishers resisted the laws, fearing that teachers would refuse to use books written to satisfy Frances Willard and her colleague in this reform, Mary Hunt. A poll taken in the 1890s did indicate that most public school teachers questioned both the facts and the theories WCTU leaders were pressing upon them. Mary Hunt, however, organized a committee of well-known scientists, including two past presidents of the American Medical Association, and she dismayed the teachers with a brilliant campaign of scientific refutation. She subsidized the writing of two books, *The Child's Health Primer* and *Young People's Physiology*. Her attack was strikingly effective, and both teachers and publishers began to respond. By 1902 the WCTU was happy to endorse as many as thirty-three commercial "temperance" text-books then available to the public schools.

Ultimately every state had a law which required temperance education. The laws were, in some areas, variously subverted, distorted, exaggerated, or ignored. But many states required teachers each year to affirm that such instruction had in fact been given. The effectiveness of all this cannot be measured, but it is clear that the agitation for these laws drew into the movement many teachers, scientists, parents, and, of course, children. However indifferent or passionate the instruction may have been, few Americans by the time of national Prohibition in 1920 had been able to escape it.

And parallel to this achievement in social control, Willard organized activities in the various reform "departments" of the WCTU, which included Penal and Reformatory Work, Work among Colored People, Work among Foreigners, Work among Railroad Employees, Work among Lumbermen and Miners, Work among Indians, Anti-Narcotics, Peace and International Arbitration, Franchise, and Social Purity. She herself headed the Social Purity Department and spent much of her energy working toward goals defined by the social anxieties of which the antisaloon movement was an inseparable part: laws to make seduction a crime, to raise to eighteen the age at which girls could legally consent to sexual intercourse—when this age of consent was in some states in the 1880s as low as seven—and to abolish prostitution.

Central to all her concerns was her increasingly creative interest in political solutions to social problems. When it was clear to her that neither the Home Protection Party nor the National Prohibition Party would ever hold power, Willard tried to take the WCTU into the People's Party, where the open criticism of urban-industrial society suggested to her that she might be welcome. She became in fact chairwoman of the first People's Party convention and used the WCTU departments to help Populists in 1892 and 1894. In 1896, however, Populist leaders felt so close to victory that they were not at all eager to lose any wet votes because of Willard's work.

By that time, however, it was unlikely that her attraction to Populism—even had Populism been successful—would have endured. Willard had been deeply influenced by the kind of Christian socialism which Edward Bellamy had made popular with *Looking Backward,* his novel published in 1887. (She was not impressed by Eugene Debs, who later led the American Socialist Party; he drank.) As she joined the Society of Christian Socialists and made some close friendships with British Fabians, she tried more and more to pull the WCTU toward socialist principles and ideals. From the platform of national WCTU conventions, she urged women to see conservative Christian morality in the policy of a guaranteed wage and in the principle of collective ownership, which, she believed, would prepare society for the time when "The New Testament will be the basis for regulating human behavior."

Though she never lost her commitment to work toward Prohibition, Willard came to take a more complex and perhaps more somber view of American society than was possible for most of her colleagues in the WCTU. In a final break with the older doctrines of Prohibition, she came to believe that drunkenness was a *result* rather than the *cause* of poverty and that social evils like saloons and prostitution were the inescapable consequence of the competitive capitalist-industrial system. This is to say that she saw morbid drinking as the *solution* rather than the *problem* itself, which was life in the urban industrial environment. These views of course were never accepted by the WCTU. She alienated some women, bored others, and at last aroused only a few to a higher social conscience. Her great achievement was the integration into the Temperance Movement of conservatives, moderates, and radicals, held together by the strength of her personality even during the 1890s.

One direction of moral "bureaucratization" in American society during the lifetime of Frances Willard was clear as more and more people demanded that their governments (for a long while this meant *state* governments) defend the essentially pietist character of their way of life. By using the power of the state, they hoped to abolish or at least to restrain the institutions which they regarded as alien or uniquely sinful and threatening: slavery, the liquor traffic, polygamy, adultery, Masonry, Mormonism, prostitution. (These institutions had nothing in common except that at one time or another in the nineteenth century certain Protestant groups felt threatened by one or all of them—and thereby regarded them as un-American.)

A critical development in American moral and political history occurred when the focus of this fear fell on Roman Catholicism. Native Americans had for generations been encouraged in this by preachers as prominent as Lyman Beecher, who, while fighting liquor and slavery, had predicted a great struggle between "Christianity" and "Popery" for the American soil and the American soul. There were many Protestants who, though lacking this apocalyptic vision, still regarded Catholic immigrants as lower-class, illiterate, and vulnerable to evil habits. Such newcomers seemed to be especially clannish in their strange ethnic identities. They seemed in need of directions to honor the Sabbath, to resist the liquor traffic, and to assimilate the bourgeois lifestyle. They seemed too much given to an open and public quality of life—they congregated in saloons—than to a private dignity and too much given to a priestly rather than a bourgeois familial discipline. This strain of bigotry was reinforced by a rich tradition of Anglican and Calvinist prejudice against Rome and by the experience of Scandinavian Lutherans, whose mother country governments had been anti-Catholic since the Reformation. It was also a mutual bigotry, for most Catholic immigrants were from cultures which had been historically anti-Protestant.

Anti-Catholic sentiments had found their partisan channels in the 1840s and 1850s when the major American political parties began to break under public demand for the government to act on matters of the liquor traffic, immigration, and slavery. Most of these issues were very much alive when in the 1870s the prohibition party clustered them in a demand that government do something about saloons, "white slavery," gamblers, and the "worthless, dangerous, disorderly, unproductive citizens" who in the United States were threatening the "purity, peace, and happiness" of the American home.

The historian Richard Jensen, in what he calls "the historical roots of party identification," has traced a conflict between "pietists" and "liturgicals" which reveals in this regard a deep relationship among certain religious identities and certain political agitations. The pietists (principally but not exclusively Methodists, Presbyterians, Baptists, and Scandinavian Lutherans) were those attracted to a revivalism and evangelism which emphasized the emotionality and the individuality of conversion more than the community of the church. They demanded of their members visible proof of individual redemption, measurably good works, and good behavior. The liturgicals (principally but not exclusively Catholics, Episcopalians, and German Lutherans) were usually those who conversely emphasized the church as an institutional community and fellowship in which creed and ritual were vital, in which "right belief" and doctrinal loyalty were more important than "right behavior." Pietists could be excommunicated for evil deeds, liturgicals for heresy.

Jensen shows that these essentially religious distinctions were more important in politics than ethnic, economic, or even cultural identities—that, for example, German Catholics voted

more with Irish Catholics than with German Methodists.
Liturgicals disliked revivals. They avoided abolitionists, even
though they might not favor slavery. They shunned Prohibitionists, even if they favored sobriety. They had usually
opposed Lincoln because he led the country into war. They
deplored the draft, and they distrusted nativist exhortations.
They were, that is to say, those who resented the intrusion of
government into what they considered to be provinces of
spirituality and private morality, where the church, not the
state, had an ultimate jurisdiction. Jensen's conclusions, in *The
Winning of the Midwest: Social and Political Conflict, 1888-96*
(1971), make it clear that there were many in-between
categories and many people who fit no categories at all. His
primary distinctions, however, are very useful to any explanation of what happened in American political life after the Civil
War, when these identities were, as he says, perhaps the most
important dimensions of political conflict.

It was, accordingly, the pietist protesters and reformers, like
Frances Willard, St. John, and their followers, who disrupted
Midwestern Republican politics in the 1880s. Pietist protesters
were inclined to join the Prohibition Party, just as earlier
protesters joined abolitionist groups, and to become increasingly hysterical in their insistence that the state protect their
lifestyle. They wanted state constitutions to do even more than
prohibit the saloon and abolish polygamy and "the social evil";
they hoped to mandate the "national observance of the Christian Sabbath" and the use of the Bible in the public schools as "a
textbook for the purest morals, of the best liberty, and the
noblest literature." (These are phrases from St. John's Prohibitionist platform of 1876.) There were of course many
reformers who shared all these views but who would not join the
Prohibitionists. The party, in fact, collapsed precisely because
most pietists would not abandon their loyalties, sanctified by
civil war, to the party of Abraham Lincoln. They instead tried to
work within the Republican ranks to achieve the basic pietist
expectations, demanding that state platforms and the candidates themselves give the party the face of pietistic

Americanism.

As their efforts increased, Republican bosses were severely strained in the 1880s to keep the party from becoming an antiliturgical party. Because the larger cities—vital to state and national victories—were usually liturgical strongholds, state party leaders had the difficult duty of preventing the party from coming apart at its rural and urban seams. In 1888 they made their most significant concession to the pietists when the national platform delicately favored "temperance and morality" and the "purity of the American home." It was almost too late.

According to Richard Jensen's study, a liturgical counterrevolt was already in motion, and it struck Republicans in the Midwest with a disaster in 1889 and 1890 that cost the party almost all the governorships and congressional delegations which had traditionally been theirs since the Civil War. In Iowa, for example, the liturgical Germans had slipped away from their Republican loyalties when the German counties voted against the Prohibition amendment in 1882, and they did not return to the party until 1896. This slippage allowed Horace Boies, the Democratic candidate for governor in 1889, to campaign against fanaticism, for tolerance and pluralism in American life, for lower tariffs, and for friendly attitudes toward the German and the Irish. His Republican opponent held only the strongest pietist counties as Boies won the election then and again in 1891.

Republicans, especially in the Midwest, were thus desperate. They complained that Prohibition did not so much prohibit drinking as it prohibited Republican victories. They had "played with firewater," Jensen says, "and they were burned." If they were to return the essential electoral votes in 1892 and 1896, they had somehow to blur their moral image without actually purging the drys from the party. With the assistance of the Panic of 1893 and of William Jennings Bryan's uncompromising pietism, and his frightening of people with the doctrine of free silver, they did indeed revert to the stability of economic issues, leaving the more ardent dry reformers for a confused moment without a visible political home.

6

A League
of Pietists

WE HAVE SEEN that the search for order in the nineteenth century brought many Americans to demand of state governments what the churches, in their disestablishment, could no longer provide—a source of firm moral authority over the discipline of interpersonal relatonships. To phrase it more broadly, they wanted precisely what the philosophers of individualism like Emerson and Thoreau most dreaded—state governments which could exert an authoritarian, pervasive, and confident moral stewardship. In the continuing disorder of America, millions of people asserted these demands, and by the time of Neal Dow's triumphs, their energies had shaped bodies of state law which described essentially evangelical Protestant or pietist societies.

But it was a nation in upheaval. There was war, more westward migration, industrialization, urbanization, foreign immigration—complex processes of disorder and social change from which arose a confusion of values that could be seen as rural, urban, western, eastern, ethnic, Catholic, Protestant, pietist, or liturgical. There was the increasingly sharp political conflict over which, if any, of these values the state should protect or defend. As the American saloon came to present an antipietist symbol, pietists became more militantly determined to have the state abolish it. They experimented with a variety of political dynamics—the Prohibition Party, the Populist Party, the Republican Party. But issues from the new American marketplace—such as free silver, tariff, and monopoly—always intruded upon their doctrines of moral stewardship. It was, moreover, soon clear to pietists that they could not crack the tight political loyalties welded into American life by the Civil War. It was also clear—during the years of accelerating industrialization, urbanization, and immigration—that neither of the two major parties would yield to an avowedly pietist morality. Indeed, they could not yield, for in taking national identities, rather than regional or cultural or class identities, they were competing for the same majorities. The major parties would in the future function more to compromise the frightful diversities and conflicts in American life than to sharpen them in confrontation.

There could, however, be a nonpartisan pietist politics. Those who understood this possibility of the bureaucratic society were for the most part the thoughtful temperance workers who in the 1890s organized and then refined what became the most effective pressure group in American political history, the Anti-Saloon League of America. This is still our classic case study in pressure politics—the use of power in every way consistent with American poltical procedures. The name itself reflected a shrewd estimation of the American middle-class conscience, which was not yet willing to accept alcohol alone as the antibourgeois symbol but was increasingly disturbed by the reality of the saloon. The league, with its background of pietist ambitions in a nation rushing toward bureaucratic manipulation, became a lens through which the various and diffuse energies of Prohibition, evangelical Christianity, feminism, social purity, and political reform could be brought into sharp focus.

The league found its structure and its potential in Ohio, where it emerged from a long and tumultuous tradition of militant reform. Oberlin College had since its inception in 1832 been a community of radicals. It was the first American college to accept women as students; it welcomed Negroes as early as 1835; it functioned as a station on the underground railway in the 1840s and 1850s, when it became a sort of overground shelter for academics who were active abolitionists. When in the years following Reconstruction the president and the faculty of the college decided to attack the saloons in Oberlin, they were not the kind of men who could be patient with polite pleading or moral suasion. They wanted relentless political action aimed at driving the saloons there and elsewhere completely out of existence.

In 1887 they determined to write a state law which would allow the local governments rather than the state legislature the option of abolishing saloons, and to lead this movement they arranged for the Reverend H. H. Russell to leave his pulpit for full-time work on the state legislature. Russell, who had come to temperance because of the afflictions of his alcoholic brother, proved to be an impressive bureaucrat, lobbyist, and manager. He brought several chruch congregations together in a Local Option League and began to show his followers that well-disciplined waves of petitions, letters, and telegrams could have a profound impact on legislators. Russell got his law. Then, after organizational work in Missouri and Illinois, he returned to Oberlin in 1893 to unite a statewide league of men and women interested in moving beyond county local option on liquor licenses to the abolition of all saloons in Ohio. The success of this unification attracted national attention and led in 1895 to the first convention of the Anti-Saloon League of America.

In devising appropriate bureaucratic techniques, Russell demonstrated keen peceptions. He learned to use the individual Protestant congregation as his basic organizational unit. He enlisted the preacher as a sort of precinct whip who accepted the direction of a highly centralized authority in Oberlin. Within the state—and later in all states—a board of trustees or an executive committee represented the several congregations and activist groups. This board appointed a state superintendent, who had been nominated by the national office in Westerville, Ohio, to conduct the programs of education, propaganda, and political action which could advance the new crusade.

The early success of the league sprang in part from the

intelligence of its leadership and in part (to repeat again) because the national temper, even among those who enjoyed alcoholic beverages, was increasingly alarmed by the abuses of the saloon. When, for example, the Progressive-Republican legislator Philip Bancroft of California sent his donation to the state ASL, he noted that "I am not a prohibitionist and do not intend to vote for prohibition, but I want to do my little to assist in your campaign against saloons." The San Francisco reformer Franklin Hichborn, who was personally wet, would help the Anti-Saloon League because, he said, "the only way to get rid of the saloon evils is to outlaw the entire liquor traffic." And the worst of these saloon evils, according to men like Jack London, was that saloons created drinkers and drunks. London felt that the quality of life in America would improve measurably when the saloons were abolished, and he felt further that it would improve extraordinarily when in the course of a saloonless era the addicted drinkers themselves began to vanish, taking their filthy habits, their bottles, vats, and crocks, along with them. Such men believed that this would happen quite naturally, with no unseemly problems of oppression or resistance, once men of goodwill had struck the fatal blow to the old-time saloon. In this mood they could drink their drinks, as Jack London did, and support the antisaloon crusade, or at least watch it move. Even as late as 1917, Senator Morris Sheppard of Texas, who was doing precisely what the ASL wanted him to do in Congress, was saying that "I am not a prohibitionist in the strict sense of the word. I am fighting the liquor traffic. I am against the saloon. I am not in any sense aiming to prevent the personal use of alcoholic beverages."

The ASL leaders with whom Sheppard worked, however, never concealed their ultimate intent, which, following the abolition of the liquor traffic, was to fashion the kind of social controls which could indeed abolish the personal use of alcohol. But the march toward a victory of "bone-dry" values, they said, would not be through the confusion and distorted loyalties of political revolution, which they identified as the mistaken goal of the older, bitterly partisan Prohibition Party. Rather it would be an inexorable "evolution" moving upon education and conventional political change toward a society in which no one would *want* to drink anything alcoholic. In the early 1900s, the first stage of this evolution was to be the abolition of saloons, and this was a goal that many people would support even though they might not for a minute believe that the ASL could ever in their own lifetimes go the full distance to the bone-dry ideal.

To approach this first stage, the ASL sponsored pieces of muncipal and state legislation which could narrow the range of saloon outrages. Local and state leagues worked for laws to prohibit gambling and prostitution, to halt the sale of liquor to minors, to close the saloons on Sundays. Few Americans would actively oppose such restrictions, and the ASL could count on the support of churches, business groups, and civic organizations. Another approach was through "high license," or the levying of fees calculated to drive the most marginal operators, who were usually the most desperate and degenerate, out of competition. Then there were "dry zone" laws designed to surround schools, colleges, and military posts with saloonless territory maybe a mile or two in diameter. The character of saloons made such laws difficult to oppose, though the laws sometimes carried an astounding potential. One such proposal, which did not pass, threatened in 1915 to close as many as 500 saloons in the neighborhood of St. Ignatius College in San Francisco.

The direction of these laws was dramatically clear in Pomona, California, where at the turn of the century only two saloons had survived the struggle among the fittest which was then being accelerated by antisaloon legislation. Each saloon was bonded for $5,000 for the licensing period of six months. The plight— one might say the sterility—of these two survivors so neatly illuminates a confluence of bourgeois anxieties in an antisaloon ethic that Gilman Ostrander's account of it should be fully quoted:

> The saloonkeeper was required to be a resident of Pomona, and, if he hired a barkeeper, the character of the barkeeper

was to be passed on by the city council. The saloon itself was required to be on the ground floor, even with the line of the street. Its front was to be more than half of clear glass. It was to be a single room with no furniture other than the bar and a single chair, on which only the bartender was allowed to sit. The saloon was to be so arranged that an unobstructed view of the entire bar could be had from the street. It was permitted to operate from 5 a.m. to 10 p.m. on week days only. No intoxicants were to be sold to any female or to any male under twenty years of age, and if the relatives of a man complained of his drinking in the saloon, his name was to be posted on the saloon wall, and he was to be refused service.

In the ASL scheme of evolution , the steps after these restrictions—which Ostrander calls "exceptionally severe"—were the "local option" laws evolved from the Temperance Movement of the 1830s and refined in Ohio during the 1880s. Local option in the twentieth century became the ASL version of popular sovereignty, the political device for allowing the citizens of local governmental units (town, city, county) to vote yes or no on the question of licensing saloons. Described as the "Jeffersonian doctrine of local control"—a doctrine for which the ASL later had no use at all—it was a critical step toward drying up the states piecemeal, toward gradually isolating wet centers and shattering wet opposition into incohesive geographical fragments. In most states it was necessary for the drys, as they had done in Ohio, to pass a state enabling act for local option, and by 1900 there were thirty-seven states with such laws. In all states the drive toward such laws was frequently integrated with a significant range of progressive legislative aims and achievements.

In California, for example, the legislature of 1911 had before it proposals for women's suffrage, direct legislation (initiative and referendum), recall, antigambling and anti-prostitution laws, and local option, all of which were supported by a wide and articulate majority of reform-minded citizens and lawmakers. As would happen in most states, the legislative alignment in California developed along the lines of classic political drama, with open and hidden compromises, massive lobbying efforts, series of frustrating amendments to amendments to amendments, all of which had to be voted in or out through the confusing layers of committee subterfuge and through final battles on the open floor. It was a struggle in which the reform-minded of both parties played a crucial role. They won in California, where the local option bill authorized elections on the question of ''no-license'' in any town or supervisoral district when petitions from 25 percent of the voters could be validated. In such elections, a majority vote could ban the saloon.

In most state legislatures, as in California, the final passage of such local option laws generated a highly combustible rural-urban conflict. Such conflicts reached their crises when legislators fought to define the ''unit'' of local option: Was it to be the town, the city, the county, or the county outside the cities? The question was really whether or not voters in rural areas would be given an opportunity to vote the cities dry. Would, for example, the antisaloon voters of the total Los Angeles County be allowed to vote the saloons out of the wet city of Los Angeles? Or, to take a broader and even more unsettling question, would the pietist, middle-class values of most rural areas be imposed upon the nonpietist, often ethnic and working-class areas of many larger cities? The answer to both these questions was usually that they would not. It was not an answer which satisfied the league, though its leaders were masters of accepting achievements short of the ideal when compromise might serve the interests of progress. The evolutionists knew that they would need time, and attacking the wet cities before 1914 was, in the scheme of things, to generate a cultural crisis which was simply premature. The rural-urban tensions within the local option legislative conflicts did not so much emphasize a polarity in American society as they indicated a rual-to-urban direction of the antisaloon movement.

Yet even at the more rural levels, where there were often no more than a few thousand people involved and where these people were often socially, economically, and religiously associated, the "saloon question" of local option sometimes burned so fiercely that for months it eclipsed all other issues of community life. In some communities, as pietists formed ranks to outvote liturgicals, it was surely the most intensely bitter and divisive issue of the century. The ASL made it so, planning for months in advance, entering each contest with carefully tested skills and techniques and providing hundreds of examples of how small towns and villages could be overwhelmed by the bureaucratic method. ASL members circulated petitions through the Protestant churches. Others, trained for the moment, went out to organize prayer districts and neighborhoods. Neighborhood captains and hundreds of volunteer soldiers skirmished in door-to-door campaigns for voter registration and for enthusiastic attendance at meetings and rallies.

Of the famous speakers drawn into the great wet-dry debates, Clarence Darrow and the Reverend Billy Sunday found the largest and most emotional crowds. A Billy Sunday revival was a cooperative effort carefully programmed by the evangelical churches for an enduring impact upon church attendance as well as upon the political question of saloons. In June of 1909, for example, the Reverend Sunday came to Everett, Washington, a lumber town of some 25,000 people, where forty saloons were open twenty-four hours a day to soothe the anxieties of men who worked in the woods with axes or in the mills with steam-powered saws. Some saloons catered openly to minors; others tightened the competition with gambling and prostitution, even narcotics. But the town also had forty churches, of which the Methodist and the Scandinavian Lutheran were the most vital and most concerned, and volunteer labor from these churches had constructed a new tabernacle for the famous preacher. On the first day of his revival he addressed more than 12,000 listeners at three meetings with his sermon called "Home, Booze, and Native Land." Billy Sunday was a master of weaving lurid references to local conditions into his standard sermon, of attacking prostitution while belaboring the saloons, and his shocking rhetoric never pulled back from uttering the words *bastard* or *whore*. In several weeks he had convulsed the town into a spasm of repentance which increased church rolls by 2,500 members and ignited a vigorous, sometimes violent, but ultimately successful antisaloon political campaign.

Clarence Darrow came to Everett shortly before election day, supported by wet businessmen who needed saloons to keep mill payrolls in their own business areas and away from more exciting cities. He was also supported by an Episcopal priest. Catholics, however, stood apart from the campaign, fearing perhaps a revival of the American Protective Association, which had been very active in that city only a few years before. Crowds numbering several hundred gathered to hear the famous criminal lawyer and civil libertarian warn them that local option was a "movement of the rich to deprive the poor of certain pleasures they enjoy." In a town of wage earners, this was a message curiously less well received than the hellfire of Billy Sunday.

In his autobiography, Darrow wrote that he had early seen in Prohibition "a fanaticism and intolerance that would hesitate at nothing to force its wishes and way of life upon the world." In his attacks on Prohibition he gave full expression to a narrow view which has endured in some measure ever since; he used the local option campaigns to identify Prohibition with Puritanism, and—in a terribly distended analogy—even with the repressions of the Salem witch trials. In his own day, he said, the Puritans, whom he identified as those who "associated pleasure with sin," had come forth from the Protestant churches to punish intelligent and civilized people who had learned to relax and enjoy gracious living. He saw here a vicious hypocrisy. In rural Protestant-land, he asserted, there had always been "more graves filled from over-eating than over-drinking, but the gluttons quietly groaned their lives away without exhibiting any hilarity or undue emotion in the process, and so were unmolested." In his famous speech called "Prohibition, a Crime against Society," he evoked the spirit of individualism against the "tyrannical and unscrupulous" majority. What Darrow apparently did not appreciate—and his message seldom won an election—was that most voters would not support the indulgent, undisciplined, and antifamily kind of individualism they associated with the city's saloons.

After the speeches in Everett, there were family torchlight parades of men and women marching together, then daylight parades of children, temperance bands, and banners which read "Protect Our Homes." In the ranks of organized labor, militant drys alarmed the wet Central Labor Council with their willingness to help the antisaloon crusade destroy several local unions of brewery workers, bartenders, and musicians. To the considerable distress of community leaders, housewives organized boycotts against wet merchants who had supported Clarence Darrow, and as election day approached there was a rash of fist fights in the streets. After pietist churches that day tolled their bells throughout the polling hours for the "death of the saloon," the returns showed a sharply divided community with a dry majority of 300—in a community where women could not yet vote. It was clear that the mill workers had banned the saloon.

In California, where women did vote in local option elections, the no-saloon areas spread rapidly. Within two years after the state enabling act, half of the supervisoral districts were dry, and 690 towns were dry. By 1914, the seemingly impregnable urban barriers to antisaloon sentiment like San Francisco and Sacramento were identified and isolated. In California, however, as in other states, the factors of urbanization, recent immigration, industrialization, and non-Protestant religious faiths provided no evenly predictable polarities in the wet-dry voting. Berkeley and Santa Barbara were dry, as were Long Beach, Pasadena, Pomona, Redlands, and Riverside. Outside of its major municipalities, Los Angeles County was dry. One can contrast these dry areas in California to the urban, Catholic center of San Francisco and thus emphasize a White Anglo-Saxon Protestant dimension of Prohibition. But the cities of Los Angeles and San Jose, both strongly Catholic and urban, would very soon close their saloons.

In Connecticut, 90 of the 168 towns were dry in 1908. In urban

Chicago, 160 precincts had closed their saloons in 1907, and the trend continued. Cities as highly industrial as Birmingham, Alabama, and Worcester, Massachusetts, were dry in 1908. In 1912 in Vermont, 225 towns voted dry, only 21 wet. In Illinois outside of Chicago, more than 1,000 townships had voted dry by 1908, when the cities began to join the movement: Rockford, Decatur, Freeport, Bloomington, Danville, Waukegan, and Springfield. In Ohio, local option dried up 85 percent of the land area. In South Carolina, all but 5 of 41 counties voted dry before the coming of statewide Prohibition. All in all, rural America— or at least agrarian America—clearly opposed the saloon. What was not so clear was the attitude in nonrural and nonagrarian areas. It would not be clear until more people, especially those in cities where the physical act of gathering enough signatures to validate a local option petition was a near impossibility, had been offered an antisaloon referendum.

The movement toward Prohibition in many states passed through a fairly typical succession of political achievements, which were actually bureaucratic modifications of democratic institutions. Direct primary laws opened nominating elections to the influence of the Anti-Saloon League, which worked for the selection of dry legislators and governors. Supporters of the league passed state local option laws, then constitutional amendments to allow voters the initiative measure. The league then sponsored initiative measures for state antisaloon legislation. Thus the evolution of Prohibition before and beyond local option depended upon several significant reforms within the American political system.

ASL leaders were fascinated by the new experiments with direct primary election laws, which took the nominating process out of the traditional and usually tightly controlled party conventions and placed it before the voting public. Such laws were becoming popular in the early 1900s, especially in the South and West; and within only a few decades primary elections were required by most states. As the movement spread, ASL workers began to refine a system of interviews, questionnaires, and careful studies of legislative records with which they could iden-tify their political friends. The word went out by mail, by newsletter, and by announcement from the Protestant pul-pits with a force that began to influence the character of American political life. Then, with great skill, the ASL used the new primary campaigns—which were experiences that might terrify even the most jaded politicians—to make the ASL endorsement a major factor in many legislative and gubernatorial elections. Thus in the state contests of the Progressive period, the Anti-Saloon League of America was often a profound influence upon the decision of which "progressive" or which "conservative" took office.

In California, for example, the election of 1910 was critical to the league's plans for that state. The Republican candidate for governor, Hiram Johnson, was a Progressive who was neither dry nor avowedly wet. He wanted simply to stay untangled from that issue and campaign against the railroads. But his career would never be so neatly simple. He needed the league's assistance, and he promised to support the league's local option bill before the next legislative session. The state ASL then worked for him rather than for his Democratic opponent, Theodore Bell, who was in fact a dry but whose heavy support from the foreign-born and from the urban centers of the state made him appear unreliable. With the help of the league machine, Johnson went to the governor's chair, where he served the league well enough (the local option law passed and the no-saloon areas were expanded), and then went on to the United States Senate.

Legislators nominated and elected with the help of the ASL were likely to be those most inclined to favor the "red-light abatement" laws which, state by state, were then breaking up organized prostitution. Many state legislatures were caught up in the "white-slave hysteria" which swept over Chicago in 1907 and from there rapidly across the nation. During the following ten years, millions of Americans came to believe that a vast and devious international traffic in young girls forcibly enslaved or trapped them—by alcohol, drugs, or blackmail—into a life of sexual degradation. The hysteria rode on a spicy melodrama, encouraged by the more lurid newspapers and their Sunday supplements, of innocence betrayed, of narcosis, or rape, or lechery, of violent abduction. It encouraged a tendency to suppose that in almost every city alley there lurked a dark and demonic procurer—usually with a thick accent—who was cleverly waiting to inject a potent drug into any girl who might for a moment relax her vigilance. Suppositions about the extent of syphilis in American life, raised with a passionate hyperbole, erupted in an essentially ethnic panic among pietist groups, whose members could believe that competitive prostitution, which surely advanced the disease in American cities, was actually an insidiously commercialized device for genocide which, if unchecked, would soon destroy them.

This was, more broadly, the hysteria of social disorder of a rapidly expanding and unpredictable urban-industrial society. The swelling pluralisms were in sharp tension. It was a hysteria of lifestyles in twisted misunderstandings and impatient conflict. Immigration had been unchecked; the ghettoes unfolded in a squalor appalling to the sober imagination. In the pietist mind, images of syphilis and prostitution rolled in vividly nativist connotations, generating a firm and impatient demand for some effective and comprehensive social control.

Thus stimulated, legislatures began to act, the first in Iowa, where a new law allowed state courts to declare brothels to be "public nuisances" and to enjoin their operators with an order of restraint. Furthermore, if a trail could establish the fact of "nuisance," the court might then issue a permanent injunction, along with an order of abatement which empowered sheriffs to close the premises (a "padlock law") for a full year. In one form or another, this "red light abatement" procedure spread to all the states before or shortly after the Mann Act of 1910 made any interstate traffic in prostitution a federal crime.

Legislators supported by the ASL were also likely to favor the state constitutional amendments which were then bringing to women the right to vote. In this integration of reform moods,

the twentieth century movement for women's suffrage contributed to the antisaloon cause probably what the saloon interests
had all along feared. Though one cannot demonstrate this with
statistics, there is almost every reason to suppose that the
women's suffrage movement reinforced the Prohibition Movement. The reverse was true as well, for it was because of the
Social Purity Movement that many women from bourgeois
homes learned that they wanted to vote. It seems clear that
women thought so, for the records of the significant women's
meetings of the nineteenth and early twentieth centuries show
that delegates wanted to vote against the saloon, against
prostitution, for direct primaries and for direct legislation, for
raising the age of consent, and for making rape a crime subject to
severe punishment. The antisuffrage interests were early convinced that women's rights were linked to Prohibition, and it is
clear that much of the money used to delay the Women's
Movement came from the brewers' associations, who had good
cause for alarm. In those states where women could vote on
such issues before 1919 (Wyoming, Colorado, Utah, Idaho,
Washington, California, Kansas, Oregon, Arizona, Montana,
Nevada, New York), all but two—California and New York—
adopted by popular vote a state law prohibiting the saloon.

The linkage between equal suffrage and Prohibition, however, was not often so simple or obvious as the brewers assumed
it to be. For example, the Women's Movement was often
distinct from the Women's Suffrage Movement. The first, a
broad movement for women's rights, was a reform movement of
social radicals whose pronouncements about individual freedoms or even free love might sound like terrible threats to the
family and cause deep chagrin to the advocates of "home
protection" through women's suffrage. Furthermore, not all
women's rights advocates were antisaloon. The leading suf-
fragist on the Pacific coast, Abigail Scott Duniway, thought
Prohibition was a great mistake. Liquor, she believed, was like a
snow storm; God created it, and people should protect themselves from it, not try to prohibit it. She blamed the drys for her
early defeats in Washington, Oregon, and California, and she

was furious with the WCTU, the "frenzied friends of prohibition" who, she believed, worked for suffrage only as a "short-cut attack on the saloon" and simply frightened the liquor interests into financing the campaign against women's rights. In her autobiography, *Path Breaking: An Autobiographical History of the Equal Suffrage Movement in Pacific Coast States* (1914), she wrote that when the WCTU was "of recent origin on the Coast . . . its rank and file were not suffragists. They never lifted voice or finger to secure their right to vote, but had often sat in the sanctuary singing 'Where Is My Wandering Boy Tonight.' when the little hoodlum was kicking up a rumpus at my suffrage meetings." Duniway argued at length with Susan B. Anthony about the infiltration of Prohibitionists into the Suffrage Movement, and she carried her arguments before conventions of the National American Woman Suffrage Association.

We see here again a significant distinction between "protest" and "reform." Some "friends of prohibition," especially after the death of Frances Willard, were sometimes so "frenzied" in protesting against the saloon that their excesses were embarrassing to suffrage leaders, who saw any women's fanaticism as a serious threat to the Suffrage Reform Movement. It is interesting in this regard that Aileen Kraditor, in *The Ideas of the Woman Suffrage Movement, 1890-1920* (1965), has found that equal suffrage leaders born before the Çivil War were more likely to be Prohibitionists (many had already been antislavery abolitionists) than were those born after 1865. Thus in the new generation of reformers—even when they were led by older women like Duniway, who was born in 1845—there were many educated women concerned with what they saw as a vital and broadly relevant modification in democratic values. They saw the saloon question as a relatively simple or subordinate question, and they were often frustrated and exasperated when the single-minded Prohibitionists seemed to exploit them or to stand in their way.

Nevertheless, any advance in suffrage reform or in political consciousness after 1900 was likely to advance the Prohibition Movement, which, in many states, faced solid walls of legislative intransigence. Even some legislators who had accepted local option—and had been rewarded with an ASL endorsement—were determined not to follow the ASL any farther into the unknown. Especially among urban lawmakers, many of them dedicated reformers, there was a feeling that popular sovereignty was fine so long as their own individual constituencies were fully sovereign. They would not support state laws which would allow their sometimes very wet districts—should they be outvoted by people in the surrounding rural areas—absolutely no option at all. Faced with this honest and unyielding resistance, the ASL recognized that the course of evolution must lie in some route around the state legislatures, and in this regard direct legislation—the initiative measure and the popular referendum—was the most nearly perfect route ever devised. These tools would, in a sense, allow local option at the state level. This would mean statewide campaigns which, like the earlier local battles, would force the issue upon the public conscience and raise tensions to the degree at which the great majority could not avoid political commitment.

It was the antisaloon vote in Oklahoma, bringing that state into the Union with a dry constitution in 1907, which seemed to give the other state Prohibition measures their momentum. In the South, many legislatures acted before the people could. But in 1914, the people of Virginia, Oregon, Washington, Colorado, and Arizona voted dry after their legislatures had refused to do so. An ASL leader then announced that the saloons of America were "more localized. . . than slavery was when the last stage of that conflict was reached." There were then 20,000 ASL speakers in the field, preaching in every part of the country.

Even in some of the most resistant regions, there were by 1916 signs of significant change. California's statewide elections on Prohibition measures had failed in 1914 and again in 1916, but the second attempt brought 67,000 more dry votes than had been registered two years before. The state ASL had a friendly, Progressive governor, women's suffrage, and a momentum in local option elections, which, by 1916, had abolished saloons in twenty-one counties and in many towns and cities. The league had, furthermore, made remarkably productive efforts to win the support of Catholic voters in antisaloon elections. Through the work of Father M. J. Whyte, a Catholic priest who worked with the league in California, the ASL would, within a year, close the saloons in Los Angeles and San Jose. In these cities, voters accepted the "Gandier Ordinance," which abolished saloons but not the sale of beer and wine for home consumption. Several cities would go as far as the Gandier Ordinance, but no farther, without major revisions in the attitudes of California Catholics. The "Gandier" victories suggested a depth of "moderate" strength that might grow even in San Francisco, which was still "soaking wet," still the "whiskey strip" in the vital geography.

In some of the antisaloon states, moreover, the impact of Prohibition laws seemed in some instances to justify even the most inflated expectations. In the state of Washington, the initiative measure of 1914 had abolished saloons as of January 1, 1916, thus giving them and their patrons an extended period of grace before absolute termination. In the last months before closure, saloonkeepers, brewers, and distillers were beset by a swarm of souvenir hunters collecting artifacts of a dying era. The State Federation of Labor was bidding a sad and bitter farewell to those members who would lose their jobs at the end of the year. Newspapers were setting full-page advertisements for mail-order liquor houses in Montana eager to provide the prepaid legal imports under the new law of three gallons of beer and wine and two quarts of hard liquor a month. The Washington law prohibited the manufacture of alcoholic beverages, which presumably meant that citizens could not make them at home, and thus the courts soon ruled. It also prohibited the sale, which the courts ruled could nevertheless occur out of state if the resident purchasers were properly licensed. Thirsty citizens repaired to their county courthouses to apply for import permits. As the year turned, the ASL announced that Seattle was the largest dry city in the world outside Russia. (To combat wartime drunkenness and to conserve food and chemicals, the czar had in 1914 issued a prohibition ukase—an event which encouraged dry socialists later to believe that sober and clear-eyed, the proletariat had been able to understand their oppression and join the revolution.)

As in most cases, the ASL definition of "dry" severely strained the metaphor. Between January and March in Seattle, sixty-five new drugstores opened to a remarkably affluent clientele. But Mayor Hiram Gill of that city, determined to make a name for himself as a reformer, attacked these new stores with an unpredicted fury. Leading his dry squad personally—shirt-sleeved and ax in hand—he fell upon those stores he suspected of "bootlegging over the counter" and reduced them to pulp and litter. His enthusiasm for vigorous and newsworthy activity led him further to destroy two major restaurants and one hotel. Public outrage over these colorful events caused the liquor interests to take heart and to place an initiative measure for repeal on the 1916 ballot. But to the consternation of wets everywhere, the dry totals in 1916 were higher than those of two years before. One of the most significant aspects of 1916 was the change that took place in urban voting patterns. In 1914, Seattle had been wet by 15,000 votes, a classic urban wet enclave surrounded and tyrannized by a dry rural majority. But in 1916 the city voted dry by 20,000 votes. Spokane had been wet by 1,500 votes in 1914 and was dry by 12,000 in 1916.

ASL statistics for the dry period indicated a dramatic decline in the number of arrests for public drunkenness and in the overall costs of law enforcement. They emphasized increasing bank deposits and decreasing tax delinquencies. The depressed lumber industry was indeed reviving, an economic development as easily related to the war in Europe as to the dry law, but this coincidence in no way diminished the popular esteem in which the law was generally held. A major event of the 1916 campaign had been the conversion of the editor of Seattle's leading newspaper, Major C. B. Blethen of the *Times*, who had studied the statistics of his city and told his story to the nation through *Collier's*. "My paper fought its damnedest against Prohibition," he wrote. But having watched the increase in saving accounts and in retail sales, and the decreasing number of arrests since Prohibition, he had determined that the drier the city became, the better business was. "It makes me sorry," he concluded, "we did not have Prohibition long ago." An editor of another paper remarked sourly that with the saloons gone the people of Seattle would surely now live longer, and that it would "seem twice as long as it really is." The reversal of Blethen, however, a militant wet and lifelong political conservative, had a deep impact in all of the urban areas of the state.

In Oklahoma, where Prohibition had been locked into the state constitution at the time of statehood in 1907, voters became even firmer in their conviction that the constitutional decision had been the proper one. Drys in 1910 neatly defeated an effort to revert the state to local option. Then and in the years immediately thereafter—years of almost incredible disorder in the new oil towns—they had every reason to suppose that statewide Prohibition was an essential barrier against a rising tide of intolerable social chaos. According to Stephen B. Oates's study of "Boom Oil" in Oklahoma, a typical ten-day period during 1913 left the following record in Ragtown, in the southwestern part of the state:

> highjackers shot and robbed two men; a woman was burned to death when Carter County lawmen . . . raided a whiskey joint; a drunken husband beat his wife nearly to death with his wooden leg; a man who had been on a prolonged drunk was found dead in a church and another died after a twelve-day drunk; a brawl broke out in a gambling casino in which two men were shot and two others were killed. When a dispute flared up in a second gambling house over alleged cheating, the winners made a run for it, only to be overtaken outside of town and beaten to death.

In 1914, in an uncommonly restrictive measure which must have been more symbolic than pragmatic, voters amended the state constitution to make public officials subject to impeachment if they were seen drunk in public.

In the South, Prohibition was so solidly entrenched that some of its uglier faces were by 1916 already apparent. The Commissioner of Prohibition in Virginia accepted the enlistment of 500 volunteers to advise him of any lawbreaking in their districts and thus ordained a host of WCTU-ASL vigilantes to work independently of organized police forces. Because blacks and poorer whites found it almost impossible to take advantage of import tax and permits—a system similar to that in the state of Washington—their plight quickly attracted a legion of bootleggers. The number of arrests and indictments among blacks and poorer whites was, accordingly, very high.

It would be wrong, however, to conclude from this that the Dry Movement in the South was a social movement to repress blacks by denying them liquor. In Georgia, local option came through the legislature in 1885, several years in advance of the really vicious laws for racial segregation. In Mississippi, a particularly good example, local option was possible after 1886. Thereafter many counties oscillated from dry to wet to dry in local strife that was hot, angry, and almost inevitably racist in tone and conduct. Both wets and drys competed for the black vote, and in the Delta counties, especially, this vote was most frequently manipulated with success by the wets. Under the circumstances, it was almost impossible for the drys not to use a racist argument which would make the Prohibitionists appear to be more antiblack than the wets. There is no evidence, however, that any of these battles ever made civil rights advocates out of the saloon or liquor interests. The broad conclusion which most whites drew from this distressing competition was not that blacks should not drink; it was that in the interests of political stability and social order, blacks should not vote. These people accordingly disfranchised most blacks with the poll tax in 1890, and the wet-dry conflict continued. Mississippi went dry by state law in 1908, but the Vardaman-Bilbo redneck revolt of "poor whites against niggers" did not take over the state until 1910.

By 1916 there was a growing feeling throughout the South that

Prohibition was a very good thing for blacks and whites alike. Newspapers rejoiced that the public drunkards had disappeared from the city streets; businessmen were convinced that the dry laws must have had something to do with the general improvement in business conditions. The old threats of the saloons to polite society seemed to have diminished so sharply that Bishop James Cannon, Jr., of the Methodist Church, the Anti-Saloon League, and the Democratic Party, noted without humor that even the practicing wets in his state were willing to support Prohibition so long as they did not have to give up drinking. Following the general elections that year across the nation, nine more states joined the dry lists: Alabama, Arkansas, Iowa, Idaho, South Carolina, Montana, South Dakota, Michigan, and Nebraska—a total of twenty-three, in seventeen of which it was a vote of the people rather than an act of the legislature which abolished the saloon.

In the South, the Midwest, and the Far West, these remarkably coordinated achievements were possible only with the use of great amounts of money. The ASL did not move on moral force alone, and it had from the very beginning found a number of ways to fund its campaigns. In the first place, local leagues had always enjoyed the considerable financial support of those who stood to realize immediate financial gain as the saloons suffered: restauranteurs who resented the saloon free lunch, employers who resented the saloon's contribution to boozily inefficient labor, employers to whom the saloon meant sullen hangovers, accidents, indifference, or even drunken insolence. Then there were, in addition, millions of taxpapers early convinced that as a matter of simple social economics—the costs of a police force to capture drunks, of jails to house them, of social workers to guide their families, of welfare costs to feed them, of hospitals and insane asylums—the saloon taxed a community significantly more than it contributed. There were also industrialists of national influence who believed that antisaloon victories made the money which men formerly wasted in saloons available for more substantial consumer goods and industrial profits. It was rumored that during the early period the great John D. Rockefeller was bankrolling the ASL in the interests of the economy and of his own Baptist convictions. And to an extent, he was; his son later said that the family contributions to the ASL were about $350,000.

The actual record of ASL financing is more prosaic than such rumors suggested, but it is also more impressive as an extraordinary triumph of bureaucratic technique among middle and lower-middle income groups. Over 90 percent of the money spent by the national organization (about $2,500,000 a year in the peak years) came in donations of less than $100. The income of the state organizations was always kept separate from the national, and these monies came in even smaller amounts, mostly from men and women who had responded during an Anti-Saloon Field Day at their church by signing a voluntary subscription card which pledged them to contribute a monthly sum, often less than a dollar.

The man who supervised both the gathering and the spending of this money was Wayne B. Wheeler, a lawyer who had joined the Temperance Movement while he was a student at Oberlin College in Ohio. When he graduated from that campus in the depression year of 1893 and began the study of law, he took a job as field secretary with the state Anti-Saloon League. Wheeler also studied the league's potential for releasing his own talents. He soon made Ohio a laboratory for ASL techniques. In Wheeler's first experience with political power, he bicycled door to door throughout his district to bring about the defeat of his state senator. Then with striking success he directed the campaign that persuaded a Republican state to vote Democratic and to defeat Governor Myron T. Herrick in 1905. His work on the legislature produced a new local option law in 1908, and thereafter he organized the campaigns in eighty-eight counties which yielded fifty-eight dry victories in 1910. He refined his methods, reviewed his mistakes, and—drawn into the national organization—trained the corps of state superintendents which the league was sending out after it had discovered Wheeler.

As general counsel, Wheeler served the league in the courts, including the Supreme Court. But as legislative superintendent he later became both the voice and the hand of the national organization. Keenly sensitive to the art of the possible, he helped draft the Prohibition Amendment, and he wrote most of the Volstead Act. Indefatigable, he wrote and spoke in a great flow of speeches and pamphlets, magazine articles, and newspaper stories that he delivered all over the United States and western Europe. At times personally cool and imperturbable, at other times warm and friendly, he was able to attract a passionate following. Described by a wet editor as a man who "works with the zeal of a Savonarola and the craft of Machiavelli," Wheeler was zealous, crafty, and, above all, successful. Another enemy said that Wheeler "would make any combination, would cohabit with the devil himself to win."

Wheeler had mastered legislative processes as well as the strengths, weaknesses, and even the schedules of hundreds of individual lawmakers. His word could arouse millions of league soldiers at any time to exert the proper pressure on the proper Congressman or Senator. Rather than ask personally for a vote, a posture which would have suggested that Wheeler lacked power, he would cover a man's desk with telegrams. "Wheelerism," as both friends and enemies used the term by 1920, meant the techniques of the hard persuasion. In both state and federal legislative chambers, it meant thousands of telegrams and letters and the threat of political annihilation to a man of soft resolve who was tempted to vote wrong in committee or on the open floor.

It brought him a degree of power equaled by few lobbyists in American history. In a sustained series of achievements, he put the 18th Amendment in the Constitution, then until his death fought a relentless and successful battle to keep it there. The Cincinnati *Enquirer*, never a friendly newspaper, called him "the strongest political force of his day." He was the polished professional, bemused at what he called the "usual and asinine" mistakes of the wets who, in his phrase, "always snatch defeat from the jaws of victory." His strength lay in his energy, his intelligence, and his confidence that "this is a moral country. . . . a legislator who votes for liquor or against prohibition votes for vice, sin, and crime." The "moral vote," he knew, was frequently the balance of power, even in wet states where Democrats and Republicans were often closely divided. And it was to the "moral vote" that Wheeler could turn. He was aggressive and severe, a man who believed in punishment and in allowing sinners to take the consequences of their sins. He approved, during the 1920s, the proposal that industrial alcohol should be dosed with poison to discourage its illicit use; if a person wanted alcohol so badly he would commit suicide, so let it be. Hard as iron, he clearly enjoyed destroying the careers and personalities of those who opposed him. Concluding an icy interview with Governor Al Smith during the Democratic National Convention of 1924, he told him, "Governor, you will never enter the White House."

More surefooted, quick, and caustic than other ASL leaders, Wayne Wheeler was a lightning rod for the league and for the dry cause; he gloried in the attacks leveled against him. He was, in total, the most nearly perfect white Anglo-Saxon Protestant Knight of the Pietist Crusade—an adversary without mercy when attacking pluralistic value systems, the master of bureaucratic organization and technique, the manipulator of social and political control. Utterly without sentimentality and finely disciplined, his own ambitions or conceits or vanities were prefectly subordinated to the destruction of the liquor traffic. He never took more than $8,000 a year from the ASL as his personal salary, and he quite literally worked himself to death in 1927.

Wheeler's achievements seem even more impressive when one considers the national prejudices he had to change and the imposing potential of his enemies. Everything the ASL did was opposed by the saloon-brewery-distillery interests, whose resources in 1913 were an estimated billion dollars. The marvelous aspect of this opposition, however, is that it was so consistently unorganized and insensitive. It is now difficult to believe that these interests made no enduring attempt in the twentieth century to impose order upon their saloons or to soften the harsh image the saloons reflected to modern society. But they did not. They made no effort to take from the saloons the connotations of debauchery, depravity, and hostility to middle-class values. Perhaps it was too late, the image embedded too deeply in the national conscience. Or perhaps the disorder which characterized the saloons, their competition, and their apparently natural affinity with corrupt politicians were in themselves evidence that the conglomerates of breweries had inherited a social monstrosity almost totally immune to bureaucratic control or manipulation. This may indeed be a kind of negative evidence that the saloons were so perversely anti–middle class in their values that they could never yield to impersonal authority, restraint, or discipline.

Gilman Ostrander says that in California the saloonkeepers were both too criminal and too stupid to be aware of even the most glaring connotations of their work or the reality of what they were in fact doing to each other. In any event, they practically ignored the entreaties of the Knights of the Royal Arch, which a few saloon men of goodwill had organized around the turn of the century with the hope that they could inspire their competitors to clean up the saloons before the ASL destroyed them. By 1912 there were chapters of the Royal Arch in many cities where the lonely few tried to win public favor by celebrating the saloon as the "poorman's club" and, with even less success, by encouraging other saloonkeepers to disassociate themselves from crime, prostitution, drunkenness, and crooked politics. Aside from a few isolated cases of heroic self-immolation, saloonkeepers simply ignored the warnings. And aside from the few Knights of the Royal Arch, the predictable attitude of the saloon-brewery-distillery interests in their organized postures was arrogant and defensive, then sullen, then often paranoid and hysteric.

There was, for example, the notorious case of the Texas brewers who put up a percentage of their annual net sales— maybe a half million dollars a year after 1905—to organize Negro and Mexican voters, pay their poll taxes, and supervise their wet voting. In this they invited self-destruction, for they could have made no more thoughtful attempt to inflate an antisaloon movement with the racist and anti-Catholic emotions that would soon again grip the nation. The United States Brewers' Association was engaged in the same activities on a national scale, but its efforts which stand out as particularly idiotic were attempts to begin a boycott against the B. F. Goodrich Company, the National Biscuit Company, and the Heinz Pickle Company because some officials of these corporations had personally supported the ASL.

In the face of such tactics, the bulk of Wheeler's opposition seems less than brilliant. However, at one time or another, or concurrently, he confronted the National Wholesale Liquor Dealers' Association, the National Association of Wine and Spirit Representatives, the National Brewers' and Distillers' Association, and the Distillers' Association of America, as well as a host of "liberty" groups, chambers of commerce, and important labor unions. Remarkably, however, these groups never joined effectively to counter Wheeler, and this was the sum total of the organized opposition. There was no independent or honestly disinterested organization of wets until well into the next decade. Before then, any such organized opposition would have been unthinkable. With this fact we are again near the heart of the Prohibition Movement and close again to a definition of the kind of social movement the temperance cause became. Organized, disinterested support of the saloon in American life in the early 1900s would have been just as unthinkable as organized, disinterested support of child labor, or prostitution, or disease in the slums.

7

Tables
of Law

AS SPEAKERS for the Anti-Saloon League explained it, the entire history of the Prohibition Movement had shown that there could be no permissibly wet enclaves within the dry Zion. The very existence of wet states presented constant and insidious threats to the order and security of the dry states,and this, to the ASL, was an intolerable situation. And since 1890, every effort of a dry state to prevent interstate shipments of liquor had been found by the court to violate the exclusive right of Congress to regulate interstate commerce. Because such rulings prevented the states from protecting themselves, the ASL insisted, they made the liquor traffic essentially a national, not a local, crime. If Congress then chose to ignore this crime, an amendment to the Constitution to circumvent the interstate commerce clause was the only way to attack it.

Accordingly, late in 1913, the Anti-Saloon League began its drive for nationwide Prohibition. Taking up their white ribbons—the symbol of temperance borrowed from Frances Willard and the WCTU—some four thousand men and women marched down Pennsylvania Avenue on December 10 to the capitol, where they petitioned Congress. Their resolution proclaimed that "*Whereas,* exact scientific research has demonstrated that alcohol is a narcotic poison, destructive and degenerating to the human organism . . ." It concluded by proposing that the Constitution be amended to prohibit "the sale, manufacture for sale, transportation for sale, importation for sale, of intoxicating liquors for beverage purposes . . ."

The movement toward this petition had been accelerated in

1913 when, to the rejoicing of bone-dry advocates, Congress had passed the Webb-Kenyon Law. This was an act to ban the shipments of "intoxicating liquor of any kind" into states where such liquors could be used "in violation of" state laws. On the face of it, the act simply provided the kind of formal protection which drys in the dry states had for years said they deserved. While it did implicitly condemn the national liquor traffic and the drunkard-making commerce, it required no appropriations of money and it carried no specific provisions for federal enforcement. It seemed to be the kind of noble, if harmless, statement one expected from Progressives and idealists, and on that basis even some wets voted for it. But President Taft, who regarded the law as both repressive and unconstitutional, rejected it. Then, in a dramatic, even stunning, victory, the drys put it through Congress again with a majority large enough to override the President's veto.

The league hailed this Webb-Kenyon victory as another evolutionary and inevitable step toward a dry nation, and its forces moved directly and confidently toward the constitutional amendment. The law itself, meanwhile, was surely headed for a major constitutional interpretation. In his most famous performance as an attorney, Wayne Wheeler successfully defended the law before the Supreme Court and thus made it possible for a dry state to close off the sources of any "intoxicating" beverages which a drinker had not brewed or distilled or fermented for himself, his family, or his friends. For all anyone then knew, such states might even ban the homemaking of all alcoholic beverages, a prohibition which almost everyone supposed to be the ideal that Wheeler and his lieutenants hoped ultimately to impose upon all Americans.

This antidrink sentiment had never been really isolated from the mainstream of the Prohibitionists' ideals. Long before the Anti-Saloon League was ever conceived, Dr. Benjamin Rush had believed that only distilled spirits—not wine or beer—were bad for individuals and for society, and this confusion about the nature of what was in fact "intoxicating" was thus laid at the foundation of the Temperance Movement. But as Rush later came to suspect all alcoholic beverages, neither he nor his followers bothered to change the word *temperance* to *prohibition,* and their casual attitude in this matter has not well served history or the English language. The movement after the 1830s was a bourgeois movement against the liquor traffic, led for the most part, but not entirely, by men and women who had rejected the lifestyle associated with any use of alcohol. But the emergence in the twentieth century of a new generation of reformers who were determined to use bureaucratic techniques to impose their pietist values upon what they saw as a chaotically pluralistic society—determined, in the interest of social discipline, to deny their fellow citizens access to any alcoholic drinks, and grimly determined, it seemed, to abolish alcohol as well as the saloon—suggests a triumph of fanaticism inconsistent with the liberal and humane temper which since the beginning had guided most temperance activities. The conversion of the Anti-Saloon League into an antidrink pressure group further suggests that real radicals had captured one of the most powerful political machines ever fashioned in American life.

But the problem here is that by 1916 in the United States, antidrink sentiment was no longer a clearly radical persuasion; it rose as much from liberal and humane considerations as it did from any other. Just as today it is difficult to understand the debauchery of the old-time saloon, so is it difficult to understand the climate of national opinion in which antidrink proposals could receive such general and solid support. Unless one has shared their experiences, one might find it remarkable that heavy drinkers like Jack London would have supported Prohibition. One might find it even more remarkable that bone-dry leaders could attack liquor without actually attacking millions of vigorous drinkers.

The essential insight, as we have repeatedly noted, is that the vast disorder of American life surely justified keen moral anxieties. Thus the "search for order" was quite naturally directed toward the official and national validation of values which could sustain the family as the vital social institution. The configuration of individual responsibilities implied by these values—duty, restraint, self-discipline—were, in an open society, often violently at odds with any tolerance for personal indulgences or moral pluralisms. Thus, as protecting the family seemed more and more urgent—more so in the disorder of industrialization and urbanization—so more urgency was focused upon the lifestyle of total abstinence.

In this regard another essential insight lies in the impressive body of scientific evidence which by 1916 supported the case for total abstinence. There were, for example, the fairly recent discoveries that alcohol does not warm the body, that it is a depressant rather than a stimulant, and that it depresses the higher mental functions as well as muscular control. Such findings had been the topics of articles in middle-class magazines for a decade. In 1915 a report on life insurance statistics held that as few as two drinks a day would shorten the life of a robust man. Highly regarded studies demonstrated to the satisfaction of many intelligent people a close relationship between alcohol and insanity. It was generally believed that alcoholic parents produced degenerate children.

Many scientists were lowering their estimates of what they regarded as harmless doses of liquor, and some prominent scientists had given up the personal use of alcohol entirely. Among these were August Forel, the Swiss entomologist known for his work on the anatomy of the brain and on sex hygiene, and Emil Kraeplin, a German psychiatrist who had investigated the influence of alcohol on mental processes. It is significant that American psychiatrists and neurologists, at a national meeting in 1914, had declared alcohol to be a poison. Physicians were prescribing less and less alcohol for their patients. Prominent educators—men such as Charles Eliot, president of Harvard—had, on the basis of scientific evidence, taken up the cause of total abstention. Moreover, investigators in the new social sciences supplied a mass of statistics to show relationships between alcohol and crime, prostitution, and poverty. Since studies in scientific management regularly stressed efficiency and sobriety, some American industrial interests, most notably several railroad companies, had actually ordered their employees not to drink at any time, on or off duty.

All these developments could be related to the best scientific thought of the age, and it seems likely that by 1916, science, even as much as organized religion, had prepared people to assume that ultimately everyone should *want* to abstain. As this assumption spread through American society, even among drinkers, it of course shaped the stratagem of the Anti-Saloon League and helped place the ASL in the position of a commanding authority in American politics.

This was clear when, following the Webb-Kenyon victory over President Taft, the league applied its full political pressure to the elections of 1914 and 1916. These elections produced a Congress in which the identified dry members outnumbered the wet by more than two to one. It appeared then to some observers that November 1916 marked a momentous victory, a signal event in national history. It seemed then certain that the dry Congress would raise the spirit of state Prohibition laws to the level of federal legislation, that the movement of a hundred years—the Antiliquor Movement, like the Antislave Movement—would indeed reach its fulfillment in the federal Constitution. Some drys supposed that the forthcoming amendment would be in the form of the Hobson Resolution (Representative R. P. Hobson, Alabama, was an ASL lecturer who spoke widely on "The Great Destroyer"), which proposed that the Constitution prohibit the sale, but not the use, of "intoxicating beverages." The resolution had failed to muster the necessary two-thirds majority in 1914. In 1916, confident of their overwhelming numbers, some Prohibitionists hoped for an even more severely dry amendment.

As their hopes became predictions, the drys were of course absolutely correct; the elections of 1916 did make possible the 18th Amendment. Yet there is reason to be critical of their optimism. It must be a pedantic criticism, to be sure, for it is based on the history of what did not happen, on assumptions about a society which Woodrow Wilson *might have* kept out of war, a society for which war could then not have become the crucible for values fused into a militant collective conscience. But without denying that the elections of 1916 were a great triumph for the ASL, one can suppose that like many popular triumphs of ideals and of the men committed to them, enthusiasms and energies come to a white heat on the day of victory but cool rapidly thereafter. In the normal course of human events, zealots tend to wander, followers to become indifferent, and the committed to slip away from their promised discipline. For the drys to have avoided this slippage in 1916 would have been most uncommon, for the attention and the energies of serious people everywhere were drawn to the death struggle in Europe. Wayne Wheeler himself later acknowledged that even after the great "barrage" of propaganda his followers had laid down against the wets in 1916, he had a problem of how "to maintain public interest in prohibition."

Furthermore, many of Wheeler's drys had been elected in states where the liquor laws were not consistent with antidrink ideals. Many a "dry" Congressman, for example, was from an antisaloon state where the importation of liquor for personal use was both popular and legal. Wheeler could not have supposed that these legislators would suddenly shift from the sentiment of their states toward an antidrink determination. And there were "dry" Senators like Hiram Johnson of California (a wet-dry state), who was "dry" because as governor he had helped the ASL through local option. As Senator in 1917, he sincerely wished that the ASL would disappear. He certainly did not cherish the thought of explaining to the Catholics of San Francisco, and then to the Baptists of Los Angeles, why he had or had not supported federal Prohibition.

And finally, in the approach to a constitutional amendment, there was a historical barrier against which the ASL and all its pressure was almost totally powerless. In Alabama, for example, citizens were gathering in public meetings to declare that while the liquor traffic in their state was "as dead as the men who lived before the flood," they would not allow the federal government to take from them what in the 1870s their fathers had taken from the federal government—the right to determine their own affairs in Alabama. Without the support of southerners in 1916, the ASL could have no national victory. And there was an uncounted number of dry Congressmen and Senators who might never yield in their dedication to states' rights, even if the issue were Prohibition.

The "dry" label of the Anti-Saloon League, then, was no surety of a dry vote. Even though the ASL had demonstrated an awesome power in American political life, there was in 1916 nothing inevitable about the 18th Amendment. It was perhaps in the cards, but the elections of 1916 did not stack the deck; the cards might have fallen promiscuously. But the President of the United States reshuffled them early in 1917.

It was because of the anxieties and the disciplines of the National Preparedness Movement that the cards fell so neatly. The course toward war led through intensified fears of disorder, through realities of sacrifice, and through urgent demands for a strong and healthy nation. Like most wars, it made people extraordinarily sensitive to their common interests, and it brought common—or dominant—values into sharp focus. The effort also sanctified bureaucratic and impersonal efficiencies to the point where almost total social control was possible. And it seemed even necessary to those who believed there could be no victories for boozy nations.

While rallying British workers to increase their productivity and save England, David Lloyd George, then Minister of Munitions, had stated, "We are fighting Germany, Austria, and drink; and, as far as I can see, the greatest of these three deadly foes is drink." His temperance sentiments were well known and widely quoted. In 1916, shortly before he became wartime Prime Minister, he said, "Drink is doing us more damage in the war than all the German submarines put together." And if the war opened vistas of sacrifice and purity, it extended the ugly channels for fanaticism and bigotry. Anything German, like beer, or foreign, like wine, or decadent, like drunkenness, could become a threat to survival. In the short period of two years, antidrink passions and antidrink laws were locked into the American experience more rapidly than even the most wildly optimistic radical of 1916 could have imagined.

When the President severed relationships between the United States and the German government, the Supreme Court that same month upheld the Webb-Kenyon Law, eliminating any further question about the constitutionality of the dry states banning shipments of liquor across their borders. Through the mood of impending war, the effect was electric.

In the state of Washington, for example, a radical WCTU-Grange alliance drove a "bone-dry" law through the legislature with breathtaking expediency. It was a sternly antidrink law which abolished the permit system for imports, except for druggists and clergymen. State ASL leaders regarded it as too radical and actually opposed its movement toward the floor of the House. But the ASL lost control. Despite its resistance, despite a cry that the bill "bears all the marks of passion," the bone-dry bill passed 75-18. In the Senate, only three members opposed the bill, and these three were recognized drys. When the law was upheld by a popular vote of two to one, it seemed to many people that an antidrink storm was sweeping across the nation. The doggedly wet editor of the Seattle *Argus* wrote that "there is only one thing for an intelligent man to do, and that is to climb on the water wagon and stay there." The aging Leopold Schmidt, founder of the Olympia Brewery, soon told his friends that Prohibition was inevitable. "It is a disease," he said, "and must run its course."

In Oklahoma, Governor Robert L. Williams tried to soften an even more fiercely bone-dry provision, one that would prohibit the importation of any alcoholic beverage for any purpose whatsoever. Hoping for a compromise which would allow an individual to import a quart of whiskey or a case of beer each month, he threatened to veto the measure. But when it passed, 89-7 in the House, 32-5 in the Senate, he allowed it to become a law without his signature. Then, in the midst of this dry storm, a group of Oklahoma Catholics placed the doctrine of the Holy Eucharist at the vital center of the Prohibition question. To test the new bone-dry law, a priest in Oklahoma City hoped to import "eight quarts of duly inspected and authorized, pure, unadulterated, fermented juice of grape . . . to be used . . . for the purpose of the celebration of the mass." The railroad refused his shipment, and the Church sought through the courts to demand it. The refusal was sustained by a district court, and while the Church appealed on the grounds of religious freedom to the higher judiciary, the case generated a bitter public dispute and revealed again the anti-Catholicism that could be invested in the Dry Movement. The Ministerial Alliance of Oklahoma City supported the law and the interpretation of the lower court, but the *Daily Oklahoman* defended the priest, contending that it was "fair to assume that comparatively few people . . . however ardently they favor prohibition, approve of making prohibition an obnoxious religious tyranny . . . If the law is literally to be enforced, it is only a question of time when the Catholic and Episcopal churches will be unable to conduct their beliefs and customs." As would frequently be the case in the near future, it was the resistance of outraged non-Catholic wets that held the Prohibitionists away from an aggressive anti-Catholicism.

In the Oklahoma case, jurists of the state supreme court soon reversed the earlier decision, saying that the restrictions of the dry law were against "intoxication," and that the wine used for religious services in the Catholic Church could not be regarded as "intoxicating" and could not therefore be prohibited. Shortly thereafter, the same court took the dispute completely out of its anti-Catholic context by ruling that the bone-dry law could not prohibit the importation of alcoholic beverages for personal use. Here for a moment it appeared that the fabric of bone-dry clauses might begin to unravel. But the storm continued. Oklahoma was among the first states to ratify the 18th Amendment.

In February, when Congress granted the President authority to arm merchant ships, it also passed laws banning the sale of intoxicating beverages in Alaska and in Washington, D.C. In March, as people read of the Zimmermann Note and came to feel that war was surely imminent, Congress amended the Post Office Appropriations Bill to forbid interstate shipments of alcoholic beverages, "except for scientific, sacramental or medicinal purposes," into any state which, like Oklahoma, forbade "the manufacture or sale therein of intoxicating liquors," whether or not these states still allowed importations for personal use.

This act, which effectively converted all the dry states into bone-dry states, was the "Reed-Randall Bone Dry Act," introduced by Senator James A. Reed of Missouri. Reed was a dedicated wet whose curiously mean sense of humor caused him to draft this measure with the intention of embarrassing his dry opponents; they could not gracefully oppose the act because it was, he supposed, what all drys really wanted. Yet neither could they gracefully support it because it was so contrary to their alleged principles of "Jeffersonian self-determination." Reed slyly enlisted the cosponsorship of Charles H. Randall from southern California, the lone representative of the Prohibition Party in Congress, who had no such principles when it came to alcohol. Randall was upright and self-righteous, a single-minded dry of the old order who would later criticize General Pershing for allowing American troops in France to drink wine and who even later introduced a law to prevent Americans anywhere from drinking anything alcoholic, even if they were living in Canton, China. Anti-Saloon League leaders stumbled over themselves, at first opposing the measure as a "wet joker," then taking credit for the Reed-Randall Bill when it passed. Antidrink sentiment in the country had clearly outpaced them.

On April 4, Congress declared war against Germany because, the President had said, "The world must be made safe for democracy." Wilson spoke also of "the sacrifices we shall freely make" in this "most terrible and disastrous of all wars, civilization itself seeming to be in the balance." During that same month, reformers successfully urged the President to appoint a Training Camp Activities Commission which, with its Law Enfrocement Division, was one of the instruments which pietist groups created from the sense of war emergency to shatter the vestiges of organized prostitution. In a pattern of action which in some ways suggests the later provisions of the Volstead Act to enforce Prohibition, the commission defined twelve federal districts. Agents for each district were men and women usually eager to gather information about prostitution, and they delivered their intelligence to municipal and state police. But the most severe instrument for this same purpose was Section 17 of the Draft Act, which flatly prohibited prostitution in the vicinity of training camps. With this, training officers could—and on the urging to reformers actually did—declare entire cities off limits to trainees until city leaders eliminated the brothels whose presence was dramatically revealed in the Wassermann tests required of servicemen. Seattle, for example, was declared off limits, and the loss of legitimate business from soldiers and sailors caused a political upheaval which evicted a permissive mayor. The threat of military closure was in itself enough to break up the last of the great red-light districts—among them the most elegant and resplendent in the world—of San Francisco, New Orleans, and New York. (The incidence of venereal disease among members of the Army fell from 108 per thousand in 1917 to 50 per thousand in 1922.) Hardly had the war started for the United States when it was clear that a definite era had come to an end.

Having thus embraced the crusade for national and international purity, Congress on May 18 forbade the sale of intoxicating drinks to men in uniform. On August 1, as the country steadied itself for the great sacrifice, civilians were crusaders no less than servicemen, and conditions less than bone-dry became conditions less than patriotic. Under the slogan "Shall the many have food, or the few have drink?" Congress forbade, with the Lever Food and Fuel Control Act, the use of foodstuffs for distilling liquor. This shut down the stills; the saloons would soon die of the hard thirst. And the drys, in their progress, had not overlooked the deadly linkage between brewers and German influences in the nation; they made them well known and notorious. On December 8, a presidential proclamation forbade brewers to brew at an alcoholic content of more than 2.75 percent, and beer was thus converted into the kind of pale temperance beverage which had been admired by Thomas Jefferson. The President also severely limited the amount of grains that would thereafter be available for legal brewing. The country had thus gone nearly dry during the first eight months of wartime sacrifice. Then, on December 22, 1917, with majorities well in excess of the two-thirds requirement, Congress submitted to the states the 18th Amendment. In the orderly and methodical way prescribed by the traditions of American democracy, Prohibition was being fixed into the principles of the nation's government.

With this passage, the Anti-Saloon League was fully marshaled, fully prepared to take advantage of the antidrink storm which had not yet subsided. In this alignment of its forces, the league had the assistance, or at least the compliance, of some of the most able men in American political life at that time: Borah of Idaho, LaFollette of Wisconsin, McNary of Oregon, Nelson of Minnesota, Norris of Nebraska, Smoot of Utah, Ashurst of Arizona, Gore of Oklahoma, Sheppard of Texas, Vardaman of Mississippi, Walsh of Montana. Beyond the Congress, twenty-seven states had dry laws and were reasonably sure to ratify immediately. Seven states held special legislative sessions for the specific purpose of ratification, and of these only the legislatures of Rhode Island and Connecticut refused. By January 1919, ratification was complete, and 80 percent of the members of forty-six state legislatures were recorded in approval. Wet or dry, the cards had finally fallen. It was "because the old-stock middle class constituted the backbone of the Progressive Movement and wielded disproportionate political power"—writes James H. Timberlake in *Prohibition and the Progressive Movement* (1963)—that "it was able to overcome the opposition of the urban masses and to impose its own standard of sobriety on the nation by law." In the deal for pressure politics, the drys—having for a quarter of a century so superbly integrated the sentiments of protest and manipulated them at a critical moment in American history—had beaten the wet bosses at their own game.

Amid evidence everywhere of worldwide disorder following the Armistice, Congress felt strongly that the period of "demobilization" was really a part of the war itself. And on the domestic front it surely was, for demobilization seemed to intensify the demands for social conformity in pietistic Americanism and confessional patriotism. In this mood, Congress refused to lift the wartime controls over the manufacture of alcoholic beverages and included an extension of these controls in the National Prohibition Act, usually called the Volstead Act, which passed through the House and the Senate in September 1919.

The bill was stopped briefly by the President, who in October vetoed it with an ambiguous message critical of what he saw as an unjusified use of wartime restrictions. The message, however, revealed no explicit approval or disapproval of the details of the act or of the 18th Amendment. And because Woodrow Wilson remained at the time totally disabled from his attack of cerebral thrombosis, no one knew with confidence what his views were about anything. He probably did not even draft the message himself. In any event, Congress immediately overrode the veto and passed into law the liquor controls which would soon define an era. They would go into effect in January 1920. That same month the government was so shaken by the sustained upheavals of war and radicalism that it fell into its time of terror by arresting 6,000 allegedly seditious men and women, most of them immigrants but also American citizens, and by herding them through the streets and into prisons. The Attorney General of the United States, who had ordered the arrests, predicted that by May 1, 1920, the country would be locked in the convulsions of a Red Revolution.

In wording the 18th Amendment, Congress had chosen to have

prohibited the "manufacture, sale, or transportation of intoxicating liquors." Representative Andrew Volstead of Minnesota, who had sponsored the enforcement act, had taken it
from Wheeler, who on his part had attempted a synthesis of the
"bone-dry" laws in effect in the several states. It was, then, a
codification of compromise, and the best approach to Volsteadism begins here with the word *intoxicating*. Despite
protest from the more radical Prohibitionists, ASL leaders in
Congress had in wording the law accepted *intoxicating* rather
than *alcoholic*, knowing full well that a radical, bone-dry
amendment, in the absence of enough bone-dry, radical states,
would never achieve ratification. Similarly, they had voted
down the effort of Senator Thomas W. Hardwick of Georgia to
add the words *use* and *purchase* to the amendment, and for the
same reasons Congress then quite deliberately avoided any
constitutional definition of what in fact might be "intoxicating."

This is a crucial consideration, for many people still regarded
"intoxicating liquors" as the "ardent spirits" of the
"drunkard-making" business, the manufacture and sale of
which they surely did hope to prohibit. Even with the remarkable rise of antidrink sentiment, however, it is quite possible that
most people in 1920 took the view that certain "alcoholic"
beverages, except for gross or morbid misuse, were not actually
"intoxicating." This was consistently the view of most
Catholic, Episcopal, and Jewish spokesmen. Governor Al
Smith of New York was the public figure who perhaps most
regularly expressed the same assumption, though others as
prestigious as Martin N. Ray, former Inspector General of the
United States Army, and Sam W. Small, an associate editor of
the *Atlanta Constitution*, repeatedly insisted that "intoxicating" and "alcoholic" should never be regarded as the same.
Small, who had for years been a lecturer for the Anti-Saloon
League, testified after the passage of the Volstead Act that in his
thousands of speeches favoring the Prohibition Amendment, he
had "strenuously combatted the charge that we sought to deny
an individual citizen his right to have and drink what he pleased;
we only denied that any man had an inalienable right to run a
barroom and conduct a commercial manufactory of drun-

kards." Lawmakers who voted for the Prohibition Amendment could thus in good conscience yield to ASL pressures, accepting the thought that the amendment should be as broad as most other constitutional provisions, and deliberately so, to distinguish it from actual legislation. They could assume, as did many of their constituents, that the matter of defining what was *in fact* "intoxicating" (just as the matter of defining what was in fact "unreasonable" in searches and seizures or what was in fact "freedom" in speech or press) was a matter for subsequent legislation and judicial interpretation, for laws and decisions which, as society itself changed, would always be subject to further revision.

These moderates were accordingly shocked when the Volstead Act defined "intoxicating" beverages as those containing over .5 percent alcohol. It forbade anyone to "manufacture, sell, barter, transport, import, export, deliver, furnish, or possess" any beverages so defined. Moreover, the law stated that such provisions were to be "construed to the end that the use of intoxicating liquor as a beverage may be prevented." Here, finally, was a national antidrink law, one to make "intoxicating" and "alcoholic" practically synonymous and to prevent the drinking of anything in any way alcoholic. But in a curious compromise that seemed more like a reversal, the law did not make the purchase of alcoholic beverages—and, presumably, their consumption—an act subject to prosecution. This left the purchaser reasonably safe from the clutches of federal agents, and it would appear, then, that the law was not really against the drinking of intoxicants. With even further confusion, another concession allowed drinkers to "possess" and presumably forever to consume such liquors as they might have laid in storage before January 1920. It would appear, then, that the law was not really against possession. This exclusion allowed a good many wealthy people the comfort of avoiding the great thirst without having to fight the government or the ASL. The Yale Club of New York, for example, had the resources and the foresight to lay in supplies of wet goods which would please its private membership for at least the next 15 years. The law also made generous concessions for liquors sold for medicinal, sacramental, and industrial purposes, and it infringed in no way with the home preparation of fruit beverages. These last liquids, of course, had a volatile potential for conversion into ciders and wines. In a fascinating circumvention, the Volstead Act held that such beverages were to be considered "intoxicating" not by their measurable alcoholic content, but by whether juries or judges would find their use *in fact* intoxicating.

Thus the Volstead Act, in both its language and its intent, stumbled through a brier of shaky assumptions, political concessions, and inhibitions. The .5 percent definition, for example, was based on the experiences of several states with what was measurable, not what was or was not intoxicating. The provisions for medicinal and sacramental beverages were, of course, reasonable concessions to entrenched ritual, tradition, and political power, but these provisions would certainly leave quantities of wine and liquor available for quasi-medical and quasi-sacramental purposes. The allowances for fruit beverages seemed a sensible way to avoid the interminable problems the government might have if it were to attack Nature even more directly and prohibit the natural laws of fermentation. But the home brewing of malts and yeasts, which could only be intended for fermentation into beer, was prohibited. This immediately gave rise to cries from the urban areas that self-serving, Bible-belt types had secured their own homemade hard cider in this section and had put one over on the city worker by taking away his homemade beer. These sections again show how loosely the word *intoxicating* would be used, even by lawyers and Congressmen, when the goal was congressional harmony rather than legal precision. The Volstead Act thus appeared as much a snarl of contradictions as a definition of a new morality.

And if it were a new morality, there was nothing at all clear about who was to impose it. Section 2 of the amendment said that "Congress and the several states shall have concurrent power to enforce this article by appropriate legislation." The section had been worded to soothe the sensitivities of the more

vocal states' rights orators, and it meant to most people that
states' rights—the integrity of local and regional autonomies,
differences, eccentricities, and values, even with the peculiarly
vivid connotations these values had taken after 1876—were to
be fully protected. This was also consistent with the tradition of
there being actually very few federal laws that were aimed
directly at individuals, and, indeed, with there being few federal
agencies designed in any way to discipline them. Before there
was even a Federal Bureau of Investigation, how was the
federal government to halt, for example, the "transportation"
of beer? Call out the army and close the borders? There was no
such army available, and few people would have been willing to
pay for its muster. It was incredible to many people that the
federal government, which had thoughtfully left their murders,
lynchings, adulteries, discriminations, frauds, and other trans-
gressions to the disciplines of their state legislatures, would ever
take a primary and oppressive interest in what they might want
to drink.

We must also for a moment consider a larger view: It may be
that the rough edges of the law were simply not a primary
consideration. As Joseph Gusfield shows, in *Symbolic Crusade:
Status Politics and the American Temperance Movement*
(1963), there are times when even futile laws are actually
ceremonial acts of great significance. In the ritual of embracing
such laws, the formal agencies of a society recognize one
configuration of cultural values and reject others, thus officially
defining a dead line between acceptable and deviant behavior.
The drawing of such lines is, of course, an act vital to social
stability and social cohesion. The most important thing about
Prohibition to many people was to have the federal Constitution
and the law of the land condemn alcohol, and, by indisputable
implication, so condemn all that the alcohol-soaked lifestyle
represented. At stake in the 18th Amendment and the Volstead
Act was the most formal and official, the most ceremonial and
ritualistic, validation of a lifestyle or of cultural values possible
in American society.

We can look backward: Validating the personal dignity

sheltered in the Bill of Rights was more important than honoring such dignity in daily practice. In the 1860s, abolishing slavery was the significant validation, not the abolition of the economic, personal, or social tyranny over blacks in both the South and the North which endured for more than a century after the passage of the antislavery amendment. The symbolic crusade against liquor and the liquor traffic was against the vision of a boozy, undisciplined, saloon-oriented lifestyle which seemed to threaten the family-oriented core of pietist America. It was Lyman Beecher's crusade for recognition of pietist preeminence. This dimension of the crusade helps explain not only why Prohibition rose from state laws and into the Constitution and why it was accelerated by war, but also why, when it became obvious that Prohibition would not prohibit, it was so difficult for Americans to repeal it.

This interpretation of social symbolism also takes an edge off the apparently rural-urban conflict which has been so important a part of older interpretations. At first glance, the voting statistics of local option and of statewide Prohibition elections do seem to define a rural-urban tension, even a rural tyranny, for it is surely true that while the rural towns and counties were militantly dry, the people of Boston, Chicago, Denver, or St. Louis, when they could vote on the issue, usually registered wet majorities. Yet it is obvious that many voters in highly urban areas also voted dry, and many rural districts were in fact very wet. What is important, then, is to know who these voters were in terms of their socioeconomic and cultural identities. From the state studies now available, it seems clear that voters in the dry precincts and neighborhoods were middle-class, white, Protestant, socially mobile, native, or thoroughly assimilated. In the wet districts, on the contrary, voters were usually wage-earning immigrants or workers whose recent antecedents were ethnic.

It was no coincidence, then, that as ethnic immigration to the United States increased in the 1890s and early 1900s, so the power of the ASL increased. For native white Protestants, it became a vital institution. Nor is it strange that Prohibition became an almost sacred cause to pietist groups like the Patrons of Husbandry or Southern Baptists or western Methodists or small-town chambers of commerce. Such groups were beginning to fear that the melting-pot function of American society, as it allegedly had functioned in the nineteenth century, was not melting well enough to protect them from the saloon. With the ASL, they believed the heat might be vigorously advanced through political action and that it might result in social control. Thus the "Americanization Movement" of these years—so properly repudiated by those who believe in the ideal of harmonious, if diverse, cultural pluralisms in the United States—dealt so ungenerously with aliens. It dealt ungenerously with all those whose values, in regard to alcoholic or sexual indulgences, were inconsistent with pietist standards. The significance of Prohibition, according to Gusfield, was that it happened as "an act of ceremonial deference toward old middle-class culture. If the law was disobeyed and not enforced, the respectability of its adherents was honored in the breach. After all, it was *their* law that drinkers had to avoid."

Because it does consider the anxieties of a pluralistic society, Gusfield's view also helps explain why the Prohibition experience of more homogeneous societies was reasonably tranquil and modestly progressive. The rulers of Sweden, to use that country again, tried to prohibit the use of distilled spirits in the late eighteenth century. But the "Temperance Question" did not become a deep social movement there until the per capita consumption of liquor had risen to alarming levels in the 1820s. Much of the same agitation had occurred in Norway, where there were sixty-eight anti-drink societies by 1845. Finnish law banned the home distilling of ardent spirits in 1866, and temperance workers in that country first sought national Prohibition in 1883. The United Kingdom Alliance for the Total and Immediate Suppression of the Liquor Traffic, the organized response to Neal Dow's lectures, grew in strength and political power toward the end of the century. German temperance societies listed 600,000 members in 1845. Even in France, where so many people were actively engaged in the traffic, a temperance organization emerged following the disasters of the

Franco-Prussian War. In all these countries, as with the temperance question in the United States, there had been before the Great War at least a century of social agitation and political experience, yet these experiences were not distorted by the deeply ugly antagonisms of cultural pluralisms that mark the development of American Prohibition.

In the collapse of the older societies of Europe between 1900 and 1919, younger, more radical, more democratic, and more intelligent leaders came forward to direct the search for a new order. They would circumvent many of the older barriers of rigid tradition in their demand for stability and social justice, and they would in this progress often see Prohibition as a critical step. When Social Democrats took over the government of Finland in 1919, they passed a Prohibition law that banned any drink that was over 2 percent alcohol. In Norway that same year, voters by referendum outlawed drinks of more than 12 percent alcohol. This law was strongly favored by the Socialist and Labor political parties. In Sweden, following a period of unprecedented disorder—hunger riots, inflation, near civil war, the collapse of monarchic political power—many Social Democrats demanded Prohibition as essential to any social stability. A referendum on the issue was narrowly defeated in 1922, after which the new Social Democratic government abolished both the profit motive and the competition from the traffic in bottled liquor by nationalizing the liquor business.

In England, agitation for local option had increased toward the end of the nineteenth century. In 1908, the Asquith government had proposed a licensing act which, over a period of fourteen years, would have reduced the number of licenses by 30,000 and thereafter have authorized local option. The bill had a majority in the House of Commons of 237, but it failed in the House of Lords. Under the wartime leadership of David Lloyd George, the government raised license fees, curtailed the production of alcohol, and, in the public houses, restricted the sale of anything alcoholic to the early evening hours. These measures, though modified after the war, brought about a significant change in the habits of Englishmen: The amount of absolute alcohol consumed in Great Britain had been 92 million gallons in 1913; it was 37 million in 1918, then 53 million in 1922.

In Canada, *intoxicating* meant 2.5 percent, and the "No-License" Movement had grown steadily since 1900. The province of Alberta had gone dry by referendum in 1915, Manitoba in 1916, Saskatchewan in 1916, and Nova Scotia, by legislative enactment, also in 1916. British Columbia went dry by referendum in 1917, at which time every province but Quebec had a Prohibition law. Quebec went dry by legislative enactment in 1919, and Canada was thus legally dry even before the United States.

In many of these countries, the initial laws of Prohibition were open to quick revision. In Canada, the dry laws of 1919 soon fell apart from economic pressures, not the least of which were the opportunities to bootleg booze to the south during the postwar depression. Thereafter, provincial laws throughout the Dominion preserved the principles of local option. For the wet-option areas, the laws established restrictive codes which to this day severely prescribe conditions for the purchase of liquor in state-owned stores and for the consumption of liquor in public places. In Norway, a referendum in 1926 abolished the older law, and thereafter the government established state stores and regulations for the times and places at which liquors might be purchased or consumed. In 1920, Scotland accepted a local option law, and "no license" apparently worked well even in the industrial towns of Kilsyth, Kirkintilloch, Wich, and Lerwick. In Sweden, a system developed for the Social Democratic government by Dr. Ivan Bratt permitted an individual to purchase liquor at the rate of one liter a week if he had a "pass book." To get this book, he had to prove that he had reached his majority, was earning an adequate income, was known as a "temperate person," and would be the only person in his family who possessed such a book. In Finland, the earlier Prohibition law remained in force until it was repealed by a referendum in 1932.

The crucial point is that during the first quarter of the twentieth century, many Europeans and North Americans came to believe that some comprehensive control of the traffic in alcoholic beverages was an urgent social necessity. When these people adopted Prohibition, it was to raise a shield against the social devastations that had followed the technology of distillation into Western culture. The point is also that when people modified their Prohibition laws, they in most instances did so with grace and intelligence. But in the United States, such modifications would come neither so quickly nor so easily.

8

Resistance
and
Social Change

~~~~~~

SOME INTRIGUING LEGENDS to the contrary, the beginnings of Prohibition did not seem so grim. Several states had
been dry for six years, several others for more than a decade.
Citizens of some regions had taken a local option before the turn
of the century, and to them the Volstead Act was only a belated
confirmation by the national government of their early wisdom.
When the war sublimated the movement for social purity into
the moral equivalent of patriotism and national defense, it swept
away the worst of the old-time debaucheries in prostitution and
gambling, and with them the worst of the old-time saloons. Only
a few people regretted the passing. William Randolph Hearst,
who often thought he knew what was best for Americans, signed
an editorial in 1919 praising the 18th Amendment because it
would abolish "half the misery of half the people." Liquor, he
wrote, "had destroyed more each year than the World War
destroyed." Possessed still by the passions of national glory and
unity, he concluded that "the suppression of the drink traffic is
an expression of the higher morality upon which we are now
entering."

This expression began with the closing of saloons and
barrooms at midnight, January 16, 1920. (Should a barroom
continue illegally as a "speakeasy" thereafter, the entire
building in which it operated might, like a bordello, be declared

"a common nuisance" and, under a section of the Volstead Act popularly known as the "Padlock Law," be closed by federal agents for as much as a year.) But following as it did the long experience of state dry laws and the years of wartime restrictions, which had never been fully relaxed, the dry morning of January 17 brought no national trauma. In major cities not already dry, the barrooms of most larger hotels had closed weeks before, and there was no great guzzle at the final hour, no ultimate orgy of binges. Thoughtful drinkers had for at least a year been laying away supplies, and contemporary writers stressed that in hotels, clubs, and private homes they found people who wanted to obey the law and usually did. Hosts serving cocktails or wine were eager tó note that the vintage and the purchase were pre-Volstead and, of course, entirely legal. Self-respecting people respected the law, and for a while at least, the nation basked in the glow of high principle. A widely-held view was expressed by an editor who wrote that he had voted for Prohibition not because he didn't "take a drink now and then," which he did and would continue to do, but because he "thought it was the best thing for the coming generation." Others recalled that the hard-drinking Jack London had before his death supported Prohibition not because he supposed it would protect him from John Barleycorn but because it meant "life more abundant for the manhood of young boys born and growing up—ay, and life more abundant for the young girls born and growing up to share the lives of young men."

There were others, however, who were totally unprepared for even a delicate passage into a new era. John Allen Krout, then a young history instructor in New York City, observed that to many Americans, "prohibition came with something of a shock." Though they were vaguely aware that somewhere out in the tall grass of the Bible Belt were people called "drys," and that these people were interested in politics, "they had not realized that the reformers were so near the goal." The "many Americans" here may well have been Krout's colleagues in the history department at Columbia, but Krout did reveal their genuine pain and surprise. Their immediate response, he said, was "to cry fraud, since it seemed impossible that the people of a great nation could be fairly persuaded to write into their fundamental law so radical a change in social custom." To many others, he noted, "it was all a mystery," something that had "emerged from remote possibility into startling reality." It was as though on January 17 the good and liberal people of the country awoke to learn that barbarians from the interior had, under the cover of patriotism and wartime emergencies, seized the government and were perversely determined to make life miserable for the good people who had always assumed that their right to drink was forever protected by the Constitution. Krout saw a problem. He immediately set himself to the task of finding a scholarly solution—see *The Origins of Prohibition* (1925)—to what he called "the riddle of prohibition."

Krout was recording the fairly typical reaction of urbanites who had seldom regarded political events or social movements in the United States as in any way worthy of more than casual attention. Especially among the more academic literati of New York, Chicago, Baltimore, and Boston, important things happened in Europe, not the United States, and this prejudice had for them obscured any real sense of what was going on in America. Their ignorance of the recent past, however, was in many ways understandable, for while the dry Congress was being elected in 1916, thousands of young men were dying in France and Russia. When the Judiciary Committee of the Senate favorably reported on the 18th Amendment, the *New York Times* placed the story on page 13. American troops were then en route to France, the Battle of Flanders was in progress, Kerensky was assuming leadership in Russia, and there was a mutiny in the German Navy. While the amendment was debated in the House, the French were attacking at Verdun, the British were in Palestine, and the Bolsheviks were bringing down the Kerensky government. Under the circumstances, as Charles Merz emphasizes in *The Dry Decade* (1930), world-minded intellectuals were giving little thought to the progress of American drys. Thus Krout wrote his book, which traced the

Temperance Movement from its beginnings through the Civil War, but which, in neglecting the twentieth century, was something less than a full explanation for those ignorant of critical issues in American political life. Nevertheless, Krout was happy to instruct his readers that the ratification of the 18th Amendment was something more than a hasty plot by rural primitives to snuff out the amenities of urban civilization. It was, rather, "the final expression of a fundamental change which had been more than a century in the making."

More than a few were not impressed, and their cries of *fraud* enlivened the early Volstead era. Their anguish was regularly enflamed by the more mindlessly impassioned nativists and Prohibitionists—both of which groups, in an age of friviolous journalism, were given inordinate newspaper publicity—whose sanctimonious platitudes and downright perversities did indeed darken the lives of men who shared the liberal persuasion. On the hysterical fringe of both there emerged from time to time—to the delight of cynical journalists—individuals who wanted to deport Catholics, disfranchise all immigrants, and shoot labor leaders along with intellectuals. Others applauded every raid of federal agents on private homes and every wiretapped telephone, demanded that the army patrol the Canadian border, asked the government to sterilize drinkers, and urged that violations of the Volstead Act be made a capital offense. In this atmosphere it is no wonder that many broad-minded urbanites came to fear for their own security and that, in their anxiety, they began to explain their misfortunes in what became a legacy of conventional legends.

Such legends held that Puritans from the Corn Country and lady school teachers from the Rocky Mountains had deviously manipulated honest patriotism to force the 18th Amendment into the Constitution while the attention of all right-minded citizens was fixed on the war. While the fighting raged in Europe, people suffered this affliction in good faith, willing to accept almost any restriction of their freedoms that was consistent with the wartime sacrifice. Then, suddenly, in the post war society of President Harding's "normalcy," they discovered a grave crisis: The malignant repressions of the wicked Puritans were actually eroding the moral fiber of a free and creative America. Prohibition, by distorting the role of alcohol in civilized life, allegedly caused Americans to drink more rather than less, and to do so with increasing morbidity. It encouraged women to drink hard liquor. It inspired new patterns of indiscretion among members of the younger generation. Prohibition supposedly cracked the very foundation of society by making it possible for those who would violate a bad law to earn an enormous amount of money—money which they used to corrupt every level of public life. It was far more serious than common political corruption, for Volsteadism allegedly created the circumstances in which organized crime could for the first time fasten its clutches upon American society. In the career of Al Capone, splendidly adaptable to legend, there was a drama which could reveal how the Prohibition laws shaped an environment of greed, envy, cynicism, fear, carnal sin, corruption, and mass murder.

When Michael Monahan, then a popular biographer, published his *Dry America* in 1921, he blamed Prohibition for everything from religious bigotry, crime, and drug addiction to a general decline in something he called "social happiness." Prohibition, he wrote, had brought upon Americans a "train of miseries and annoyances quite surpassing any with which we were actually threatened by the war itself." This view has been remarkably durable. As recently as 1966, Robert Lewis Taylor, another popular biographer and a Pulitzer laureate, carried the same theme through his book about Carry Nation. He concludes—apparently without caution and completely out of patience—that the 18th Amendment launched "an orgiastic and prolonged era of hard drinking, immorality, racketeering, gun molls, gang wars, political corruption, bribed police and judges, poisoned booze, speakeasies, irreligion, emancipation of women to fresh vistas of impudence . . . short skirts, saxaphone-tooting . . . and additional decadence." On the night of January 16, 1920, says Taylor, "the country had gone to bed fairly sober; next morning it awoke, grabbed a red tin New

Year's Eve horn and blew it without interruption for fourteen years. . . ."

This note of high irritation is still often reflected in the work of writers who lived through the period, even those who write college textbooks for American history courses. For example, Samuel Eliot Morison's *Oxford History of the American People* (1965) indicates that during the 1920s "every city became studded with 'speakeasies' to replace the saloon, almost every urban family patronized a local bootlegger. . . . Bravado induced numerous young people to drink who otherwise would not have done so." Prohibition, writes Morison, encouraged "the building up of a criminal class that turned to gambling and drugs when Amendment XVIII was repealed." It changed the tastes of respectable people from wholesome beer and honest wine to the deplorable and depraved concoction known as bathtub gin. Woman, says Morison, who was emancipated "by Amendment XIX, enthusiastically connived at breaking Amendment XVIII. . . . Hip-flask drinking certainly helped the revolution in sexual standards. . . . And it encouraged hypocrisy in politics." The moral of the legends was abundantly clear. As Monahan wrote in 1921, "To believe that Prohibition will stand is, in my view, to believe that the Republic has lost her way and is without the guiding light of her noblest traditions." To work for repeal was to save the nation.

There are today few reasons to believe that these legends, even those so recently embellished, are more than an easy and sentimental hyperbole crafted by men whose assumptions about a democratic society had been deeply offended. To suppose, for example, that the principle of the 18th Amendment was generated by wartime hysterias—even though the Volstead Act itself reflected the tensions of an unhappy epoch—is, as Krout tried to point out, to ignore temperance legislation across a century of American history. To suppose, further, that the Volstead Act caused Americans to drink more rather than less is to defy an impressive body of statistics as well as common sense. The common sense is that a substantial number of people wanted to stop both their own and other people's drinking, and that the saloons where most people had done their drinking were closed. There is no reason to suppose that the speakeasy, given its illicit connotations, more lurid even than those of the saloon, ever, in any quantifiable way, replaced the saloon. In fact, there is every reason to suppose that most Americans outside the larger cities never knew a bootlegger, never saw a speakeasy, and would not have known where to look for one.

The statistical evidence to support this takes more than a footnote. The most recent figures are those assembled by the task force of scholars from the Department of Health, Education and Welfare who prepared for Congress the special report entitled *Alcohol and Health* (1971). This report shows that the annual per capita consumption of alcoholic beverages in the United States—conveniently converted to gallons of absolute alcohol—stood at 2.60 for the period 1906-1910, which was the period before the state dry laws had any national impact and the period which must be regarded as "before Prohibition." After Prohibition, in 1934, the figure stood at 0.97. In 1940, by which time the effects of repeal had surely pervaded the national drinking habits, the figure was only 1.56. It would be difficult to overemphasize the significance of this change: Americans after Prohibition were drinking less than at any time since they had learned the technology of distillation, and the marked change had surely taken place during the 1920s.

And there is even more evidence. In 1932, Clark Warburton's study, *The Economic Results of Prohibition*, made estimates of per capita consumption during the dry decade—an uncommonly slippery problem in historical detection. First he analyzed the verifiable reports on the legal production of alocohol that might have been diverted to illicit use. Then he examined the reports on arrests for drunkenness. Finally he reviewed the statistics on the national death rate from alcohol-associated diseases. His synthesis was conjectural and his projections were admittedly rough, but they were refined in 1948 by the century's most prominent and indefatigable researcher in alcohol studies, the late E. M. Jellineck. Even more recently, Joseph Gusfield has reexamined both these studies and concluded that "Prohibition was effective in sharply reducing the rate of alcohol consumption in the United States. We may set the outer limit of this at about 50 percent and the inner limit at about one-third less alcohol consumed by the total population that had been the case . . . [before Prohibition] in the United States."

Another illuminating calculation from *Alcohol and Health* is that during the period "before Prohibition," about 37 percent of the absolute alcohol consumed in the United States was in distilled spirits, the remainder in beer and wine. In 1940 the percentage of spirits consumed had risen to 43—an indication that the Volstead era may have helped in some measure to turn tastes toward distillates, though across the period of a full generation this does not seem to be a really significant change. In 1970, when the per capita consumption was 2.61 gallons, the percentage of distilled spirits was 44.

There is, furthermore, an abundance of evidence in social statistics from the 1920s indicating that Prohibition could not have encouraged drinking among most Americans. John C. Burnham has recently reviewed these statistics, in "New Perspectives on the Prohibition 'Experiment' of the 1920's" (1968), to show that arrests for drunkenness fell off remarkably during the Volstead era, as did the public expenses for jailing drunks. There were marked decreases in the incidence of diseases associated with alcoholic psychoses, and for several years, Burnham shows, articles on alcoholism simply disappeared from the periodicals of American medicine.

Burnham also makes pointed suggestions about the origins of Prohibition legends. He shows that as rumrunners opened supply lines from abroad in the late 1920s, liquor was indeed increasingly easy to get for those who wanted it and could afford it. Most people who remember Prohibition at all have generalized about this later period, not the early years when liquor was really scarce. But even when we understand this flow in the late 1920s, it is important to know who drank what the rumrunners were running in. When liquor was available, it was only under conditions of considerable risk and considerable expense. Irving Fisher showed in 1928 that the average price of a quart of bootleg beer was 80 cents (up 600 percent from 1916), gin was $5.90 (up 520 percent), and whiskey was $7.00 (up 310 percent), when the average annual family income was about $2,600.

These conditions easily associated the act of drinking with affluence and defiant individualism, making it a symbol of conspicuous consumption as well as of conspicuous rebellion. Thus the fashionably cynical, rebellious, and marvelously witty critic H. L. Mencken recalled in his essay "The Noble Experiment" only two isolated instances during the entire period, 1920-1933, when he could not find a drink if he wanted one. (In Pennsylvania, in 1924, he learned finally that "Sea Food" was the euphemism for beer, and that same year in Ohio he turned in great distress to rumrunners from Canada.) And Burnham shows that the affluent and defiantly colorful individuals like Mencken and his friends were more likely to impress journalists than were the mass of wage earners, for whom booze was usually too expensive. Thus when they reported that "everyone" was drinking, or was drinking more than ever before, journalists were recording merely what was to them the most visible and interesting, not the most representative, American experience. After Martha Bensley Bruère surveyed social workers across the country during the Prohibition era, in *Does Prohibition Work?* (1927), she concluded from their experiences that Prohibition did work quite well. The wage-earning families were drinking much less than before, and they had, furthermore, significantly improved their living conditions. Warburton's 1932 study supported this conclusion with a rough estimate that wage-earning families in the United States during the 1920s had about a billion dollars more to spend on consumer goods than they would have had without Prohibition.

Burnham's article is also a refutation of the "almost universal public belief" in a crime wave during the 1920s. The best studies in criminology, he indicates, give no evidence of any "wave," though across the decade there probably was a slowly rising level of criminal activity. People believed the "wave" was real because of impressions left by journalists who saw a lot of crime, reported a lot, and—in the age of instant communication—were irresistibly tempted to romanticize it. Among competing newspapers, crime became the most welcome kind of "hot news," and it was eagerly fastened on the front pages. This is not to deny that there has always been a great deal of crime in the United States to see and to publicize; it is only to suggest that Prohibition did not make it any easier than it had been before to bribe a policeman, or commit a murder, or corrupt a friend of the President.

We can attack the principal legend directly. Though the Volstead Act was bound to raise the levels of opportunity and expectation among any criminals who could organize their skills and resources to exploit it, the cloud of soft fact surrounding the career of Al Capone seriously distorts the history of organized crime. The business which Capone came to dominate—the Colosimo-Torrio-Capone conglomerate—had for a generation aggregated the production and distribution of illegal goods and services around Chicago. An essential part of its history is that it had for years been based in the gambling and prostitution which could thrive only in the presence of the urban saloon. The progress of integration, in fact, began when John Colosimo, a precinct captain who could deliver the immigrant vote in the First Ward, linked together his first chain of brothels and saloons. It was said later in Chicago that when Johnny Torrio bought a shut-down brewery in 1920, it was with the idea of converting it into a brothel. As it later occurred to him that he might use it as a brewery, he began to explore the possibilities of Volsteadism. Capone, who worked his way up the ranks before the Volstead Act, did indeed become more prosperous, more influential, and perhaps more ruthless than any of his predecessors. But surely he would have become so anyway, without the advent of Prohibition. His dark distinction lay in his method of forcing organized crime in Chicago to shake down, to consolidate, to conglomerate—witness the 550 gang-style murders in Chicago between 1920 and 1930. Joseph Gusfield remarks that the St. Valentine's Day Massacre shows how Capone "brought the severest of all sanctions to bear against 'unfair competition' . . . seven executives died in defense of free enterprise." But that they died in any way associated with Prohibition was only incidental.

Because of the very nature of such dealings and the character of the men gripped by them, we shall probably never have an accurate statistical portrait of Capone's entrepreneural achievements. It is clear only that he was an extraordinarily shrewd businessman. In the mechanics of bootlegging beer or booze, however, there is reason to suppose that the costs were nearly equal to the profits, for Capone himself estimated that his payoffs to policemen and to other public officials ran to thirty million dollars a year. This may be close to the sum of corrupt money formerly pumped into the Chicago system by saloons and prostitution. Furthermore, it is clear that Capone regarded the running of beer, over which he exercised a virtual monopoly, as a fortuitous adjunct to the traditional whore-driving, gambling, racketeering, and bribery which had sustained the organization long before the Volstead era. His outrages were certainly not the beginning of organized crime in the United States, and to see his career as the consequence of a liquor law is to simplify a profoundly disturbing circumstance of American cultural pluralisms. Capone and his lieutenants came out of subcultures which were indigenous to the massive urban growths such as New York and Chicago, and these men took brilliant advantage of an institutionalized commerce in illegal goods and services.

If among the drinkers of the 1920s young people—as legend had it—were drinking more than ever before, the phenomenon is not easily open to quantitative investigation. Which young people, and where, and when? The National Education Association sponsored a survey in 1929 which indicated that drinking among high school students was decreasing each year. This doesn't tell us much, for we have already learned that in 1929 the price of bootleg booze had put it beyond the reach of all but the most affluent. However, a profusion of literary evidence makes it difficult to ignore the image of "flaming youth," and one can suppose that some young people were indeed finding in liquor something more than indifferent recreation. But the problem of learning why and how young people were attracted to interdicted and mood-changing drugs is surely complex and ambiguous. One immediately wonders what forbidden fascinations young people in the United States in the 1920s would have found if the Volstead Act had not given liquor an augmented burden of illicit connotations.

The answer seems to be that they would have found liquor. In 1931, the Alcohol Information Committee published a book by Earl L. Douglas, called *Prohibition and Common Sense*, which, because it was a sort of intellectual's diatribe against the wealthy classes and their arrogant defiance of the Volstead Act, was easily lost in the flood of wet and dry propaganda. However, Douglas did accurately point out a circumstance which the legends overlooked—namely, that the comportment of "drinking" or "flaming" or "rebellious" youth was in no way uniquely American. By reading novels from abroad, Douglas learned that Europeans were confused by precisely the same kind of rebellion, and he properly concluded that it was absurd to associate these experiences in the United States with Prohibition.

This conclusion now seems beyond dispute. In *Long Week-End: A Social History of Great Britain, 1918-1939* (1940), Robert Graves and Alan Hodge show that polite society in postwar England was startled by a rebellion of young people and by challenges which are strikingly familiar: night clubs that became speakeasies of a sort, selling mixed drinks after the legal hour, provoking raids and padlocking; returning soldiers addicted to alcohol; cocktail drinking, a new form of "alcoholic abuse" then deeply disturbing to British physicians; radios in public houses—they made drinking too popular; the lack of parental control among middle-class young people who were finding in liquor, automobiles, sex, and "jazzmania" a lifestyle terrifying to the older generation.

Thus a central consideration for any social historian of this period is that middle-class young people in the United States and in Western Europe were rejecting the social conventions, ideals, and values of their elders. They were for good reason disenchanted with the pious idealism of the Wilsonian era. They were, as are young people of any generation, hypersensitive to the possibilities of opportunity and freedom implicit in a new technology. They were fashioning a new lifestyle, the snarled symbols of which were radios, automobiles, contraceptives, electric machines, instantaneous news media, a bold literature, a new music and new dance, perhaps even a new perception of what the quality of life might become. They were establishing their individual identities through rebellious behavior, which, though marginally acceptable, yet brushed the dead line of counterculture: instant, rather than delayed, gratifications; indulgences and excesses, rather than loyalties and responsibilities; impulses, rather than duties; the peer-directed, rather than the conscience-driven comportment. The raised glass rejected any authority higher than the individual pleasure. And it was easy. If a young person in the United States chose to transport or sell a bottle in the back seat of his automobile, this was a matter for which the risks were far outweighed by the promised rewards in prestige and status. Martha Bensley Bruère noted in her social work that drinking by young people was "an adventure, a gesture of daring, a sign of revolt, an illusion of power, part of the game they call life." This is to note a very great deal indeed, for to see life as a *game* rather than as a *duty* is to see more than a metaphor; it is to see values in convolution.

This use of liquor as a holy water in the ceremonial validation of individual identity can also help explain why women—in the United States, Canada, and Western Europe—seemed to be drinking more during the 1920s than ever before. Again, who knows for sure? What statistics? Possibly the circumstances were that women in the lower socioeconomic classes actually got less than before and that middle-upper income groups got all they needed for the purposes of conspicuous consumption. At any rate, it was a phenomenon—like voting, birth control, divorce, and working in the city—that had much more to do with the liberation of women from sex-role assignments and from duties, loyalties, and obligations than with the laws against selling liquor. This is a phenomenon we shall examine more fully before the end of this chapter.

It now seems certain that the many legends about Prohibition arose not so much from social distortions caused by the Volstead Act as from the deep social turmoil of the decade, and that the legends were given currency by those who for many reasons hoped that the Volstead Act would somehow disappear. Moreover—it is important to emphasize—they were discordantly amplified by the spirit of sensation-seeking journalism. Even the *New York Times* seemed more interested in bizarre murder and high foolery than in national issues or substantive news. As Frederick Lewis Allen pointed out, when many people lost interest in foreign affairs after 1920, newspaper editors became infected with "a contagion of delighted concern over things that were exciting but didn't matter." This was an apparent compulsion to headline the often phony dramas of Babe Ruth, Jack Dempsey, Red Grange, John Charles Scopes, and the Queen of Romania, and to see ticker-tape parades, crime, noise, and public vulgarity—most of which seemed to occur in New York City or Chicago—as more newsworthy than events which might have illuminated the nation's passage into the twentieth century.

However, to challenge the legends is not to dismiss their premise—which was that as the decade lengthened, the Volstead Act prohibited less and less. Nor is it to dismiss their implied question: If Prohibition did not effectively prohibit, should it then not have been repealed? This was a very basic question, but it arose from a sort of quicksand of soft logic.

What, in the name of clarity, did "effective" mean in regard to criminal law, and how "ineffective" must such a law become to justify its repeal? Laws against dueling, gambling, adultery, murder, and larceny have never been totally "effective" in "prohibiting" what many people have always hoped they could prohibit, and there is reason to suppose that many people were willing to grant the same ambiguity to the laws of liquor prohibition.

But this again is quicksand, where any working hypothesis has but soft footing. Some of the drys, especially those of the older abolitionist passions, were so flushed by the Volstead achievement that they did indeed suppose that the law would stop all use of alcoholic beverages; that the country would see an immediate end to crime, poverty, and greed; and that they temselves would usher in the millennium. After 1920, these people would darkly resent the very existence of any drinker. Others more moderately supposed that the law would indeed abolish the saloon and would surely inhibit drinking, and that these developments would mark a signal revision of national morality. Such expectations would be deeply offended by the presence of urban speakeasies and the notorious effectiveness of international rumrunning. Still others might more generously conclude that in closing the saloons the law had made a fine beginning, but that the making of a truly dry nation would require perhaps more lifetimes than their own. Dry leaders as influential as Senator William Borah said that a fair trial for Prohibition would take at least twenty-five years. It was, therefore, unlikely that any precise criteria for "effectiveness" could meet the expectations of all those who supported the ASL convention delegates in 1927 when they resolved to thank "Almighty God that the people of this nation, in our day and generation, have placed in the fundamental law of the land, by means of the Eighteenth Amendment, the great principle of sobriety."

To thank God for the principle, of course, was not to demand of Him the immediate reality, and it is almost impossible to distinguish precisely between the hope and the expectation. To find a view of "effectiveness" less colored by the triumph of 1920, it may be better to look again to those who for a generation had worked toward its coming. To take specific footing, there are in the writings of E. J. Wheeler, a pamphleteer of the middle period, certain standards which offer both clarity and the chance of precision. Wheeler wrote for the party in the 1890s, and in 1894 he published a short book called *Prohibition: The Principle, the Policy, and the Party*. The purpose of Prohibition, Wheeler said, was "not to reform the moral conduct of the individual, but to relieve society of the burdens and damages imposed upon it by drink." There was a fine sophistry in disclaiming "moral" and embracing "social" purpose—as though Prohibitionists supposed that the dangers imposed on society by drink had little to do with the moral conduct of individuals. But this is no great matter; it is better not to take the logic as seriously as the feelings of those who used it. They meant what they said, which was that boozers were doomed anyway, that even with a good Prohibition law the unrepentant could probably still find ways to drink themselves to death, and perhaps they should; but the law did not have to recognize the legitimacy of any public facility conducted to stimulate or to gratify their passion. If all went well, the drinkers would shortly depart, taking their traditions and appetites with them. Wheeler and Prohibitionists like him—good Puritans indeed—simply had little faith in the salvation of any drinker or the possibility of the proposed law making him any more honest, virtuous, or self-disciplined. They did suppose, however, that the law would have its effect ultimately in shaping a dry society.

But measuring the extent to which people drank or did not drink after such laws had been passed many be the best way to measure the impact of Prohibition. The evidence we have already examined makes it clear that Americans drank less during Prohibition. We have also looked directly to the "burdens and dangers" that Wheeler had in mind to determine if some were actually relieved by Prohibition, and we have seen that the incidence of public drunkenness and of diseases related to alcohol did, to a remarkable degree, indeed decline. We can here add yet another item. When Professor Irving Fisher of Yale in the late 1920s studied North Carolina as representative of states where there was very little public criticism of the Volstead Act or of the 18th Amendment, he found most people there convinced that Prohibition had so reduced the incidence of public drunkenness and of drink-related social problems that the Volstead Act could be credited with the happy facts of their low taxes, decreasing rates of mortality, low incidence of automobile accidents, and decreasing rates of hospital admissions.

Sentiment in North Carolina, one might object, cannot fully explain the hold of Prohibition north and east of what was still rural America. But this sentiment, in only a slight revision, can be traced upward into the highest levels of the industrial elite in the American power structure. Professor Herman Feldman of Dartmouth showed that most American industrialists—at the time of his research, before the Great Crash—still favored Prohibition because for them it meant more money. Paychecks formerly pumped into the saloons were being converted into radios, automobiles, movie tickets, food, clothing, and real estate; neither the bootleggers nor the speakeasies presented any serious threat to the efficiency of industrial production. Prohibition, in short, seemed clearly related to higher productivity and general prosperity. Social statistics, at almost any point where they can be opened, suggest that Prohibition at least for a while worked well enough to satisfy most people. By these measures, then, Prohibition was something of a success, and—to answer the question implied in the legends—at least until 1930 the case for repeal rested in no overpowering reason.

But what then of the "burdens and dangers" to society which were imposed *by* Prohibition and might in themselves have been serious enough to condemn it? We have already discounted the legends of a "crime wave" and of drunken youth. But there may indeed have been a social burden in the tension and anxiety of men and women who found individual identity in defying the law, and this anxiety may have played an important role in the undoing of Prohibition. There is the possibility, too, that prohibiting the traffic in alcohol may have turned some people to other additive drugs. By 1920, however, most such drugs were already severely proscribed, driven underground where they were more difficult and much more expensive to acquire than booze. There is the matter of marijuana, which, though not usually regarded as an addictive narcotic, did come into popular use during the 1920s. Smoke parlors, some of them similar to opium dens, emerged in New York City, where one could get "high" on marijuana for twenty-five cents. Undoubtedly some former drinkers and some steady drinkers learned to use the drug, but it is unlikely that they took it instead of booze when, especially in New York, the booze flowed so easily.

A more real burden would have been the crime—even if there were no "wave"—in bootlegging, rumrunning, and speakeasy entrepreneurship. This was at times certainly onerous, and, wave or not, it caused people to strain their social tolerances. But it is clear that only a few people perceived this crime as a problem which called for dramatic social responses. Most widely felt crises in American society will generate not only social awareness but also major public expenditures, and this was never the case for crimes associated with prohibition. Whether or not the crime actually constituted a real crisis, ASL leaders did not want to suggest that Prohibition was ineffective. They used their power to keep both protest and appropriations well below the threshhold of public frustration. The crime was deplorable, but the response to it was mostly verbal.

The economic burdens imposed by Prohibition were unemployment and the subsequent financial disasters, personal and institutional, which followed the closing of distilleries, breweries, and saloons, and then the loss in revenues that liquor interests had formerly contributed to the public treasuries. These were considerable. But it was argued that industrial growth after 1921 quickly absorbed the unemployed, and that in regard to taxes, the declining expenses of policing public drunks and clearning up the wreckage of their drunkenness in destitute families, disease, and industrial accidents more than compensated for the loss. At any rate, the vigorously expanding economy before 1929 seemed for most people proof enough, as the drys contended, that prosperity followed Prohibition.

Here we must register some important qualifications. First, most people knew also that Prohibition was generally more effective before 1925 than after, and that following this initial period increasing numbers of people became confused about the burdens they had escaped and the burdens the 18th Amendment seemed to impose upon them. Second, it is clear that Prohibition was by all measures more effective in the states where there had been dry laws before the war. And third, in the states with a dry tradition as well as in those without one, there were striking rural-urban differences. Usually the rural areas defended Prohibition to the last, and the urban centers were generally the centers of wet practice, sentiment and leadership. A fourth consideration is, as Martha Bruère's studies showed, that in these urban areas the Volstead Act pretty well shut off the low-income groups from their traditional sources of alcohol, and the new sources made it very expensive. The saloons did close, and very few speakeasies ever became "poor men's clubs" with working-class associations.

In any event, we must conclude that by these indications— burdens lifted, burdens imposed—Prohibition was at least *partially effective.* But we cannot here beg the broader question: Why then was it not more effective or less effective? That is to say, what were the problems of making it more effective, why were these problems not solved, and what barriers were there during the 1920s to the spread of support for Volsteadism?

To begin with the problems of enforcement, these were indeed stubborn. They may very well have been beyond solution. Congress thrust them upon the Treasury Department, where the new Prohibition officers would suffer not only from inexperience but from federal political patronage, from the confusions inherent in the "concurrent clause" of the 18th Amendment, and from all the flaws in the Volstead Act itself. The technical problems before the Prohibition Bureau of the Treasury Department were both varied and perplexing. Prescription alcohol and sacramental alcohol tempted physicians,

priests, dentists, and druggists to become sophisticated bootleggers for their friends. This was not a great leakage, but it was
one very difficult to police. For example, the demand for
sacramental wines increased by 800,000 gallons during the first
two years of Prohibition, a circumstance which caused a
spokesman for the Federal Council of the Churches of Christ in
America to suggest that "not more than one-quarter of this is
sacramental—the rest is sacrilegious." There was a more
severe problem in the manufacture of beer of a fairly high
alcoholic content, which was legal under the Volstead Act if the
purpose was to make "near beer," a "dealcoholized" version
of the real thing. Here really enormous amounts of beer were
diverted to bootleggers before they could be rendered adjectly
pusillanimous, and trucks loaded with beer traveling the streets
in broad daylight were a common sight in many large cities.
Then there was industrial alcohol, which, when legally man-
ufactured, could easily be turned to the bootleg trade. Furthermore, smuggling along the open borders of the country was a
violation which would have required a huge standing army to
police in any effective way; and even a modest degree of
interference with smuggling along the coasts would have
required a two-ocean naval blockade. Finally, there were illegal
stills, home breweries, and bathtub gin mills by the hundreds of
thousands which presented a challenge so unnerving it could be
neither defined nor contained.

The awesome magnitude of these last two problems,
smuggling and home manufacture, seemed to raise doubts
concerning the sanity or the intelligence of the dry leaders
who opened them. Given any understanding of human nature, especially in America, what in the name of reality
could they have supposed would happen? But these leaders
were not unintelligent, nor did they suppose that an army would
patrol the borders, or a navy the shorelines, or a massive
national police force the nooks and crannies of every private
residence. Most Americans, they assumed with reason, wanted
Prohibition. Of those who did not, they supposed, surely only a
few would be so defiant as to break the law. And if a few did

break the law—we are back with E. J. Wheeler—how could this rupture Prohibition? The purpose was to protect society, not to change individual morality or to assure individual salvation.

The essential mechanics of these expectations were made clear in a pamphlet published by the Treasury Department, *Public Cooperation in Prohibition Law Enforcement* (1931). According to this rather exquisite projection, the drys themselves assumed that local groups, probably in association with the Anti-Saloon League, would, as the old antivice crusaders had done, act as intelligence-gathering units, feeding information to the police or to the Prohibition Bureau. Thus—and typically—when an honest citizen in his usual reconaissance detected the presence of a bootlegger or a speakeasy, he would inform his ASL leaders, who would in turn alert the District Prohibition Administrator, whose patronage appointment would have been secured by the nomination of local drys. The administrator and his agents would then plan and execute a "raid," and in the process of searching and seizing they would surely uncover "lists" of individuals and places—rumrunners, middlemen, "ring'leaders"—from which the administrator could identify the sources of supply and go on triumphantly to smash a "ring." Beyond this happy scenario, dry expectations were supposedly based on an assumed self-interest. Railroad executives would cooperate to avoid any complicity in the crime of transporting, building owners to avoid the Padlock Law, real estate persons to protect neighborhood property values, individuals to protect their families.

Under pressure of these expectations—which were perhaps naive but not altogether unintelligent—members of the dry Congress during the 1920s adopted a policy of avoiding the problems of enforcement, minimizing the costs, and urging caution at every suggestion of vigor or change. Investigation into the character of enforcement, the dry majority implied, would serve no useful purpose; worse, with the wrong direction it could create opportunities for wets to expose certain inevitable practices which in the light of inevitably sensational publicity might generate unseemly public criticism. Congress should no more investigate drinking in the United States than it should investigate adultery. When questioned pointedly about the law violations, most dry leaders responded by indicating that the need was not for troops or guns or ships or prisons but simply for more respect for the Constitution.

One has here a striking reminder of certain theories of social deviance—especially those presented by Kai Erikson in *Wayward Puritans* (1966)—that criminal activity, which usually stirs the dominant group to common outrage and thus to an exciting sense of group identity, may actually serve the interests of social stability; that the agencies designed to check deviance frequently are so poorly equipped for their assigned chores that they function more to illuminate the character of the deviance than to exterminate it—which may also serve social interests; and, finally, that the exertion a community makes to control a crime—the physical capacity of its courts and jails, for example—is a fairly good indication of how seriously the community regards the deviation.

Thus Congress in 1922 gave the Prohibition Bureau $6,750,000 for a force of 3,060 employees, including agents, clerks, and stenographers. The bureau divided the country into federal districts, each of which was headed by a Prohibition Administrator at a salary of about $6,000. Field agents under him were paid about $150 a month. Often an entire district would be without automobiles, boats, or any of the tools of crime detection. That this deployment of minimum force was a mere token—a symbol of dry confidence rather than of tyranny—was soon apparent to those who were attracted to the illicit trade. They learned, for example, that in the 20th District of the Prohibition Bureau, which included the Pacific Northwest, 20 agents faced all the problems listed above in an area where the Canadian border could hardly be policed at all. The Pacific Ocean and Puget Sound, with the many islands and adjacent wooded beaches, provided a foggy and usually private paradise for rumrunners who supplied bootleggers from

California to Seattle. Anyone with a small boat could enter the business, and many came equipped for big business, since the risks were slight compared to the fabulous rewards.

When the resources of the Prohibition Bureau were generally recognized, nearly a hundred bootleggers and rumrunners attended an open convention in a Seattle hotel in 1922, where, without undue hilarity and under Robert's Rules of Order, they adopted resolutions setting "fair prices" for liquor and establishing a code of ethics "to keep liquor runners within the limits of approved business methods." In the district for New England there were only 91 agents, in the district for New York City only 129, in all of Oklahoma only 18. The U.S. District Attorney for New York City said that he needed at 1,500 to do any king of job at all. Moreover, most of the agents were untrained, and many were simply incompetent.

Under these circumstances, what is remarkable is that Prohibition was as effective as we know it to have been. The expectations of the Prohibition Bureau, however, were soon distended. When John F. Kramer took office as the first national Prohibition Commissioner, he vowed intemperately that the law would "be obeyed in the cities, large and small" and that liquor would not be sold, "nor given away, nor hauled in anything on the surface of the earth, or in the air." But within two years, he told delegates to the national Anti-Saloon League convention that the federal government could never do the job alone. If Prohibition were in fact to prohibit, he said, then state and local officials would have to enforce the law.

Most of the states had laws patterned after the Volstead Act, some of them even more severe. Vermont, for example, had a law requiring persons arrested for liquor violations to reveal the source of their liquor. Indiana made it illegal for a jeweler to show cocktail shakers in his display windows. But here again we see more confidence than tyranny:Legislators usually found such laws easy to pass so long as the drys did not ask for significant appropriations. Many state governors early determined that their state police, who had enough to worry about with their regular duties, would not be available to chase rumrunners or close speakeasies. Most of these governors were men usually overwhelmed by their own problems with budgets and politics. When harassed by the uncompromising drys who wanted really effective enforcement, they sought shelter in positions of adamant sophistry: Since Congress had passed the Volstead Act and increased its own police powers, they reasoned, then Congress could very well use these new powers if it really wanted the Volstead Act enforced. The law, after all, was aimed at individuals, not state governments. They referred questions and complaints about liquor violations to the nearest office of the Prohibition Bureau and attempted to remain politically aloof from the real problems of either the wets or the drys. By 1926, state legislatures in the United States were appropriating annually a total of only $698,855 for Prohibition enforcement, an amount estimated as approximately one-eighth of that which the same governments were spending to police their laws for the control of fish and game. Some states were spending nothing at all.

At the level of county government, it was unlikely that the problems would differ in any real way. The sheriffs, as elective officials, were obliged in all their activities to consider the attitudes of their constituents, and most were careful not to offend any significant body of public opinion. They were forced, as it were, to develop delicate maneuvers for acting dry while protecting the wet, and this usually meant that they fell with a special fury upon the politically weak—the vagrant bootleggers and lonely moonshiners. Thus one prosecuting attorney noted in his annual report that "The few convictions for liquor violations were of visitors or those to whom no jury could have had sympathy. Our own bootleggers are small retailers who, if convicted at all, the juries seem to have a feeling that the possession of intoxicating liquor of such inferior quality, is enough punishment, in itself."

What the county governments could not do for Prohibition, the larger city governments seldom attempted. After the war, city governments faced a host of vexatious problems which grew more demanding with each year: schools, sewers, traffic, utilities, labor, crime, taxes. These problems had to do with immediate municipal well-being and could not be ignored.

Councilmen thus hoped that "concurrent enforcement" meant an escape for the cities from the dissipations of money and time that would surely have followed any full-scale attempt to keep liquor outside city limits. The alternative slowed even the most radical imagination. If a city wanted to stay dry, it would need an army of policemen, maybe even a police state; if it expected these men to remain honest, it would have to pay them salaries high enough to encourage honesty. Hardly a councilman in the country was willing to consider methods of raising such revenue. The popular attitude was that articulated by ASL leaders—that Prohibition was a moral issue, to live or die not in municipal budgets but in the public conscience.

And it does seem clear that the character of municipal enforcement contributed to the fatal erosion of enthusiasm for Prohibition. Sadly, it must have been, urban Prohibitionists learned that illegal booze, just like gambling and prostitution, could find warmly hospitable undergrounds and prosper in the urban environment. Thus bootlegged liquor, like outlawed sex and card games, easily inclined policemen and politicians toward the view that laws can't change human nature. Many speakeasies did prosper in the larger cities. Many bootleggers did pay their customary "license-by-the-bribe" fees and made their rounds without fear. In an era of relaxed "normalcy," they were more often greeted with an indulgent smile than with moral alarm. No one could with any accuracy estimate their numbers. Such defiance was particularly grievous to many devout Prohibitionists, because it was in the big cities that they chose to measure the "success" or the "failure" of the 18th Amendment. The rural areas had been mostly dry before the Volstead Act, and what remained in 1920 to "prove" was whether or not a national law could dry up an urban center which had not before yielded to local option.

In most of Chicago, it seems, the impact of the Volstead Act was to raise to 75 cents the cost of the whiskey highball which had sold for 15 cents in 1919. And there were in that city uncounted numbers of people who regarded the price, rather than the purchase, as the outrageous crime. In 1926, a Prohibition agent in New York City estimated that there were 100,000 speakeasies in his metropolitan district, and it seems clear that few people who were willing or able to pay the high prices were ever really thirsty in Boston or New Orleans. At the same time, an investigation by the Department of Justice in San Francisco showed that rumrunners and bootleggers had made liquor of almost any quality or quantity available there in restaurants, drugstores, and open barrooms.

In Washington, D.C., when General Lincoln C. Andrews of the Prohibition Bureau told Congress that by 1926 his agents had seized almost 700,000 illicit stills, he estimated that at least half a million persons were employed in the production of moonshine booze. When Mayor William E. Dever of Chicago the same year told a committee of Congress that perhaps 60 percent of his police force was actually in the liquor business, he added that he could do nothing about it. This was no casual admission of Volstead's failure in that city. In 1923, Dever had begun a determined effort to clean up Chicago. In three days his police arrested seven hundred violators of the Prohibition law, and Dever had announced that he would have a dry city even if this meant dismissing every officer in the entire police department. There was no reason to question his integrity, or sincerity—or failure. In 1926 he could not say for sure "whether there are five thousand or twenty thousand stills in Chicago." He said, moreover, that honest efforts to enforce the dry laws were destroying the city, and he asked for some way out. He hoped "to pass the burden of this great subject on to somebody else, or else from the aid of constructive legislation to be relieved of its annoyance." So while it is true that many Americans never knew a bootlegger, never entered a speakeasy, and would have found it difficult to identify one, still others never knew an environment in which bootleggers and speakeasies were not an enduring presence. In the urban ghettoes, especially those of French, Italian, and Slavic ethnicity, Prohibition may have seemed something of a mystery; few people could understand how pietists could take it seriously.

These circumstances bring us into a new focus of consideration—that Prohibition was a *partial failure*. This was

surely not a happy consideration for most Americans in the
1920s, and we must now raise the question of why they tolerated
it. Why did they not demand that the law be either enforced
effectively or summarily repealed? We have already seen that
some of the problems of enforcement were perhaps beyond
solution, at least in the 1920s; but we have also seen that the drys
had persuaded political leaders, at least for a while, to regard
these problems as something less than a national crisis. It would
in this instance be difficult to underestimate the weight of that
persuasion or of the sustained power held by the Anti-Saloon
League in American political life. The word continued to go out
each week from the pulpits. Friends of the ASL were highly
visible—Senator Borah of Idaho, for example, was becoming
the country's most popular and possibly most influential public
speaker. Perhaps the clearest measure of the league's influence
is that the elections of 1928 returned a Congress with the
greatest dry majority in American history. Thus the ASL and its
dry voters were a firm barrier to any political movement against
Prohibition, and this barrier was a conspicuous feature of the
moral landscape in most parts of the nation.

Furthermore, among the highest levels of the prestigious elite
of the decade were men like Henry Ford and W. C. Durant of the
automobile industry, and John D. Rockefeller and William
Randolph Hearst, all of them fully aware of the partial "failures," and all of them at mid-decade still eager to support
Prohibition. Indeed, when things began to go sour in the next
few years, both Hearst and Durant, in a quaint tradition of
stewardship, sponsored contests and awarded prizes of $25,000
each to authors of the "best" plan for salvaging the 18th
Amendment. In a similar vein, the Motion Picture Producers
and Distributors of America, Inc., determined in 1926 that
recent movies had dealt too frivolously with the Volstead Act,
and members instructed the president of that organization, Will
H. Hays, to strike from films any "word, phrase, clause, or
sentence that directly or indirectly encourages the slightest
disregard for the law." In films made thereafter, liquor was not
to be "brought in unnecessarily in any way which might be
construed as being for an ulterior purpose or which in any way

promotes disrespect for the law.''

Americans could, then, live harmoniously enough in the presence of ''partial failure,'' and to many people even the often gross inadequacies of Volstead Act enforcement during the 1920s were not in themselves reasons to abandon Prohibition. But this dike-plugging by the Hays Office suggested twhat everyone knew at the time—that the barriers to anti-Prohibition sentiment were holding less and less well. Repeal was then only a few years away, and the questions we should now consider are why and how the Repeal Movement gained momentum. This may be our most important question, for we have now considered the long history of temperance agitation and rising expectations, the enthusiasms across a century of increasing numbers of drys, the success of their ambitions, the apparent willingness of Americans to live contentedly with the ambiguities of partial success or partial failure—that is, we have considered the barriers to wet sentiment as late as 1928. What then happened in the United States to Prohibition?

From the very first, it is true, some people were, like Michael Monahan or like H. L. Mencken, indeed convinced that Prohibition was a disaster for the nation. Yet they did not call for repeal with any confidence. Most of them regarded repeal as unthinkable: No amendment to the Constitution had ever been repealed, and it was clear that most Americans were happy enough with the partial success—or partial failure—of the 18th. And some of the deepest pockets of wet resistance seemed to yield when New Jersey finally ratified in 1922 and when in 1924 the voters of Massachusetts finally approved a state enforcement law to supplement the national Volstead Act. Yet others clearly did not yield. Connecticut and Rhode Island never ratified, and in Maryland there was never a state provision for enforcement; officials there consistently refused to cooperate with federal agents. And things began to slip. In 1923, the New York Assembly voted to repeal that state's enforcement laws, and the measure was signed by Governor Alfred Smith. This was a critical event for the future of Prohibition. In New York, thereafter, enforcement was largely a matter of public games in which, to the amusement of almost everyone, a few agents pursued the vast multitudes of manufacturers and sellers. In 1926, slightly more than 48 percent of the voters in California favored repeal of the state's dry laws; in Montana, a clear majority did in fact repeal them. That year in Illinois, 60 percent favored a state request to Congress that the Volstead Act be modified. At the same time in New York, voters favored similar measures by over 70 percent. By 1926, then, a movement was obvious in several quarters. But it was not a Repeal Movement. A nationwide poll conducted by the Newspaper Enterprise Association that year, with the cooperation of 326 member newspapers in 47 states, indicated that only about 30 percent of the people wanted outright repeal, but about 50 percent favored some form of modification, some easy kind of upward revision in the Volstead definition of "intoxicating beverages" which would allow beer and wine.

Some historians have found an explanation for the subsequent conversion of a moderation movement into a repeal movement in the currency of legends about crime and youth; in the failure of governments to enforce the law; in a growing conviction that this failure would ultimately undermine respect for all laws; in the prestige given to these ideas by "one of the most effective publicity campaigns of modern times" led by the Association against the Prohibition Amendment (AAPA), the repeal organization of very wealthy wets who assembled the money and the skills to "beat the Anti-Saloon League at its own game"; and finally in the enormously accelerated shift of public sentiment after 1929, when it could be persuasively argued that Prohibition deprived men of jobs, deprived governments of revenue, and contributed to economic cataclysm. Surely a great barrier broke with the beginning of the Great Depression, and one can with that moment mark a rising tide of public sentiment so strong that it pulled up the drys, the modifiers, the indifferent, the undecided, and the repealers into a wave which washed away not only the ruins of Volsteadism but also the very spirit of the 18th Amendment. To some social critics, this irresistibly swelling demand for repeal was an unfortunate development. Even Andrew Sinclair's often "wet" historical interpretation of the period concludes that modification might have saved the 18th, and that repeal was a "fanaticism" justified neither by immediate circumstances nor by any healthy concern for the future of the country.

It is true that there was a sort of "fanaticism" of repeal that impelled a fabulously financed and eminently skillful manipulation of public opinion about Prohibition. But surely this interpretation overvalues the power of conspirators and the tendency of public opinion to level grievances against a law and its supporters without reason. It is a view which does not help us at all to understand repeal or Prohibition in a wider context. It does not illuminate the development of liquor legislation and morality in Sweden, for example, or in England, where there was no AAPA and where major changes occurred before the depression. Nor can the view help us account for the long-term persistence of various state or regional efforts in the United States after repeal to find a socially acceptable formula for moderation—the determination of several states to keep the profit motive out of liquor sales, or the fact that in some regions it was illegal to sell hard liquor by the drink until after World War II, or the tenacious grip with which the people of Oklahoma clung to their Prohibition law until 1959 and the people of Mississippi until 1966. Repeal was by no means the very end; it was not a social fluke or a moral retrogression. Because of the enduring strurgle of many people after repeal to define how much or how little liquor control was consistent with the circumstances of life in the second quarter of the twentieth century, one could indeed support the counterview that Prohibition was "fanaticism" and repeal was the real beginning of "moderation."

Our most important consideration, however, should be this: If liquor laws reflect the character of a nation's anxieties, then to understand repeal is to approach the shifting moral and spiritual values which overwhelmed Americans during the first quarter of the twentieth century. Of the participants in this turmoil, Frederick Lewis Allen was certainly among the most percep-

tive, and when he wrote *The Lords of Creation* in the early 1930s
he was pondering what he called the "quantum change"
between 1897 and 1920 in the quality of American life. He noted
carefully the material dimension of that change—the electric
technology and techniques of mass production; the breathtaking advance in urbanization and industrialization; the new
sources of wealth, power, and prestige; the new pluralism and
complexity. Such vast dislocations brought down his "lords of
creation"—the last heroes of Protestant stewardship in the
Rockefeller-Carnegie-Morgan tradition—by destroying their
influence and their self-confidence. Then, in a brief but precise
definition of Progressive energies he noted also the spiritual
impact of these dislocations. What was taking place in the early
twentieth century, before the 1920s, he wrote, "was a complex
and pervasive change in the intellectual and emotional atmosphere of America: the spread of a contagious desire to purify
politics, win justice for the poor, protect the helpless, and
subdue wickedness in general by statutes, regulation, and moral
conversions."

Surely a central fact of American society at that time was that
after almost a century the West had been conquered and
assimilated; the Frontier was finally closed. The impact of its
closing would surely shape the material and spiritual future. If
the opening of the West had exposed Americans of the
nineteenth century to an extraordinary level of tensions,
anxiety, stress, and disorder, then the closure must have fallen
heavily upon the Americans of the twentieth century. The
opening had shattered a sense of community. The closure
encouraged its mending; national energies could again be
internalized, and this was a process Frederick Lewis Allen was
defining. It was a rise of moral sensitivity from isolated
concerns to the level of urgent public questions, bringing into
moral focus some of the more outrageous social abuses of an
undisciplined industrial society, which, having lost its sense of
organic unity and social goals, had encouraged the sense of
freedom that justifies economic exploitation: the tyranny of
trusts; the ruthlessness of wage slavery, child labor, industrial

accidents; the plight of blacks, Indians, and Orientals; the serfdom of women; the corruption of government; the social pollution of saloons and slums. As the frontier closed in the 1890s, the moods of protest and then the energies of Progressive reform were the first clearly spiritual phases of the quantum change.

The next distinct phase was a rapidly rising sensitivity to the possibilities of a human life liberated from Victorian, rural, and agrarian confinements. The expansive scope of services available in the new society opened vistas for the gratification of impulses and for self-fulfillment which in the nineteenth century even the counter-culture had only furtively glimpsed. The individual, increasingly unfettered from family disciplines, could define his realization and identity in terms of his wants and desires instead of his duties and obligations. The velocity of this change soared in stunning increments, for during the 1920s technology created new instruments of change which were both the carriers of a new lifestyle and the symptoms of it: automobiles, radios, telephones, movies, confession magazines, advertising, a new psychology, a new literature—each with its previously unthinkable opportunities for communication, leisure, interpersonal relationships, individuality, and freedom.

The Repeal Movement rode on all of these instruments, and we should briefly examine at least a few of them. For some years before 1920, a number of Americans had been reading Freud, Jung, and Havelock Ellis, drawing what they regarded as the liberating conclusion, for better or worse, that when one repressed a "natural" instinct or impulse, his own poor health would be an inevitable consequence. Thus a new psychology—weighted with theories of glandular imperatives and with the promises of individual fulfillment implicit in psychoanalysis—provided an intellectual base for the ideal of self-realization (often in bitter contrast to family-realization) and for the practice of self-indulgence. Indeed, some readers drew from this psychology a rationale for what formerly had been regarded as depraved behavior—the comportment of impulse and excess. And what John Burnham calls the "narcissistic preoccupation'' with the idea of ''the hidden self'' was quickly integrated into literature and art and into studies of medicine, social work, and industrial efficiency (where a specialist might stimulate the ''self'' to control the worker). It was seized with indelicate enthusiasm by bureaucratic-minded sales engineers searching for better techniques to sell the products which were streaming in profusion from the new technology of mass production.

A popular book by H. A. Overstreet in 1925 was called *Influencing Human Behavior,* and it had a chapter on ''The Appeal to Wants,'' which must have been eagerly received by the advertising business. According to Otis Pease, in *The Responsibilities of American Advertising* (1958), specialists in this field were coming to see themselves—like clergymen, teachers, and attorneys—as intellectuals, as professional manipulators of ideas. Indeed, some saw their role in the great chain of production as absolutely vital to a society in which to unload consumer goods was to advance economic progress, if not civilization. They saw their social function, in fact, as the creation of new *wants* where before there had been only *needs* or *inclinations.* Thus an executive of the General Motors Corporation noted in a speech during the 1920s that ''The old factors of wear and tear can no longer be depended upon to create a demand. They are too slow.''

What was faster was an image of the ''good life'' which could promote consumption by obscuring the value system to which the old factors of wear and tear were important. Advertisers, accepting the techniques as well as the moral implications of the new psychology, began the traffic in models of this image, a traffic in emotions, hidden feelings, and symbols that became the substance of the new persuasion. The model made clear certain prerequisites for the good life, and we see them in the newspaper and magazine printouts of national advertisers across the decade: a willingness to consume rather than to deny, a fashionable taste in recreation and dress, and a seductive sexuality. One should buy soap, perfume, clothes, gadgets, radios, automobiles, cigarettes. To be willing to consume was to be individually free; to be fashionable was to be impulsive; to be sexually impressive was to be independent, liberated, daring, rebellious—it was to fashion a lifestyle for which drinking was the preeminent symbol.

This image was carried to even the remotest rural areas and rural minds by middle-class magazines (whose articles increasingly favored repeal) and by newspapers (increasingly wet). This was a time when competition among them, as we have noted, was forcing even the most staid editors to forsake truth for sensation and grasp for stories of crime, adventure, grotesqueries, and sex, singly or in titillating combinations. To compete for national advertising money was, of course, to compete for circulation, and this drove the urban newspapers deeper and deeper into small towns, where they would work to dissolve the barriers of distance, ignorance, and prejudice which had for so long isolated millions of Americans. By 1930, hardly anyone could avoid a daily image of the advertisers' wisdom.

Movies of the 1920s—afflicted by perhaps even more competitive frenzy—quickly embellished the image with their own symbols as they projected the satisfactions of the impulsive life. Among the intriguing heroes and heroines of movie fantasies, Americans saw that glamorous people escaped lives of quiet desperation by being defiant, indulgent, and amoral, qualities which could be dramatically characterized by an individual's liberation from the older fixations against drinking and sexual freedom. It is very clear, as Andrew Sinclair's study of repeal shows, that in the plots and characterizations of the most popular movies, moral courage and individuality were associated with drink and sexuality, and the good and strong people in these projections were more liberated than the weak or villainous.

The more profound expression of this rebellion against pietist values was of course projected in the serious literary art of the decade. The Hemingway heroes, for example, seek the good life in an honestly direct approach to fundamental instinct and pleasure. Food, sex, and liquor, says Andrew Sinclair, became a sort of holy trinity. Hemingway, indeed, stressed the purity of this candid pursuit: In their deeply moral aversion to hypocrisy, deviousness, pretense, greed, and even ambition, his most attractive characters project a life purified of the kind of motives and morals which had led the world to industrial debauchery and urban squalor, world war, and spiritual repression. Thus the efforts of artists neatly complemented the thrust of the bureaucratic society toward a new and boggling Reformation: in the name of morality, to stimulate impulse and to justify indulgence. In the name of progress and civilization and social discipline, the old values of restraint, duty, and denial had to be undone.

A signal, if nonliterary, event in the second phase of quantum change occurred in 1928 when Henry Ford announced his intention to produce a Model A and when half a million Americans were so desperately eager to have this vehicle that they made down payments for it without yet having heard the price or seen the product. It was, indeed, much more than a product, for the availability of automobiles to middle-class families determined the nature of subsequent social change in ways yet staggering to the historical imagination. Having learned that automobiles existed, Americans had to possess them, both as conveniences and as profound symbols. A recent study suggests that in the late 1920s most Americans came to feel that owning an automobile was more important than owning a home. When families could have motorized wheels, individuals acquired a new mobility, both geographic and social—or had it thrust upon them: individuals to an encapsulated and mobile privacy, nuclear families to a new nuclear, suburban isolation. This privacy and isolation changed the structure of geographic community or destroyed it; likewise it shattered the patterns of interpersonal relationships in friendship, neighborliness, courtship, marriage, and community. It was an explosion of social atoms, each of which would thereafter reestablish its own personal moral orbits on the basis of new configurations in freedom, opportunity, and anxiety that had never before been experienced. This is to say that the automobile, perhaps more than any other factor in urban-industrial life, had made modern individualism possible.

Thus the powerful family anxieties inspired by the saloon—those so vivid in *Ten Nights*—were shortly reduced to mild irritations. On the eve of the Great Depression, there were actually few necessary chores, rituals, or defenses that middle-class urban families were by any circumstances compelled to perform together, few reasons for the bourgeois family to stand firm in unity and loyalty as the most vital shelter against social disorder. The modern family was less the institution for social discipline; it was more the institution for the individual fulfillment of husband, wife, and children. The children were more and more involved outside the home—the growth of public high schools is one measure of this—and the impact upon them or their out-of-home environment became more and more pervasive. The family served then not so much to protect and train children as to develop, refine, encourage, and prepare them for a final liberation from the tide of family-determined goals, prejudices, comportments, and traditions. Through a century of profound change, the bourgeois values of internalization, discipline, privacy, individual dignity, and self-identity had moved the family toward a remarkable mutation: What was important to the new family and the modern society was individualism.

Within the urban-industrial family—a social unit more companionate than tyrannical, more intimate, elective, open, indulgent, permissive, and creative—the modern woman need no longer protect or defend her function as guardian angel, no longer fear the comportment of the old lifestyle, the Victorian tyrant, or the Victorian saloon. The more modern Mrs. Joe Morgan would not live in stark terror that Joe—were he so quaintly perverse as to prefer the tedium of exclusively male drinking and drunkenness to the excitement of movies, radios, parties, dances, and automobiles—might come home dead-drunk and flat broke from Slade's barroom. She could take a job from a friend of Henry Ford, buy factory-made food and clothing, practice birth control, and send those children she may already have off to the public schools. It was not, then, impossible to get along without Joe. She could divorce the lout, then go herself to the polls to vote for officials who would tax the villainy out of old Simon Slade. Mrs. Morgan might herself take a martini now and then, for she was not entirely without anxieties, and she was as much at liberty as anyone else to fulfill her wants, seek her personal gratifications, and relax her own tensions.

In the older society—one with a sense of community, one like the communities of Maine in the days of old Hate-Evil Hall— even Joe Morgan would have rejoiced that others were concerned about his drinking and were protecting him and his family and the total society from his compulsion or his excess. He would expect it. But in the family-based society of *Ten Nights* he would not expect it, for there was but little community, and only his sad-eyed daughter would beg him to leave off iniquity and sin no more. In the society of individualism, there was no community and not much family. Joe Morgan, the individualist, and Mrs. Morgan, the liberated, would resent any challenge whatever to the freedoms with which they had so carefully defined their sacred identities.

Individual freedom: We see here in quantum change a ragged end to the stewardship which had been a social cohesion in the pietist Republic. In the collapse of Wall Street and the ignominy of the industrial lords after 1929, the tradition lost all its authority. From Neal Dow to Woodrow Wilson, Rockefeller, J. P. Morgan, and Herbert Hoover, the solemn guardians of capitalism and social virtue seemed to have been so insufferably pious, self-righteous, and stuffy—and so very wrong.

In the 1820s, Americans had rushed toward freedom from Old World orthodoxies, traditions, and age-old confinements; in the 1920s they rushed toward a freedom from bourgeois obligations and restraints. We see then the steady but often bitter erosion of the bourgeois family values which the old stewards had presumed to protect: duty, delayed gratification, unity, loyalty, continuity. The individual cast off his moorings, and we see the beginning of a lonely glory. We chart it in the creative literature after 1890: Mark the utterly bourgeois family concerns of William Dean Howells, who could not bear to see the play *Damaged Goods*, then the dislocated and confused individuals of the young Stephen Crane, then the fierce if hypersensitive egos in the existentialist heroes of Ernest Hemingway. Mark the anguished spirituality of nostalgia for a lost family-community in Thomas Wolfe: "Naked and alone we came into exile . . . into the unspeakable and incommunicable prison of his earth. Which of us has looked to his father's heart?"

Which, indeed, in the new society, would want to look? (The new psychology justified attacks upon both motherhood and fatherhood.) Roland Berthoff, in his conclusions about *An Unsettled People,* describes prospects for a cold atomic world:

> the social institutions of the new age were to be simply the sum of the personal ties among their individual members. The "church of one's choice," the family held together mainly by the inclination of its members, the suburban community of physically detached houses and socially isolated households—such anti-institutions . . . became the asocial norm of American social aspirations.

Thus in the 1920s the American family was becoming just such an anti-institution. Disestablished like the early American churches, it went aimlessly afloat in the new society. The course of quantum change had dislocated it from the productive economy. The new urban-industrial civilization had relieved it of obligations to provide economic skills, of its responsibilities for child (but not infant) care, and of its central role (before Sunday schools) in religious education. The agency-society had relieved it of its obligations to care for the sick, the aged, the indigent, the orphaned. When the "head'of'household" ceased to vote for the family, it was dislocated from its political establishment—another developmental point we can mark on the dateline of progressive disintegration. We mark here not the *disappearance* of all family values, of course (though it often seemed so); nor do we imply any moral retrogression. The development of moral freedom has moved our mark from the church-of-one's-choice to the sexual indulgence-of-one's-choice to the family-of-one's-choice, and surely to the drink-

or-drug-of-one's-choice. This was the unraveling, the *disintegration*. Social discipline was unhinged from the family nexus and passed to the agency-society that was, through wants and impulses, learning new techniques of control.

Now to paraphrase Frederick Lewis Allen: What was taking place in the 1920s, the decade marking the second phase of quantum change, was a complex and pervasive alteration in the material and spiritual environment of America. We see it in the spread of nuclear family isolation and in the spread of a contagious desire to glorify the individual and the values of indulgence and impulse, often at the expense of traditional social and familial harmonies. We see it in a desire not so much for social justice—as was the case during the first phase—as in the demand by individual men and women for individual civil liberty and want-gratification. We see it in a desire not so much to protect the helpless as to protect the defiant. And in the repeal of some statutes and the creation of others, we see a desire to define a new private and a new public morality.

By a periolous irony, this new morality was remarkably close to that of the old counter-culture which had sustained the saloon. But the saloon was indeed dead. The Prohibition laws did not stop all drinking, but they certainly strangled the old drunkard-making business and pushed into obscurity the old-time public drunkard. And as Jack London had hoped, people during the 1920s came to see saloon drinking as a decadently quaint old custom. It could not revive—so curiously like Prohibition itself—because it was not consistent with the urban-industrial styles of freedom and control for men and women. In the new society, the saloon could serve no useful individual, economic, sexual, or social function. Like so many other institutions, it had been utterly disestablished not only by law but by movies, radios, assembly lines, and automobiles, by the new psychology, new advertising, new sex-role differentiations, and new structure and function of family life. There is, then, an even deeper irony: Because the saloon was dead, Prohibition could be repealed.

This was the character of trends in the society that supported the Repeal Movement. This movement did not require the devious manipulation of public opinion aspired to by the Association against the Prohibition Amendment, though such manipulation was a part of the total culture and certainly provided acceleration. It was not necessary to convince Americans that Prohibition was no great success, for they had moved beyond this consideration and toward a reorientation of values, toward a new line between the acceptable and the deviant. It is useful in this regard to think for a moment about a more recent quantum change that we can see in the movements to repeal laws against adultery, gambling, homosexuality, and drug use. It is unthinkable that the pietist Republic should not have demanded these laws. It is equally unthinkable that a new society should not repeal them, for people will not forever hold to a code of public or private morality developed by men and women, most of them long dead, to fuse a paradigm of social values which have lost their function.

In this light it seems that the repeal movement was carried to its crest on the idea that Prohibition was simply inappropriate to the circumstances of life in the new society. This idea was indeed brought to the level of social urgency by the Great Depression, as were many other rebellious notions. In the failure of American capitalism, Americans lost the vision of the Progressive age, and in the second phase of quantum change, the age of Liberalism, there was much in American society to be repealed besides Prohibition. A society whose frontiers had been closed had lost geographic and social safety valves and needed then to look to the problems of the individualism it had already generated—and to the problems of how this individualism might function within the necessary harmonies of a closed system. For example, the National Origins Act of 1924 was a repeal of the melting-pot ideal, a repeal quite necessary if the disharmony of nativist anxieties of a hundred years was ever thereafter to subside. Because immigration could not thereafter threaten the supremacy of white Protestants, immigrant drinking comportment was less an occasion for pietist anxieties, and a Catholic could then be nominated for President.

Later and more vividly, the Indian Reorganization Act in 1934 would repeal the persistent idea that non-WASP cultural minorities should not sustain their own cultural integrity. Many of the principles of primitive business practice would be repealed, for businessmen in a closed society cannot assume that society will forever sanction a predatory system.

The list of repeals becomes an inventory of such adjustments in the name of internal harmony: repeals of the restraints against organized labor, against social planning and social security, against the federal government's taking a role in economic management; repeals of restraints on divorce, on birth control, on access to public education; repeals—yet later—of barriers to the advance of nonwhite minorities in society, industry, and government. This is a chronicle of the long and noisy deflation of pietist capitalism, of its bourgeois values and of its superstructure of ethnocentrism, for which Prohibition was but one symbol.

9

Repeal
Politics

AS EARLY AS 1922, the Association against the Prohibition Amendment had entered national contests to the extent of endorsing congressional candidates—and thereby handing the vastly more powerful Anti-Saloon League an accurate list of its foes. In 1924, when the AAPA both endorsed and opposed office seekers, it found 262 candidates for the House of Representatives "unsatisfactory." The ASL easily helped 219 of these get elected anyway. After the elections of 1926—the year when, as most historians believe, it was first obvious that a majority of the voters had deep misgivings about the Volstead Act—Congress was drier than at any earlier time. This paradox again underlines the power of the Anti-Saloon League in American political life. It also emphasizes a deeper complexity of American politics: that the wets failed to win in 1928, when the new society of individualism was already well advanced, shows again that Prohibition was seldom an isolated or organic issue and was instead intricately related to the complex nature of politics and social change.

Most participants, and certainly those from the Anti-Saloon League and the Association against the Prohibition Amendment, understood the profound conflict which faced the Democratic Party following the collapse of Woodrow Wilson. It was a conflict symbolized and personified by William Jennings Bryan and Alfred E. Smith—a clash of cultural values, ideals, and lifestyles. The conflict has been variously described as a struggle between the country and the city, the nativist and the immigrant, the liturgical and the pietist, the old America dedicated to the preeminence of white Anglo-Saxon Protestant values and the new America shaping an alternative social model in the ideal of harmonious cultural pluralisms. Though the struggle indeed demonstrated all these dimensions, it was not yet a struggle between the progressive and the liberal, the family and the individual. The new liberalism had as yet no politics and no hero. It was, however, a struggle in which the wet–dry antagonisms of a hundred years clearly played a central part.

In all of Christendom, as H. L. Mencken might have said, there was no more illustrious defender of white Anglo-Saxon Protestant values than the man whom Mencken called the "Fundamentalist Pope"—William Jennings Bryan. As presidential candidate, as Cabinet member, as the great silver-tongued orator, he had since the early 1890s raised his silver voice against the encroaching pluralisms of the urban-industrial society. If there was the purity of silver in the ideal of monetary reform, it was but a reflection of the vital purification—sanctified earlier by Lyman Beecher—which was to make the country safe for pietist values. Bryan had articulated a deep distrust of high finance, urban lifestyles, and racial amalgamation. He had in fact been the prototype of the culture-hero since 1896, when his candidacy had helped shape a new cultural alignment in American political life. As Paul Kleppner's study *The Cross of Culture* (1970) shows, Bryan's campaign drew many pietists into the Democratic Party and drove away many liturgicals, who were "repelled by the evangelical fervor of the Bryan crusade." His ideal even then was to use the party for the moral reconstruction of the nation; and in 1916, when he had abandoned his presidential ambitions, he was still determined to make the Democratic Party the party of virtue, peace, the Sabbath, and Prohibition. The nation, he prophesied, "will soon be saloonless for evermore and will lead the world in the great crusade which will drive intoxicating liquor from the globe." In the 1920s he attacked liquor with the moral outrage he had earlier generated for

Republicans or Wall Street conspiracies.

This was a posture most politicians tried to avoid as the political hazards of Volsteadism became increasingly apparent. Republicans soon mastered the evasions. Bryan, however, disdained them. In 1920, the Democratic National Convention became a field of glorious battle in which Bryan fought against the candidate, James M. Cox, whose wet record as governor of Ohio offended him, and against a party platform that was as equivocal as the candidate himself. He lost both battles. But the margins of loss—as well as the volume of clamor—meant that the convention of 1924 would be even more explosive. By then the question of the party's identity was more urgently before the delegates, to be defined uproariously in terms of Prohibition or modification, Catholicism or Klanism, urbanism, or agrarian verities. The 103 ballots for the presidential nomination in 1924 were, in a way, a measure of the extent to which Democratic delegates recognized a deep cultural conflict. Throughout the ordeal it was Bryan's pleasure to see the nomination withheld from Governor Alfred E. Smith, but Bryan himself could not award it to his favorite, William McAdoo, or keep it from John W. Davis, whom he had resisted because of Davis's Wall Street connections and political expediency on Prohibition.

Bryan's death in 1925 did not diminish the party's rush toward some confrontation of the forces he represented and those he abhorred. Governor Smith had then taken unto himself all those energies working to give the party an urban–industrial–working-class image, working, actually, to advance the ascendancy of counterpietist values in American life. And when these values were indeed ascendant, their heroes would be as harshly inhospitable to the ideal of pluralistic harmony—they had little use for dryness or Sabbatarianism or social purity—as had ever been the heroes of Beecher-Bryan Americanism. By the 1920s, Smith's background as a Catholic, a vigorous working-class ward politician, a spokesman for the immigrant culture, and the successful, popular governor of the nation's most polyglot state had thrust this personification upon him. In his own character and personality, Smith made the differences between this

background and that of the traditional Democratic political
figures of the South and West as dramatic as possible. He was,
without apology, wet and Catholic. As a New Yorker, he
immediately aroused all those Democrats who thought that a
Tammany ward boss could never understand their problems. As
a Catholic, he aroused the nativist tradition still smoldering
from a wartime inflammation. And as a wet, he was notorious.
He had allowed the New York Assembly to repeal the state's
"Little Volstead Act," and the drys thereafter hated him. He
was said to have served liquor in the executive mansion at
Albany. The editor of the *Nation* wrote in 1927 that Governor
Smith drank as many as eight highballs a day—an assertion
difficult to believe now, but one which confirmed the fears of
many drys. It led to Smith's being referred to, widely and
rudely, as "Alcohol Al." Though his delegate strength in 1928
was enough to hand him a first-ballot victory without a
prolonged argument over Prohibition, Smith, like Bryan before
him, was soon playing the role of culture-hero.

But he was, of course, not of the old counterculture,
and he often tried to articulate the difference. The old
competitive traffic in drunkenness was dead, he emphasized, and this was Prohibition's great achievement.
The saloon, he said, "is and ought to be a defunct institution," and he seemed to believe that such statements established him securely as a defender of "temperance." But
from this base, he attacked the Volstead Act by claiming
that its definition of "the alcoholic content of an intoxicating beverage" was "admittedly inaccurate and unscien-
tifi." He promised to propose, as President, his own
"scientific" definition, one that would permit the manufacture and sale of wine and beer. He later raised for public
consideration his apparently sincere belief that the 18th
Amendment did not, in his words, "prohibit alcoholic beverages; it prohibits intoxicating beverages." This was a
tenable position, even an eminently intelligent one. It
would in fact be validated in law within four years, and in
1928 the country needed a referendum of some sort on

precisely this interpretation.

But in his 1928 acceptance speech, Smith went far beyond the common sentiment be calling for a "fearless application of Jeffersonian principles" to the matter of Prohibition. This meant states' rights, and it was not in 1928 a happy phrase for the drys. He further proposed an amendment to the Amendment which would allow those states where the people so voted to authorize the manufacture of "alcoholic beverages"—still not clearly defined—and the sale of them through state-owned dispensaries. This prospect may have aroused the faithful wets and their thirsty friends, but it did not sound like wisdom in most other Democratic circles, where the highest hope was that the issue of Prohibition would somehow go away and not divide them. Josephus Daniels, a fervent dry, still supposed that the Teapot Dome Scandal might emerge as the issue which could drive Republicans out of office in 1928. He predicted to Franklin Roosevelt in New York that the Democratic Party "would not only be defeated, but humiliated if the prohibition issue is paramounted." Though Smith himself had said earlier that the "liquor question" would not be "the great issue" of the campaign, he seemed determined that it should in fact be so. It was a theme of seven of his thirteen major speeches, and it was the exclusive topic of his Milwaukee address, in which he emphasized that Prohibition was "the most demoralizing factor in our public life."

Smith's refusal to conceal in any way his real feelings allowed no security for those who nursed misgivings about his liturgical loyalties and about the impression he left that the urban-immigrant culture was central to his character. When he chose John J. Raskob to manage his campaign, the misgivings of pietist Democrats were further aggravated by the fact that Raskob was a former Republican, a wet, and a Roman Catholic. He was the man who could swing the millions of dollars that some other eastern industrialists, impressed by Smith's economic conservatism as well as by his wetness, were willing to drop into the Democratic campaign. The implication for the older Bryanites was that these men—wet, Catholic, urban, and fabulously wealthy—were about to take over the party and the White House and deliver both to Jews and Catholics who were determined to overwhelm the traditions of the Protestant Republic. During the Campaign of 1928, the Reverend Bob Jones was speaking throughout the South to crowds wherever he found them: "I'll tell you, brother, that the big issue we've got to face ain't the liquor question. I'd rather see a saloon on every corner of the South than see the foreigners elect Al Smith President." Such attacks became so widespread and so vicious that many people have ever since supposed that the campaign was a sort of metaphorical anti-Catholic pogrom.

The Anti-Saloon League, as a federation of evangelical pietists, was surely well situated to generate fears and hatreds of the liturgical lifestyle—and to take advantage of such fears and hatreds. The correlation between the rising numbers of immigrants and the rising numbers of saloons in the 1890s was well known to the leaders of the ASL. But the founders of the league had organized their movement to assert a social discipline, and their technique had been to attack saloons, not immigrants or Catholics, Republicans or Democrats. This was a central consideration which they never allowed their followers to forget. They hoped to present the appearance of a united front of churches against the saloon, and they sometimes needed the votes of dry Catholics as much as they needed the votes of dry Protestants. To have people suppose that the dry cause was simply an anti-Catholic cause would have seriously distorted their intentions.

Among the friends of the Anti-Saloon League in the nation's capital were good Catholics like Senator Randsdell of Louisiana, Senator Walsh of Montana, and Senator Ashurst of Arizona. It was always clear that the league had allies who were both antisaloon and Roman Catholic. Father J. J. Curran was for twenty-five years a vice-president of the national ASL. There was, furthermore, a group of dry priests called the

Catholic Clergy Prohibition League that gave the ASL valuable support. Bishop Lenihan of Montana expressed the view—greatly appreciated by the ASL—that Prohibition would contribute to the "spiritual progress of the Catholic Church" in America.

However, it is true that other leaders of the Church regarded the dry laws, and attempts to implement them, as immoral and unjust. Catholics were never unified on the issue, and they saw no reason why they should be. Some were personally dry but could not support laws which they regarded as offensively repressive. Others were against saloons, and would vote that way, but were not against drinking. Many of the Catholics in California had shown that they were opposed to the use of hard liquor and to public drinking but not to the personal use of wine and beer. What they all seemed to agree on was that no Catholic should say anything that might be interpreted as encouraging anyone to disobey American laws. Thus Catholics were generally as cautious as Anti-Saloon League leaders to avoid any act or statment suggesting that the Prohibition Movement was some form of revived religious persecution.

This, at its best, was the relationship between Catholics and the ASL until the death of Wayne Wheeler in 1927. The league then fell under the heavy-handed direction of James Cannon, Jr., a bishop in the Methodist Church, a league principal of long standing, and a Virginia political boss who had also assumed Bryan's position as leader-of-the-pietist-faith in the Democratic Party. In this dual role of ASL and Democratic leadership, Cannon led the protest of those who hated everything that Al Smith seemed to represent. Like Lyman Beecher, Bishop Cannon was so deeply bigoted that he simply could not regard the Roman Catholic Church as Christian. He had called it "the Mother of ignorance, superstition, intolerance and sin." Thus the elevation of a wet Catholic as a candidate for President was to Cannon an appalling event, the worst thing that could happen to the Democratic Party or to the United States of America.

It may also have been the Bishop's opportunity to reach for really great power. In any event, his immediate response was to use the league to distribute hundreds of thousands of copies of an anti-Catholic attack upon Smith, who, according to Cannon, was "bigoted" and typical of "the Irish Roman Catholic hierarchy of New York City." In a boldly partisan departure from ASL principles, Cannon organized the "Democrats for Hoover" for a campaign in the previously solid South.

As party leader and pietist crusader, he carried the message that Smith drank "from four to eight cocktails a day" and that he planned to deliver the American government over to "the kind of dirty people that you find today on the sidewalks of New York." According to his biographer, Virginius Dabney, in *Dry Messiah* (1949), the bishop drew upon the latent anti-Catholicism in the nation so skillfully and aggressively that he spread a conflict which was "tantamount to a religious war." Agitated by the pronouncments of both Smith and Cannon, the blight became a distinctive feature of the campaign, especially in the South and the border states, where the estrangement of dispirited Democrats—the "dry" vote, the "bigot" vote, the "rural" vote, the "progressive" vote—became a critical factor. In a stunning reversal of political history, Cannon delivered five southern states to Hoover; all the border states went Republican.

Some historians have seen the election of 1928 as "the last major victory of the country over the city, of the old American over the new." But this is surely to play with myth and symbols, to invest American political life with a depth of unconscious artistry which is more often in the eye of the beholder than in the energies of the participants. It seems today that the role of culture-hero played by Al Smith, the platitudes of Herbert Hoover, and the bigotry of Bishop Cannon represent the bizarre and peripheral anxieties rather than the essence of political conflict. Though there are many complexities of Al Smith's defeat that do not bear on this study, it seems clear today that his defeat did not occur principally because he was wet or urban or Roman Catholic. Even before there were immigration quotas, the issues of the American marketplace always outweighed nativism in American politics, and there is no reason to suppose that this was not the case in 1928.

David Burner, in *The Politics of Provincialism* (1968), says that Smith provided "startling instances of urban provincialism" on the part of a leader who hoped to win a national election. And it does seem startling that in a major radio address to the nation on the eve of the election, Smith dwelled almost exclusively upon his narrow achievements as governor. Burner points out, furthermore, that however profound or alarming the issues of Prohibition, nativism, and anti-Catholicism may have seemed in 1928, they cannot obscure what was surely the overriding political issue of the entire decade. This was not a lifestyle, a personality, or a regional identity; it was the vigorous expansion of American industry associated with Republican policies. Many historians of the period feel today that whatever he stood for or however skillfully he molded the forces of opposition, no Democrat could have defeated Herbert Hoover in 1928.

This was not, however, a conclusion available in 1928 to Herbert Hoover. The Republican victory in the South had been a momentous departure, and Hoover felt deeply indebted to the dry Democrats and to Bishop Cannon. And even more imposing was his obligation to the Prohibitionists of his own party and to the man Hoover always regarded as "the leader of the drys," Senator William E. Borah of Idaho. As we have already noted, Borah was becoming the most popular speaker in the country, and, consequently, one of the most influential. Many people saw him as the most able constitutional lawyer in the Senate. Because he could so quickly arouse public opinion, he was surely one of the most powerful men in the nation. Journalists called him "the orator supreme," and some compared him to Daniel Webster. Though in sheer eloquence there was a basis for this comparison, Borah was not, like Webster, the great compromiser; he was the insurgent, the independent and restless conscience responsible to himself alone. In a book about the congressional insurgents of the decade, Ray Tucker wrote, "There are four distinct political factions in the United States—Republicans, Democrats, Progressives, and William Edgar Borah."

Borah had never allowed his sympathy with the Prohibitionists to so lock him into the posture of the dry ideologue that it would diminish his great prestige. His international reputation was based firmly in his opposition to Woodrow Wilson and his role in shaping foreign policy. Yet, like many sensitive drys, he felt the social tremors weakening Prohibition in 1926, and he set himself to reinforce it. Early that year he was insisting that voters had a right to know where their candidates and their parties stood. The more he spoke and wrote about it, the more he drove the issue directly into the center of partisan politics. (At about the same time, William G. McAdoo was pressing Democrats in the same direction, stressing that in enforcing the law the federal government was not *assuming* powers which belonged to the states, it was *exercising* powers which the states, in ratifying the 18th Amendment, had imposed upon it; that a state's refusal to enforce the law was virtual nullification; and that candidates—especially Smith—should make it clear whether or not they stood for anarchy.)

Though Republicans could not thereafter ignore the issue, almost all of those who might have opposed Borah kept their silence, fearing that any attack upon him would be a personal as well as a party disaster. Of the notable leaders, only Nicholas Murray Butler, president of Columbia University, accepted Borah's challenge. Confronting Butler in a classic debate before a distinguished audience at the Roosevelt Club of Boston in April 1927, Borah quoted Washington on the Constitution and Lincoln on temperance. He defended Prohibition as consistent with his dedication to states' rights, which, he said, included the right to be protected from the liquor traffic. His responses to Butler were sharp, quick, and eloquent—he was at that moment surely the "orator supreme"—and the judges of the debate declared him the winner. In the context of Republican power brokerage, it was a brilliant victory, and thereafter Borah demanded that the Republican Party vigorously defend the 18th Amendment.

Early in 1928, Borah determined to make or break Herbert Hoover. His device was to request a frank expression of the candidate's views on Prohibition—and then to make public his request to Hoover before Hoover had a chance to respond. Under these circumstances, Hoover, replied in February that "I do not favor the repeal of the 18th Amendment. I stand, of course, for the efficient, vigorous and sincere enforcment of the laws enacted thereunder. Whoever is chosen President has under his oath the solemn duty to pursue this course." And in concluding what would be his enduring statement on the matter, Hoover phrased the expression which he would reiterate several times during the campaign and which would be widely misquoted thereafter. "Our country," he wrote, "has deliberately undertaken a great social and economic experiment, noble in motive and far-reaching in purpose. It must be worked out constructively."

Having hooked his candidate, Borah moved upon the Platform Committee of the Republican National Convention. Beating back the moderates with Hoover's statement and with his own opinion that a "moderate" plank would be "like a woman of moderate virtue," Borah got the dry plank he wanted. He then put his full energies to the task of getting Hoover elected. It was Borah, not Hoover (the engineer who had never run for public office and who was at best a fumbling campaigner), who challenged the Democrats and who consistently answered Al Smith. Speaking across the country in a series of major orations, Borah was clearly the principal Republican spokesman. Journalist Ray Tucker regarded Borah as the man who had placed Hoover in the White House, and Borah may indeed have done more for Hoover than did Bishop Cannon. Though he was offered the State Department, Borah would in victory accept nothing for himself. In this refusal he tightened the bonds he had thrown around the new President.

Consequently, Hoover's problems were not only what to do about prosperity but what to do about Senator Borah and

Bishop Cannon. Though as men they had little in common but their dry sentiments, both took lunch regularly in the White House. When Cannon announced that the election had been a great referendum and that "the enemies of the Eighteenth Amendment have been ignominiously routed," Hoover could not object. With Borah and Cannon looking over his shoulder, Hoover gave the drys their pound of rhetoric, and having allowed them to pilot his campaign train, Hoover had to go where Borah and Cannon were determined to take him.

Hoover was then a captive—or at best a reluctantly indentured servant—of a cause for which he presonally had little passion. His biographers say that he did not really believe that true temperance could ever be achieved through legislative action. He had never defended the Volstead definition of what was "intoxicating," and this reserve had given his sometimes wet admirers a slender reason to suggest that he might not oppose a rigorously scientific redefinition. Nevertheless, with the advent of the Volstead era he had disposed of his splendid prewar collection of fine wines. Though the word *experiment* in his stiff pledge of allegiance to Borah was probably loaded with a painful ambiguity, and the phrase *worked out constructively* could be taken kindly by even the moderately wet, he later made it clear that he would stand by the Volstead Act. With the two pilots aboard the campaign train, he was to say of the 18th Amendment that there was a duty "imposed upon the President to secure its honest enforcement and to eliminate the abuses which have grown around it; I wish it to succeed."

Thus, on the eve of the Great Depression, hardly anyone could have predicted the scope of disasters which during the next four years were to befall the once victorious drys. There had indeed been shifts in public opinion, especially since 1926. The resistance movement had its cause, its martyrs, its evidence, its champions. But in the churches and the legislative halls, the labor temples and the chambers of commerce, these shifts had done little to dim the hopes of the drys that they would live to see a dry and law-abiding nation. The shifts could also seem like a mirage on a dry horizon: The new President was bone-dry, and Congress in 1929 numbered more dry members than it had when the Volstead era began. No one really knew what the Resistance Movement meant, and there was little evidence anywhere to lift the vision of the wets beyond some slow, eventual compromise or modification of the Volstead Act. To most people it seemed that Prohibition would surely survive the generation.

Nevertheless, when Hoover took office, the government's efforts to suppress the liquor traffic were beset with a host of vexatious problems. Underlying them all was the political fact that voters demanded public officials who could mutter the traditional phrases about "upholding" the Constitution and defending the laws, but the same voters apparently assumed no official would ever do anything really drastic about "enforcing" them. There was a delicate balance between the words *uphold* and *enforce*—we have seen it as a willingness to live with "partial failure"—which Will Rogers turned to a classic quip about people who are dry so long as they can stagger to the polls. One can see that many Americans wanted to protect their ideology as it was embedded in the Constitution through the 18th Amendment. Yet at the same time they were increasingly uneasy about petty-minded agents and self-serving politicians whose use of the law was repressive, meddlesome, and violent. Fully aware of this, Hoover had reiterated in his inaugural speech another campaign pledge, carefully calculated to appease both wets and drys,"to appoint a national commission for a searching investigation of the whole structure of our federal system of jurisprudence, to include the method of enforcement of the Eighteenth Amendment and the cause of abuse under it."

Two months later he created the Commission of Law Enforcement and Observance, to which—cautiously following the advice of Bishop Cannon—he appointed a prestigious group of citizens under George W. Wickersham, who had served the Taft administration as Attorney General. In the character of Wickersham's early pronouncements, both wets and drys found encouragement to believe that some intelligence would be brought to bear upon the problems of American Prohibition. But their patience was not rewarded. Except for a bland and unanalytical interim report in 1930, Wickersham and his committee set about their work and effectively disappeared for a critical two years. The drys, meanwhile, were demanding action.

In response to their pressure, and with a sincere desire for a more businesslike efficiency, Hoover did end an outrageous era of patronage abuse by bringing the Prohibition Bureau under the purifying influence of Civil Service. He also brought into the bureau highly competent men who promised to direct their attention away from petty bootlegging and go after the major violators. They promised more intelligence, less drama. In their support, Hoover made the solemn observation that "no individual has the right to determine what law shall be obeyed and what law shall not be enforced. If the law is wrong, its rigid enforcment is the surest guarantee of its repeal. If it is right, the enforcement is the quickest method of compelling respect for it."

The law he had in mind had been handed to him by the Anti-Saloon League on Coolidge's last day in óffice. With the "Jones Five and Ten Law," Bishop Cannon was determined to protect the integrity of the Volstead Act by making it absolutely clear that Congress would not tolerate the kind of flagrant violations that were almost everywhere apparent. But he was not only asserting a demand for sterner social control; he was also defiantly raising to a prominent visibility the antidrink ideals which the ASL had usually handled with great delicacy. The Jones Law amended the Volstead Act by raising the maximum penalties for first liquor offenses, initially six months in jail or a fine of a thousand dollars, to new maximum sentences of five years or ten thousand dollars, or both. Throughout a spirited debate on the measure which brought both the wets and the drys to full voice, some Senators linked it to a malicious "philosophy of hate." But a majority followed Borah and voted for the bill, which Senator Wesley L. Jones carried successfully to the House and to the President. It went into effect in March 1929, and the new administration seemed quite willing to put it to the test.

The cutting edge of the law was that it raised a first offense, as well as any succeeding offense, to the status of a felony. And according to federal criminal code, a person who knew that a felony had been committed but who failed to report it was by this failure himself committing a felony. Thus, under the Jones Law, anyone who bought a bottle or a drink—or who had seen a bootlegger or a speakeasy in operation—could be charged with a felony if he failed to disclose what he knew to federal authorities. Jones, or Cannon, had indeed shaped a vicious instrument. It created an almost incalculable number of felonies which could be associated with the Volstead Act. In attempting to strengthen enforcment, the ASL had turned it into an absurdity. It seems clear that the Jones Law was a symptom of explosive moral frustration. The line between acceptable and criminal behavior, functionally but fuzzily drawn by the Volstead Act, had become so blurred by 1929 that it could no longer clarify social distinctions. And the guardian drys, in a surly mood, were attempting to both sharpen it and move it toward the enemy.

The protest which followed was immediate, national, bitter, and abusive. Senator Jones found himself attacked without mercy in newspapers, in state legislatures, in Congress, even in the federal courts. The impression spread that Senator Jones and the Anti-Saloon League wanted to jail everyone who might on occasion be tempted even to taste bootleg booze, that the Jones Law was a vindictive and sinister move against anyone who in any way opposed Prohibition.

This impression reflected the unhappy national experience with the years of futile attempts to enforce Volsteadism. According to Treasury Department figures, the federal government by 1929 had used the Volstead Act to arrest more than 500,000 violators, some 4,000 of whom were then serving sentences in terribly overcrowded prisons. The courts had backlogged so many Prohibition cases that the congestion was causing a serious judiciary crisis. These figures were so high that to many people they surgested actual social chaos. Local governments, even the federal government, apparently could not effectively regulate criminal activity. If the bureaucratic society was held together by control agencies, then surely the most imprtant of these agencies was being frustrated by Prohibition. And a crime "wave" of this magnitude might not be a wave at all—it might be a rebellion of major proportions. Because the Jones Act was seen as a political performance to satisfy the Anti-Saloon League, Prohibition violators after 1929 could be seen as Jones Act protestors, participants in anti-Volstead rebellion which was creating thousands of political prisoners.

The depth of this protest was apparent in the defection of William Randolph Hearst, who, in the old tradition of elitist stewardship, had in his wisdom early determined what was good for the common people and had accordingly been among the most enthusiastic supporters of the 18th Amendment. In 1929 he decided to lead the rebellion. A man accustomed to speaking to and for the nation from the pulpit of his editorial offices, he had long assumed that he should have been—and except for national perversities would have been—President of the United States. In his own fierce megalomania, he was also a severely temperate man who did not in good humor suffer the self-indulgence of others. He was known to have imposed strict limits upon the amount of liquor available (in his presence) to guests at his great castle in California, a prejudice which reduced some of his most famous vistors to smuggling bottles into their bedrooms. Yet as late as 1925 he had editorialized that the Volstead Act was working "well enough." The so-called "crime wave" of the decade, he indicated, was merely the sort of thing that follows any war. Prohibition, he said, "has not failed . . ." And he gave Hoover his unqualified support in 1928. But after the Jones Law, Hearst sensed that something was very much awry.

The Jones Law, he wrote in 1929, was "the most menacing piece of repressive legislation that has stained the statute books of this republic since the Alien and Sedition laws." He condemned those lawmakers, who, between pulls on their own smuggled liquor, "pass a law imposing five years penal servitude and a $10,000 fine upon any citizen who takes a drink."

He claimed that it "adds persecution to prohibition, and in our principles of government substitutes fanaticism for freedom." He then blamed the Volstead Act, as amended by Jones, for having extended drinking to women, increased drinking among all age groups and classes, created criminals, corrupted judges, and encouraged government agents in "un-American methods of spying and sneaking and snooping and keyhole peeping." In a dramatic turnabout perhaps calculated to create a great splurge of journalistic excitement—which it did—he lamented that the Volstead Act had "hindered the cause." It had created intolerable criminal conditions, intolerable political conditions. And it had "done nothing after ten years' trial to advance the cause of temperance."

Hearst was then fully engaged as the great creator of news, the role in American life which he had played so skillfully. Using the vast resources of his publishing empire to ask "What Can Be Done?" Hearst held the Volstead Act in the heat of constant publicity. "The Hearst $25,000 Temperance Prize Contest" attracted 71,248 entries, the best of which, according to the Hearst Prize Committee, came from a judge in New York City who called for continued Prohibition of hard liquor but for modification of the Volstead Act to allow state dispensaries for wine and beer. This sounded like a principled and sensible temperance program to Hearst, whose prejudices it neatly reflected. There was nothing radical, nothing that would tamper with the Constitution. Hearst then publicly urged the plan, and late in 1929 he published his views with an account of his contest in a book called *Temperance or Prohibition?* When, after a few months, his efforts seemed in no way to have influenced either the President or the Congress, Hearst lost patience and advocated the complete repeal of the 18th Amendment.

Many people were concluding meanwhile that the politics of the dry decade may have been even more corrupt than the politics of the saloon era. In some states, the Anti-Saloon League had disciplined legislatures in quite the same way that the old saloon barons had done before 1916. Political and judicial appointments had been handled with the same expediency. The Prohibition Bureau itself had been a plush system of political patronage for the ASL and its friends, and it was painfully clear that special interests were privileged to use public agencies for their own political purposes. Conspiracy theories were increasingly popular: The drys had "bought" the 18th Amendment with $50 million treasury while patriotic voters were fighting in the trenches of France. The Anti-Saloon League had bribed editors to print dry propaganda. Church-based political bosses, it was rumored, controlled candidates and determined who would take public office. They misused congressional mailing privileges to sustain their strength, and they conglomerated a lobby of dry moralists more powerful than any pressure group in congressional experience. Moreover, to many observers this all presented the appearance of a dark union of church and state in a Congress-ASL-WCTU oligarchy which could dictate policies of the most vital national concern: law enforcement, taxation, and federal-state relationships.

And as they were surely slipping in public estimation, some of the dry leaders seemed to become even more harshly fanatical. Henry Ford announced in 1929 that if the 18th Amendment were ever repealed, he would stop manufacturing automobiles; he would refuse to pay people wages "which the saloons would take away from them." That year Bishop Cannon was still attacking New York City by leading a movement for an amendment to the Constitution which would have excluded aliens from the population counts used for the basis of congressional apportionment. And during these same months he was working on a law which would unequivocally make the purchase of liquor a crime. Cannon called the Repeal Movement the "whiskey rebellion," and he proposed that the President use force—he meant call out the army and the navy—to suppress it. In 1930, however, ministers of his own church accused him of gambling in stocks, of adultery, and of various other malfeasances, and people almost everywhere were coming to see him as a self-indulgent hypocrite rather than as a dedicated crusader. As a leader of dry pressure groups, he was ruined.

The years had in no way softened the relentless fundamentalism of the nation's leading Presbyterian, the Reverend Mark Matthews, who continued to delight his parishioners with thunder over loose morals, smoking, cosmetics, modern novels, Sunday golf, and liquor. Though in sophisticated circles of the new society he was increasingly regarded as a rather quaint and crabby character, he still had the authority of a pillar of morality and the voice of a Puritan father. The law, he shouted, was sovereign and eternal and "ought to be enforced if every street in America had to run with blood and every cobble stone had to be made of a human skull." Prohibition, as it had for thirty years, touched the recesses of his personality and caused such distortions that one wonders if most poeple did not think him demented. One of his letters to Senator Wesley Jones is a fair example:

> The whiskey on the one side, the narcotic evil on the other side, the immoral question of the other side, the false, rationalistic, atheistic, bolshevistic, damnable Russian propaganda on the other side are all combining to make of this land and sacrificing it with as much glee as the demons of the Roman forum sacrificed the Christians of ancient days. . . . Give me position and power and let me do something.

Jones's reply was to stress his "confidence in the substantial people of the country" and to blame everything on the newspapers.

The *Literary Digest*, which then had a record of impressive accuracy in its predictions of how the presidential votes would fall in 1924 and 1928, polled the public in 1930 about Prohibition. The results indicated that about 30 percent wanted modification, about 30 percent no change at all, and about 40 percent total repeal of the 18th Amendment.

But the hour was overshadowed by measurably more serious matters as a decade of high-velocity change climaxed in the impact of the Great Crash and the Great Depression. Markets collapsed, mills and factories closed, banks failed, and the number of people losing their jobs each week reached 100,000. The need for relief was the focus of urgent discussion everywhere, and the skid roads began to fill with drifting men. As the gloomy lines of the unemployed seemed to grow without end, the public mood was fearful, ugly, and impatient. That bootleggers were hiding in back alleys became a matter of small significance, but that federal agents, the favorites of entrenched politicans, were paid to chase them became more and more intolerable. A new thought was rapidly overtaking a new society: Perhaps repeal was a way to get the country moving again.

To shape this thought, magazine and newspaper writers found a dazzling array of economic statistics. The National Association of Manufacturers persuasively called for beer to boost markets, put idle men to work, and relieve businessmen of tax burdens. Pierre S. Du Pont wrote that a liquor tax "would be sufficient to pay off the entire debt of the United States. . . . in a little less than fifteen years." Grain growers were urged to contemplate the return of beer. Sharpened almost daily by the increasingly harsh realities of the depression, the economic arguments for repeal cut across just about every thread of logic still supporting the 18th Amendment.

The most specific efforts toward bringing repeal into the center of politics were led by people who had much to gain and who could best afford it—the very well-to-do. The Association against the Prohibition Amendment was by far the most effective organization working for repeal, and it was directed by several dozen millionaires, among whom the principals were John J. Raskob, the Du Ponts, General William H. Atterbury from railroads, H. B. Joy from automobile manufacture, Charles H. Sabin from investment trusts, Edward S. Harkness from oil, and a host of former brewers and distillers. These men in turn organized groups of millionaires in each of the forty-eight states—men who, like themselves, were wet in principle or who at least supposed that repeal had a potential for increasing purchasing power and employment. They were often men who were also keenly aware of the promise which liquor and beer taxation held for reducing their personal or corporate obligations to state and national treasuries—some said at least ten million dollars a year to the Du Ponts alone. And they had money to spend to save money. After its initial efforts in 1926, the AAPA spent about a million dollars a year on repeal, and this was in addition to the publishing costs, paid personnel, and routine expenses which large corporations can so easily conceal.

The motives of these men were usually obvious and did not escape criticism. Their opponents in Congress spoke bitterly, accusing them of being a part of a "deep-laid plot of heartless millionaires to shift the tax burden from their pockets to the cravings of the helpless." The AAPA leaders, however, suffered only mildly from such attacks. They could retaliate with the support given them by outstanding members of the nation's business and intellectual communities—widely publicized repeal statements from such men of distinction as General John Pershing, Alfred P. Sloan, Jr., Harvey S. Firestone, Nicholas Murray Butler, Walter Lippmann, and John D. Rockefeller, Jr. Rockefeller's stand was particularly significant inasmuch as he had been a leading prestige figure, a solemn authority in American life who, like William Randolph Hearst, had been a part of the movement to achieve the 18th Amendment.

And the repealers, in one of the more brilliant political strokes of the first decade of equal suffrage, enlisted their wives as well. In 1929, Mrs. Charles H. Sabin formed the Women's Organization for National Prohibition Reform. This group enrolled a large number of wealthy socialites who, in colorful caravans of expensive automobiles, joined the movement for repeal. They were inevitably ridiculed as "Sabin's sob sisters" and "cocktail-drinking women," and even more luridly as "Bacchantian maidens, parching for wine." But through a most significant social mutation, these jaded affronts to feminine dignity were, by 1930, ludicrously antiquated phrases which probably did Mrs. Sabin more good than harm. Resistance to Prohibition had, among the upper classes, become stylish. Surely a major revolution had occurred when attractive and socially prominent women could support the cause of drinking—and in doing so, speak as individuals, for individualism, not women for family protection.

There was, accordingly, in the substance of Mrs. Sabin's organization also much to learn about the social symbolism of the revolution. Forty years before, when the dry cause had been supported by most progressive Americans, Frances Willard had attracted the college-educated, upper middle-class women of that generation, the wives of physicians, professors, lawyers, industrialists, and men of commerce. In 1930, Mrs. Sabin had these women—or their daughters. The WCTU at that time presented the appearance of dry, pinch-nosed puritans who sat almost silently in the ashes of ancient discontents. They were, Joseph Gusfield's study shows, the aging wives of small farmers, neighborhood morticians, and chiropractors, the mothers of tradesmen, store clerks, and ministers of minor distinction—pacesetters and tastemakers of a world that lay far behind them.

In 1931, George Wickersham's Commission on Law Enforcement and Observance finally submitted its report to the President. Though it was seen by some drys as a repudiation of the AAPA, the Wickersham Report would ultimately help the AAPA rather than hinder it. In drawing conclusions from its lengthy study, the commission flatly opposed any modification of the Volstead Act and any movement toward the repeal of the 18th Amendment, and in this the drys could rejoice. But in its investigations of law enforcement, the commission found that there was in fact no effective enforcement of the Volstead Act, and the details of these investigations were delightful to the increasingly wet newspapers. Other conclusions were that substantial federal appropriations, as well as the cooperation of the several states, would be absolutely necessary if there were ever to be any effective enforcement. Inasmuch as these necessities were also impossibilities, the Wickersham Commission had found essentially that the situation was terrible but that nothing could be done to correct it.

This disparity between findings and conclusions added a wave of impatience to the general public confusion. Then, as if to add an absurd dimension to the entire affair, Hoover submitted the report to Congress without comment. As Virginius Dabney shows in *Dry Messiah* (1949), the only approach to understanding this farce is through a fairly wide-spread impression at the time that Hoover had influenced Wickersham not to draw conclusions which might offend Bishop Cannon. If this were so, it was the last time that the President would bend to keep his peace with the Bishop. With the depression on his shoulders and the election at his throat, Hoover was ready to break his long indenture.

But as the campaign approached, leaders of the Repeal Movement brought forth the United Repeal Council, which included the AAPA, the Women's Organization for National Prohibition Reform, the Voluntary Committee of Lawyers, and the American Hotel Association. Though not a part of this council, both the American Legion and the American Federation of Labor joined the movement. The critical event before the council was the election of a Congress and a President in full sympathy with a plan for repeal. This meant, surely, that there was no reason for the AAPA to give money to Republicans, for even as Hoover, in accepting the nomination, had called for repeal, the depression had clearly burdened him with more liabilities than any man could carry through a national election. AAPA money would go to Franklin Roosevelt and the Democrats and help fund the politics of a new wet-liberal-urban-industrial-pluralistic coalition.

As governor of New York, Franklin Roosevelt had an occasion been against the saloon. But he had also been in favor of enforcing the law, in favor of having no dry laws to enforce, and always for the federal Constitution. It was well known that his wife, Eleanor, whose father had before his death been an alcoholic, was an absolutely dedicated dry. She had in 1924 attended a convention of women who were protesting the weak enforcement of the Volstead Act. Even early in the 1930s, she refused to serve wine at her dinner parties, and she made it difficult for her husband to find a highball, which he occasionally enjoyed. Roosevelt's reluctance to dry out the family and his own politics irritated her, but he would do nothing to modify the ambiguity of the problem. He did not regard it as very important. What was important to him was to avoid the ideologue's position, wet or dry—to avoid, until he knew where it would take him, the issue which had served Al Smith so poorly. As he moved craftily toward the presidential nomination, he was determined that there should be no "Democrats for Hoover" in 1932.

Nor would he offend the wets of his party with any gesture toward the bitter drys. When in fact the Methodists did push him in the matter early in 1930, he told them that he was "heartily in accord with enforcement of the laws of the State"—at a time when his state had no Prohibition laws to enforce. After taking the public pulse in the summer of 1930, he cautiously let it be known that he favored the repeal of the 18th Amendment and the restoration of states' rights to the problems of controlling liquor. This position may have been difficult to distinguish from that of Al Smith in 1928, except that while Smith had taken up the role of the wet liberator, Roosevelt stressed, on the contrary, that under his policy many areas would remain bone-dry. This was the "moist," or "damp," position, in contrast to the hard-eyed wet or dry dedication. Roosevelt received a few protests from the Democratic South, but there were no serious ones. The fact was—and he used it for all it was worth—that all other candidates for the nomination were "wetter" than he was and that dry delegates to the convention were practically bound to support him. From a state as dry as Utah, he heard that his moistness was quite acceptable, and for reasons which he had of course anticipated: Times were so bad that even Mormons hoped repeal might bring some relief from the depression.

When the National Democratic Convention opened, apparently the only Democratic politicians who did not understand this were those who still supposed that as a wet hero Smith might yet become President. With superb control and timing,

Roosevelt used his moistness to hold dry delegates in his camp until it was certain that Smith could not capture the nomination. When the Smith-Raskob wing tried to smear Roosevelt with a dry label, Roosevelt reiterated his 1930 position, but with a brilliant refinement: Those states which under his proposal would choose to allow liquor again should do so in such a way as to increase their revenues and reduce their taxation. His view was consistently on the depression. On this note, even the hard-eyed drys could not comfortably oppose him, and events then closed rapidly around the future President. When his delegates tried to raise a moist plank into the platform, the convention rejected it for simple, outright repeal, which Roosevelt's enemies hoped might embarrass him. Roosevelt responded to this in his acceptance speech by announcing warmly that "This convention wants repeal. Your candidate wants repeal. And I am confident that the United States of America wants repeal." He became the symbol of liberalism, relief, and confidence. Repeal would go with relief, recovery, and reform.

Before Congress met in January 1933, the United RepealCouncil had its plan. It had phrased the 21st Amendment to the Constitution, which would repeal the 18th. The council's hope was to achieve the new amendment in such a way as to circumvent the various state legislatures, where, it feared, dry legislators from rural districts (because rural districts were represented with a strength so inconsistent with their actual population) might present a serious barrier to ratification. Repeal leaders had estimated that in existing legislatures, as few as 132 dry state senators in only 13 states would have the votes to defeat the amendment. To prevent this, constitutional lawyers proposed—for the first time since the Constitution itself was ratified and for much the same reason—that Congress should call for ratifying conventions in each state. Delegates would be elected for the specific purpose of considering the 21st Amendment.

A repeal resolution embodying this idea was approved by the

leaders of the AAPA and carried before both chambers of the Congress. The immediate action repealers had hoped for, however, was stopped in the House, where the resolution failed by only six votes. Then, in the Senate Judiciary Committee, a group of western progressive Prohibitionists—among them Borah of Idaho, Ashurst of Arizona, Walsh of Montana, and Dill of Washington—tried to frustrate the AAPA by insisting upon the traditional avenue of ratification. It was their plan which first went to the floor of the Senate.

But the council's lawyers and AAPA leaders knew their Senators and did not anticipate any prolonged congressional battle. They drew up a general measure which the various states could, with appropriate local changes, use to call their own ratification conventions. Jouett Shouse, then president of the AAPA, sent the proposed bill to friends in each state so that even while Congress debated, the legislatures then in session might prepare the way for the state repeal conventions. Congress approved the AAPA resolution on February 28. By this time the convention bills in most states were ready for passage. Shouse's timing and administrative skills had beaten the clocks of legislative adjournment, and his smooth coordination of national and local efforts may have advanced the actual fact of repeal by as much as two years.

Meanwhile, in anticipation of the 21st Amendment, many legislatures had early in 1933 already repealed their state dry laws. Congress sharply accelerated the movement by modifying the Volstead definition of "intoxicating" to permit the sale of beer after midnight, April 4. As the billows of suds began to wash across the nation—an event covered like a New Year's Eve by NBC radio—officials of state and local governments made eager plans to spend the forthcoming taxes. Some states, however, awaited a popular vote on new systems of liquor control, and in Oklahoma a referendum on a measure to allow beer was set for July 11. Though the measure passed with an almost two-to-one margin, thirsty citizens were momentarily frustrated by Governor "Alfalfa Bill" Murray, who ruled that beer would not be legal until he had officially proclaimed the results of the referendum. He was in no hurry. The governor had earlier told the wets to "go to hell" when he had learned that the election would cost a lot of money that the state did not have, and on election day he was sullenly aware of his prerogatives. "Oklahoma will not have beer until I say so," he announced after the polls had closed. Before retiring that evening, he declared a state of martial law and called out the National Guard to protect the thousands of carloads of beer then resting in railroad yards across the state. After a late and leisurely breakfast on July 12, he did finally verify the election and call off the guard. Citizens were drinking even while the beer was being unloaded.

In most states, already wet with brew, the convention bills called for the voters in each legislative district to elect as many delegates as they had representatives in the legislature. Candidates campaigned across the summer, and these months saw the last great duels among the heroes of Prohibition and repeal. The month of August was enlivened by motor caravans which carried prominent women from Mrs. Sabin's organization into several states, where they spoke, paraded, and distributed repeal literature. Except for a few candidates, however, no one worked very hard, and real enthusiasm was hard to find. In the election of convention delegates, the trend toward ratification was overwhelming by August, and it was finished in December 1933. The repeal vote nationally ran at almost 73 percent. In all but three states, even the rural vote was more than 50 percent for repeal. The 21st Amendment would have carried without a single vote from the wet, urban centers.

Thus the AAPA, like the Anti-Saloon League before it, had manipulated the mechanics of nonpartisan, pressure-group politics with consummate skill. When Peter Odegard wrote his *Pressure Politics* in 1928, he then regarded the Anti-Saloon League as one of the most effective pressure groups ever organized in American life. It had indeed been so. But during the 1920s—riding detached from the broadly-based reform programs which previously had given it strength and complexity—it became vulnerable to the fanaticisms and even the corruptions to which most single-issue groups are prone. Then the depression ripped its strongest armor, washing away the moneys that for a quarter of a century had been regularly gathered from millions of middle-class salaries and wages. The league sank with breathtaking speed.

By 1933, the AAPA had proved that it could be even more effective than the ASL with the manipulations which had given the league its power and fame. But as a signal event in American social history, repeal was much more than a skillfully-wrought political achievement. It represented a great change in American life. The Prohibition Movement—in its ideals, its enticements, its politics, its frenzies, its coercions—had been a movement toward a new order, toward a new social stability profoundly rooted in bourgeois values. In 1933, the change away from that order could not have occurred without an equally profound shift. Repeal, like Prohibition, was the mark of a new society.

10

Legacies
of Prohibition

〰〰〰〰〰〰〰〰〰〰〰〰〰〰〰〰〰〰〰〰〰〰〰〰〰〰〰〰〰〰〰〰〰

IN *THE DRY DECADE*, published in 1931, Charles Merz explained that the Repeal Movement had become a nullification of federal legislation and official morality. He described it as a rebellion on the part of many people who finally refused in any way to honor a law held almost universally in contempt. Merz compared this rebellion, as the wets had for years compared it, with the reaction of Americans, especially in the South, to the Reconstruction laws which reformers carried through Congress after the Civil War. This is to a degree a useful analogue, for it reveals a certain similarity in the efforts of Americans to suppress racism and intemperance. But at best it has a narrow validity. There is surely little to be learned from comparing racism to drinking or drunkenness, and surely history has no need for another shaky analogy.

It is true that Charles Merz did not work this particular analogy very hard. But he did, at least by implication, suggest that because the efforts to suppress racism and the efforts to suppress intemperance were both failures, Americans should have learned from the history of the one experience what to anticipate from the other. This is the unfortunate distortion. Though racism has not been suppressed, slavery is dead; this is surely because of the Antislavery Movement, and since 1865 racism has been measurably diminished in American society. Though intemperance has not been abolished—and there is here no further implied comparison—the movement against it did abolish the saloon, and this in turn has made the public drunkard at least less common than he was during the nineteenth century and something less of a social hazard. There is every reason to believe, as we have seen, that even with their inadequacies, the various state dry laws and the Volstead Act were, in part, causes of the substantially reduced consumption of alcohol among Americans.

What is unfortunate, then, is that many people have come to explain both Reconstruction and Prohibition as decades of experiment and failure, as periods when the efforts of misguided reformers were abandoned to a historical slag pile by a disillusioned society whose values were inconsistent with sustained repression. It would be nearer the truth to explain that while the American experiences with racism and intemperance were in most ways dissimilar, neither racism nor intemperance was, or now is, necessarily incompatible with American values. But the institutional structure of racism before the 13th Amendment and the institutional stimulation of public drunkenness before the 18th Amendment were incompatible with the values of the societies which ratified those changes.

A distinctive mood of the new society—the society which repealed th 18th Amendment—was shaped by the feeling that in a saloonless society, public drunkenness would never again approach the proportions of a social crisis. Indeed, as we have already noted, this widespread feeling made the success of the Repeal Movement possible. And while the repealers themselves were often eager to assist their state governments in designing laws to prevent the return of the "old-time saloon," few of them expressed any enduring anxiety about the less dramatic forms of intemperance. After the Crash of 1929, Edgar Kemler wrote in *The Deflation of American Ideals* (1941) that the traditions of "proper" behavior sustained by the older society seemed irrelevant to hard times and to hard economic decisions which would shape the future of the nation. To Kemler's friends, at a time of great distress, these traditions seemed even to be a barrier against effective social action. "Proper" men like Woodrow Wilson and Herbert Hoover had failed because they had arrogantly mixed their personal ethics with political and economic objectives, because they had determined to "lift men to higher things," and because their vision was thus distorted by "self-righteousness and moral superiority." To a good New Dealer, according to Kemler, high moral indignation was the sure sign of political bankruptcy; it made significant social reform quite impossible.

With the repeal of Prohibition, Kemler wrote, "sin was returned to the jurisdiction of the churches where it belongs." Thus liberated from the institutional moral restraints of the pietist republic (this was a conspicuous liturgical triumph), New Dealers were free to refine the agency-society without confusing morality with the techniques for relief, recovery, and reform. It seemed beautifully efficient. The agency-society was in control, not the churches or the families, and there could finally be truly objective analyses of social problems and truly scientific solutions. In this confidence, New Dealers like Kemler disdained both the ideals and the lifestyles of their predecessors. They talked openly with prostitutes, used shocking vocabularies, drank cocktails. They tried to show that a liberated comportment—an honest surrender to impulse, a self-generous indulgence, an identity of individual wants and needs—was an essential characteristic of the scientific and civilized man. The Volstead Act, as did the Mann Act, became the butt of jokes. The implications of both were not ideals with which a liberated person cared to associate himself. This was the legacy of the raised eyebrow, the snicker, the sneer—at someone's abstinence.

Even before repeal, drinking had become the comportment of protest, the existential identity of the individual against the system. The defiant rebel with his pocket flask had become an almost irresistible symbol of dignity, courage, manhood, and liberation from hypocrisy and pigheaded repression—a symbol which could elevate drinking into a sacrament of true individualism. After repeal, advertising specialists brought to these symbols an increasingly delicate and effective illumination. The techniques were necessarily subtle, for after 1933 the Federal

Alcohol Control Administration was severely sensitive to obvious associations in advertising copy of liquor or beer to women, children, health, sex, religion, or group drinking which might even seem "excessively convivial." Accordingly, ad copy of the 1930s suggested a hearty masculinity by associating drink with the horse race, the hunt club, the vigorous sportsman, the daring adventurer. They showed drinking as integral to the fashionable life—to the world of the wealthy, the proud, the elite. These associations, rising from values essential to conspicuous consumption, projected a new linkage of images which—like the saloon-based images of a previous generation—were seared into the American mind until they became coordinates for a new American conscience.

Drinking man was the man of physical action and triumph, distinguished in his masculinity and in the demonstration of its symbols. Drinking man was keenly aware of his uniquely complex individuality; he nurtured it, guarded it, exercised it, polished it. His indulgences were deep, yet honest, always consistent with health and spiritual equilibrium. His impulsiveness was mature and humane and firmly true. He was not a man who would ever beat his, or anyone's, wife or children. He was never irresponsible. His life was never overshadowed by loneliness, which in the society of social atoms was a grievous affliction. By the fact and the style of his drinking, he could attract not only sexual partners but loyal friends. Drinking man was a man's man, intelligent, discreet, always thoughtfully sensitive to the possibilities of lifestyle in the new urban era. Drinking woman was her own person, liberated yet compassionate, firm-minded, yet ready to yield to the proper stimulation. She knew, as though intuitively, the symbolism of intimacy and of intimate experience which could be carried with the raised glass. Thus Drinking American was warm, friendly, convivial, physically attractive, distinctively upper-middle or upper-class in taste, demeanor, and comportment.

In an easy passage, advertising values became movie values. Achievements in romantic love became the most common Hollywood theme; gangsters and cowboy heroes found individual, rather than social, fulfillment; the immediate gratification of wants became stylish and fashionable. In the plotlines of the 1930s, it was usually the clowns and fools and villains who got drunk—or who did not drink at all. For the good people, drinking was the symbolic action suggesting sexuality, a finely sharpened identity, a cool sophistication. But even more significantly, the movie star cults were becoming lifestyle cults. Around stars such as James Cagney, Clark Gable, Tyrone Power, Greta Garbo, Jean Harlow, Mae West, and Humphrey Bogart this cultism carried the potential of a new and startling institution: People could *learn* a lifestyle—not at home or at church, but at the movies. This was becoming a revolution of extraordinary dimensions.

Women learned from Garbo how to embrace, how to express sexual anguish, how to dress, how to drink, and how to smoke. From Mae West they learned smartly and wittily how to defy convention. The Reverend John J. Cantwell, Catholic Bishop of Los Angeles, expressed a militant dismay when he saw that "talking pictures" could actually "teach" a "philosophy" which could undermine "the sanctity of the home." Hollywood's response to the Legion of Decency was the Production Code for purity, which may have kept Greta Garbo and Mae West out of some movie-set bedrooms but which also may have encouraged the directors of their films to invest their styles of taking a drink or of holding a cigarette with an even more unnerving symbolism. Women imitated their movements. their gestures, their aura of liberation and individual freedom.

And so with the masculine heroes, Gable, Power, Bogart—one cannot imagine them *not* drinking. They drank convivially, in pleasant cocktail lounges or at elegant cocktail parties where one might escape from the urban-industrial world of anxiety and high personal tension. Or they drank in barrooms, hardly distinct from old-time saloons, where the overtones of sexuality could reveal the constantly libidinous core of American drinking. Or they drank alone, reflectively calm and quiet, using alcohol in carefully measured applications to the raw edges of their many spiritual wounds. For the Bogart character, especially, life was serious and the kicks were hard. A man suffered, and he surely *deserved* his honest indulgences. He need not apologize. He drank like a man who had earned it; he smoked like a man who had found in the smoke some critical expression of his manhood. When the ultimate moral question before many people in the new society was what kind of person they should be, the Bogart model of a *drinking and smoking person* was enormously attractive to serious people kicked around by life—of whom there were many. Movies of the 1930s were, of course, profuse and diverse, and there were many other models—few of them, however, with the stamp of serious artistic conception. Hopalong Cassidy, the western hero, did not drink; nor did Judge Hardy. And when actor Lewis Stone played this part in the Andy Hardy movies he found that his characterization as a stern and sober WASP knight was so fixed in the popular mind that he could not in comfort drink in public, even while dining out as a private citizen.

To understand that Prohibition brought about a substantial revision of American drinking habits is not to deny that alcohol thereafter was a problem among substantial numbers of Americans who used it regularly for deeply compelling reasons. There is no account of the creeping dependence more moving than Jack London's. In the last years of his youth, London knew that he was doomed; and in the last of his nights of drinking, he laced the cup with morphine. According to his friend Upton Sinclair, in *The Cup of Fury* (1956), compulsive drinking decimated American literary circles as Sinclair knew them: witness Stephen Crane, Eugene O'Neill, Sherwood Anderson, Hart Crane, Scott Fitzgerald, Sinclair Lewis, Ernest Hemingway, William Faulkner. Most recently, Theodore Roethke tragically dramatized the wreckage, and then John Berryman. Witness also the literary artist as the explorer of freedom, as the conspicuously anguished individual in the straitjacket of a harsh society, as the defiant rebel against stifling conformity and an imposed morality. In the twentieth century, the traditions of individualism have shaped a literary lifestyle which has often become a form of conspicuous self-destruction.

After repeal, some Americans drank in that legacy. Others drank to excess because they had personal problems, and this was surely a serious pathology. Still others, however, had personal problems because they were such serious drinkers. And there were those who, as they do in many societies, responded morbidly to a tight, complex paradigm of personality, boozy friends, and a boozy lifestyle. But an alarming number of Americans drank too much because drunkenness, as a ritual of certain American subsultures, became a liturgy of protest against the cruel heat of the melting pot. Drunkenness served to validate certain non-Protestant, or nonwhite, or non-Anglo identities. Irish-Americans, for example, had this problem. According to the recent study *Alcohol and Health*, the percentage of heavy drinkers among them was more than among the Irish in Ireland. American Indians suffered grievously— more, even, than poets. Nancy Oestreich Lurie explains that Indians drank to morbidity not because they lacked self-esteem or needed to escape reality (as some sociologists suggested) but because they had to demonstrate that they were Indians. Getting drunk was *to be* an Indian. The stereotype demanded that the good Indian be a drunken Indian when no better means of "validating Indianness" was available. This was a devastating validation. Calvin Trillin reported in 1971 from Gallup, New Mexico, that when a Yugoslavian expert on alcoholism visited that unhappy town, his early observations were that drinking was the same "all over the world." This was before he had confronted the utter destructiveness of Indian drinking—the stupefied bodies, the two hundred Navajos laid out comatose in a concrete drunk shelter, the deaths from exposure and automobile accidents, the horror which makes drunkenness in Gallup, according to Trillin, "something like a medieval epidemic." The vistor later remarked that "in a Socialist country, this could never happen."

With repeal, the federal government gave up most of its prohibitions, though there was surely a strong element of control in heavy federal taxation. Some states abandoned all their liquor laws in 1933 and accepted liquor "wildcatting" and the consequent drink storms, at least for a while. Others restricted the hours of sale and through other codes attempted to prevent the new drinking establishments from assuming the character of the old-time saloon. Still others authorized state dispensaries to separate the liquor traffic from the profit motive and from competition. Some let in beer and wine but not hard booze. Some reverted to the earlier patterns of local option. In most cases the idea was that in preventing the resuscitation of the saloon, states could prevent public drunkenness, and thus society would have solved its problem. Of course, *individuals* might thereafter have problems, but these were surely a matter for the concern of social agencies, not state legislatures. Even when the frequency and the nature of drunken accidents on the highways took an increasingly bloody toll, most states were extremely relectant to impose liquor laws which might encourage the bootlegging that would then suggest that they had not "learned" from Prohibition.

The dominant view then was that Prohibition had been simply foolish from beginning to end. Problems of morbid drinking, in this view, were like problems of gambling and prostitution—the "moral by-products," not the root causes, of poverty and social inequity. Thus, by concentrating a scientific attack upon poverty and social inequity, reformers assumed they could cure crime and drunkenness without having to contaminate themselves in the moralism of the older generation. The results were not convincing.

One should note in contrast that the Social Democratic Party in Sweden was concurrently structuring comprehensive public welfare programs, and its efforts did indeed diminish crime, poverty, delinquency, and disease. But they did not diminish public drunkenness, the persistence and the extent of which seemed to threaten every other reform achievement. Rather than live in a nation of fully-employed, well-housed, well-educated, and well-fed drunks, the reformers accepted the older moralism that drunkenness is a social evil which must be attacked directly. They then begin the exceedingly strict regulation of the sale and public consumption of all alcoholic beverages. Harsh "temperance" laws specified how much a person could buy each month, and under what conditions, and even dictated how much restaurants could serve him with each meal. In the interests of social progress, the Social Democrats during the 1930s made it extremely difficult for a person to become a dedicated drinker.

In the United States, as in Sweden or Yugoslavia, the most distinctive circumstance of morbid drinking was not the presence of poverty, or personality problems. or identity crises. Such disorders usually found expressions totally unrelated to alcohol. The primary condition was simply that liquor was plenteously available and that its heavy use was socially acceptable. Thus, in the *Quarterly Journal of Studies on Alcohol*, a researcher who had conducted experiments in "induced chronic intoxication and withdrawal in alcoholics" supported a hypothesis that "alcoholism represents a process of physiological addiction and that this process is similar to addiction induced by other pharmacological agents." In *Science*, researchers Virginia Davis and Michael Walsh noted that many opium addicts have a personal history of alcoholism, and they demonstrated that alcohol produces a "metabolic aberration" which "could then lead to the endogenous production of addictive compounds." They concluded that alcohol and morphine present patterns of physical dependency so strikingly similar that "the real distinctions between the two drugs could be only the length of time and dosage required for development of dependence."

Though not all researchers in alcohol science accepted this conclusion, there seems to be little doubt that the Prohibitionists were to this degree entirely right: Through some physiological or psychological mechanism—the precise aberrations or linkages are not yet perfectly clear—alcohol is by any definition a dangerous drug which in many individual cases does in fact become addictive.

Our topic is, then, at least in part, the problem of narcosis, drug addiction, and drug control in American history. What historical parallels are there between American efforts to control the addictive drug alcohol and the efforts to control other narcotics? We must explain the conspicuous historical circumstance that widespread use of both *aqua vitae* and opium in Western civilization began in the latter part of the eighteenth century, and national prohibitions of them both occurred in the early part of the twentieth.

Both drugs had for centuries been evident on the occult margins of classical medicine. The first clear references to the psychic glories of the opium poppy are Sumerian, written about 4000 B.C. The word *opion*, however, is from the Greeks, for whom the poppy juice was an all-healing, universal remedy. In the late seventeenth century, Thomas Sydenham, often called the father of English clinical practice, prepared for his patients a mixture of wine, spices, and opium, which he called *laudanum*. It was through laudanum that most Englishmen were to have their first experience with the dried resin of the "joy flower"— and during the very same period when English distillers were flooding the country with gin.

In the United States, by the 1830s both powdered and liquid forms of the more potent morphine were readily available for medical or nonmedical use. Thus men and women who swore off the alcohol habit in the early years of the Temperance Movement could gratefully turn to the powders, or to compounds of alcohol and morphine, and usually with the best wishes of a physician. There were no restrictions on their manufacture, sale, or possession. Apart from the high favor it received as a cure for alcoholism, morphine brought impressive relief from the vexatious problems associated with menstruation, menopause, and aging. Physicians recommended it for almost every known malady. In an era before there were any effective curative medicines, morphine at least did something: It was a happy anodyne for sheer physical suffering; it brought a measure of quietude to fear and distress; it soothed the turmoil of inevitable frustrations. It might also be taken as casually as tobacco, for it evoked a warm mood of patience, serenity, and tolerance.

Both proportionally and absolutely, the consumption of

opium and morphine in American society during the nineteenth century was higher than in any other Western nation. And the amount rose steadily. The injection of morphine by hypodermic syringe became a principal technique of military medicine during the Civil War, and many veterans continued to use the drug long after they had healed their wounds. The annual per capita consumption of opiates in the United States—expressed in grams of crude opium—rose from twelve in the 1840s to fifty-two in the 1890s.

This was no cause for general alarm. According to a medical paper presented in 1889, a person converting his alcohol habit to a morphine habit might take three grains a day, the equivalent of thirty grains of crude opium (which, incidentally, in twenty days would have cost him a total of fifty cents). Thus the annual per capita ingestion of even fifty-two grams (about nine hundred grains, or approximately the amount a person would consume in a month if he were daily taking the thirty-grain conversion) was no measure of implied criminality or social decadence. It sustained an estimated 250,000 addicts—compared to the inestimable millions of "heavy" drinkers who regularly drank alcohol to excess and were, in fact, addicted. The opiate habit was not uncommon among women, among the aged, and, to a degree, among the indulgent rich. A writer for the *Catholic World* noted in 1881 that in the United States the use of opiates was confined largely to the educated classes who wanted to disassociate themselves from the lower-class connotations of liquor and drunkenness. Among those who took up the use, addiction was no more necessarily inevitable than with the use of alcohol. The striking difference, however, was that among those who became addicted, the affliction was not necessarily morbid or obsessive. Addiction could, on the contrary, be controlled and disciplined. An individual with the habit might maintain it for decades at a daily level, say, of three grains of morphine—which was in fact the level of maintenance held by Dr. William Stewart Halsted (1852-1922) after his thirty-fourth year and during the years when he was chief of surgery at the Johns Hopkins School of Medicine.

What is most remarkable is that reformers who were so
acutely sensitive to national moral problems in the late
nineteenth century were so indifferent to the use of opiates. This
can be explained only by the circumstance that opiates, unlike
alcohol, had never been associated with the comportment of
social irresponsibility, lust, or violence. No one supposed that
opiates could inspire the fierce and often savage comportment
of inflated masculinity and individualism which Americans had
consistently drawn from the booze bottle. In contrast to the
brawling, foulmouthed lechery of common drunkenness, the
passivity and euphoric introspection which characterized
opiate consciousness had not yet presented any obvious threat
to the individual, his family, or society. "Wine robs a man of his
self-possession," Thomas De Quincey wrote in *Confessions of
an English Opium Eater* in 1821; "opium sustains and reinforces
it." There was indeed no reason—before the Harrison Drug
Control Act made him a criminal—why the person addicted to
opiates, despite his misfortune, could not fulfill his family
responsibilities in good conscience and still in some corner of
the day find his quiet and private hour. In fact, as the rigidities of
Victorian family life tightened to the point of emotional suffoca-
tion, and as the dislocations of industrial America broke
painfully through the most essential sureties, it may have been
that the taking of a few grains of morphine during a quiet hour
each day was entirely consistent with the obligations of a sane
and responsible man to maintain a high threshold of frustration.

How, then, do we explain the apparent congruence of the
Antinarcotics Movement and the Antidrink Movement? In
1875, just as the Women's Crusade had opened the first great
temperance campaign in California, the government of the city
of San Francisco prohibited opium-smoking dens. In 1887, the
federal government prohibitied Chinese, and only Chinese,
from importing opium. These laws did not evolve from the
Temperance Movement, yet a certain relationship is clear: Both
movements had ethnocentric cores. Actually, the anti-opium
laws attempted to ban only the smoking of opium, which was

common then only among Chinese. The laws were classic pieces of racist legislation.

But within the next decade, the first real stirrings of an Antinarcotics Movement did begin. After the 1870s some reformers noted the sharp rise in the annual per capita consumption of raw opium. This rise, as David Musto's recent study, *The American Disease: Origins of Narcotics Control* (1973), shows, did not, as one might first suppose, reflect a pattern of immigration. It correlates only with the rise of national advertising and with the enormous new markets for patent medicines. It caused alarm because some physicians were at the very same time just beginning to deny opium its panacean eminence. The medical case against opiates, in fact, paralleled the case then building against alcohol. As a series of new insights into bacteriology made it possible for them to identify the causes of several diseases, an elated generation of practitioners began to criticize the indiscriminate prescription of narcotics, including opiates and alcohol, as a crude and even dangerous custom of their unsophisticated elders. Deploring the high per capita consumption of opiates, the young men, in their new professionalism, blamed the rise squarely on the trademarked frauds. And an increasingly popular prejudice among the new physicians (at least among those who were not themselves addicts) was that the use of any narcotic could lead to an irrepressible craving, which in turn could lead ultimately to complete moral and physical degeneration.

The prejudice was both unkind and unfortunate. On the eve of scientific medicine, this bit of nonscience was taken in absolute seriousness by the pure food and drug muckrakers who were even then sounding the alarm about fraudulent cures advertised in almost every magazine and newspaper. Many of these proprietary medicines were, like the ancient and classic compounds, presented in the flamboyant tradition of panacea—balms for almost every conceivable affliction; and, like laudanum, they were often so heavily laced with narcotics that they could indeed become addictive. As journalists revealed this fact, they ignited the first national concern about the use of narcotics. In the 1890s they inspired several state laws which required a physician's prescription for the purchase of pure opiates. For the following few years one could say that the patent medicines at least allowed an addict to obtain his opiate without admitting a loathsome habit to a pharmacist and to a physician. The time, however, was short; in 1906, federal laws required such compounds to carry an honest labeling of their ingredients.

As knowledge about narcotics spread around the country, the Reverend Charles Brent, then Episcopalian Bishop of the Philippines, alerted reform groups to the similarities between opiates and alcohol; it was his observation that both "enslaved" their victims. Brent, a curiously pure liturgical, had no objection to alcohol; his case rested in a passionate condemnation of "heathen" behavior in "weaker" races. It is possible that he had been appalled by the reaction of most opium smokers, who, within minutes after the first puff, fell into a state of dreamlike serentiy which was not at all consistent with their duties as capitalists or Christians. This was precisely why few WASP Americans ever chose to smoke it. Brent, however, may have assumed that use of the opiate in any form was equally dramatic. However this may have been, Brent was seeking support for national and for international control legislation. He drew friends of the Anti-Saloon League and the WCTU to a casual interest in the proposed Harrison Drug Control Act of 1914.

The Antinarcotics Movement, such as it was, had neither the urgency nor the depth of the Prohibition Movement. When the Harrison Act became law in 1914, it provoked no debate, no militancy, no great emotion. It was presented to Congress as a diplomatic opportunity for the country to demonstrate leadership among the nation-members of the recently organized Hague International Narcotic Control Convention, where Bishop Brent represented the United States, and where the United States should not embarrass Bishop Brent. The passage was so quietly ceremonial that it is not even listed in the index of the *New York Times*.

The sadness we can see here is that the Harrison Act, even

more than the Volstead Act, left a legacy of enduring spiritual malignancy. By fixing severe limits on the amount of opiate a patent medicine could contain, and by otherwise prohibiting the traffic in opiates except for medical purposes, the law abolished the legitimate traffic. When the Supreme Court ruled in the early 1920s that prescriptions for addictions were not legitimately medical practice, the interpretation meant simply that addiction thereby became a federal crime—a strange triumph of pseudoscience, racism, and mild hysteria on the part of a few people and of indifference on the part of most others. The court thus lowered narcotics use into the underworld, forcing addicts to migrate to the urban centers of illicit supply. It also forced formerly decent and responsible citizens who had acquired an unfortunate habit to become aggressive and violent criminals. It made addicts conform to the image of nonscience; as they robbed or cheated or prostituted themselves to support the illicit price, they did indeed become debauched, corrupt, and depraved. In 1923, as many as 75 percent of the women in federal penitentiaries were Harrison Act prisoners.

Though the law never recognized it, medical opinion shifted swiftly. Dr. Lawrence Kalb, Sr., the famous public health official and drug expert during the 1920s, left a memorable metaphor when he remarked that while whiskey maddens, opium soothes, and that "there is more violence in a gallon of alcohol than in a ton of opium." Prominent scientists today— see Edward M. Brecher, *Licit and Illicit Drugs* (1972)— conclude that the experience of controlled opiate addiction, though indeed a misfortune, is yet in every way more benign than alcohol addiction.

Licit and Illicit Drugs is a remarkable study, and it makes a case for the Volstead Act which is not at all a bad one: There are millions of Americans who, so long as alcohol is available to them, cannot stop drinking it. Alcohol addiction is "utterly destructive of the human body." Alcohol underlies the most serious criminal problems in modern America: drunken driving, homicide, suicide, and the many others acts of deliberate or negligent violence which are more often than not alcohol-related crimes. The weight of evidence is impressive—as it was in the 1830s. The counterbalance—the same scientists conclude—is that few moralists of any persuasion suppose that the United States could survive the national withdrawal syndrome, and fewer would ever propose it. Prohibition will probably never again be a political issue or a social movement.

There is a final consideration. Some psychiatrists today assume that addiction to drugs of any sort is much more than a physiological process. Thomas Szasz, for example, sees powerful addictions as part of "an internally significant dramatic production" in which the "patient-victim" is the star. Only when he has decided "to close down this play and leave the stage," according to Szasz, will the patient find the grip of the habit broken.

For the historian, this is a revealing hypothesis. If morbid drinking is a compulsive role playing in which drinking is a central function, what roles have Americans, in the presence of disorder, found most satisfying? And why? Of all the drunks in American history and literature (this is a guess, not a statistic), from the colonial bum to Neal Dow's relative to Huck Finn's father to modern case studies, the role of Drinking American seems to be the role which symbolizes freedom and self-determination. Drinking is rebellion and individuality, and the act of drinking says to the world, "I bow to no king and to no priest . . . I do what I want . . . I deserve my indulgences, and my life is my own. . . . What I do is important." Drinking Man is freeman and freeholder, Jacksonian Man and Mountain Man, determining that what he wants is thereby moral. He is Cowboy Man and Gangster Man, determined to be the creator of his own circumstance, the master of his own soul. It is the role of moral freedom, vital to the American experience. But it is also the role of moral nihilism, known in the New World since the time of James I as the Antinomian Heresy. It is a role perhaps less understood by pietists, who have glorified it, than by liturgicals, who have learned that it is something to fear. We see it more in literature than in history, because history has focused upon the prohibitors but not upon the drunkenness which they hoped to prohibit. We need a history of Drinking American.

Many fascinating insights might come from studying drunks rather than Prohibitionists, and the first of them might lie in the dynamics of addiction. Leon Wurmser wrote recently in *The American Scholar* that he sees three layers of existence in which compulsive behavior becomes embedded. The first is a "lifestyle" which encourages an unwillingness to accept limitations or responsibilities—a sort of antibourgeois environment of goalless drifting in which neither work nor leisure is a significant value. The second layer is that of "prevailing feelings"— usually those of rage, boredom, or tension. Drugs, including alcohol, he says, enter at this second level to relive tensions, but they can bring a kind of gripping relief which obscures the problems at the third level, which is a deep loam of "unconscious conflicts" where a wish for omnipotence and greatness is countered by a persistent sense of helplessness.

Where do these feelings come from? Wurmser's answer is striking: "I have never yet seen a compulsive drug user who did not come from a family with massive problems." The most fundamental of these problems, he writes, arises from disorder, from a sometimes violent vacillation between permissiveness and discipline and from a chronic inability to find a tranquil balance of love and limitation. This sounds like social history as much as it sounds like personal history. It might well define the problems in transition both toward and beyond the values of the bourgeois American.

What, then, do we know about the reasons why certain societies become drunken societies? Did Americans become excessive drinkers because they inadvertently addicted themselves to distillates, because they were psychoneurotic, or because they found in distillates some desperately needed relief from the social disorder that surrounded them? Most researchers in alcohol science agree that people drink in excess to relieve tensions. Most historians agree that to be human is to have tensions. Tensions feed upon a sense of lost security, and in few societies have people lost their sense of community so swiftly or so permanently as in American society during the nineteenth century. Intemperance in the United States, and the Prohibition Movement which followed it, were carried around by the virus of social disorder.

Acknowledgments and Sources

IN A STUDY of the Prohibition Movement published in 1965, I was happy to reflect many ideas from the exciting research on Prohibition which had then only recently appeared, particularly Andrew Sinclair, *Prohibition: The Era of Excess* (Boston, 1962); James H. Timberlake, *Prohibition and the Progressive Movement* (Cambridge, Mass., 1963); and Joseph R. Gusfield, *Symbolic Crusade: Status Politics and the American Temperance Movement* (Urbana, Ill., 1963). In this present study I have tried to reevaluate these ideas and to integrate my reevaluation with the new approaches to social history which are now having a profound influence on most thinking and writing about the American past. For my purposes, the most significant of these recent approaches have been Roland Berthoff, "The American Social Order: A Conservative Hypothesis," *American Historical Review* 65 (1960): 495-514; Philippe Ariès, *Centuries of Childhood: A Social History of Family Life* (London, 1962); Dwight B. Heath and others in David J. Pittman and Charles R. Snyder, eds., *Society, Culture, and Drinking Patterns* (New York, 1962); Robert H. Wiebe, *The Search for Order* (New York, 1967); Joseph Gusfield and others in John Braeman, Robert H. Bremer, and David Brody, eds., *Change and Continuity in Twentieth-Century America: The 1920's* (Columbus, Ohio, 1968); Craig MacAndrew and Robert B. Edgerton, *Drunken Comportment: A Social Explanation* (Chicago, 1969); Gilman Ostrander, *The Rights of Man in America* (2d ed., Columbia, Mo., 1969) and *American Civilization in the First Machine Age, 1890-1940* (New York, 1970); John Lukacs, "The

Bourgeois Interior," *American Scholar* 39 (1970): 616-630; David Noble, *The Progressive Mind* (New York, 1970); Douglas T. Miller, *The Birth of Modern America, 1820-1850* (New York, 1970); Roland Berthoff, *An Unsettled People: Social Order and Disorder in American History* (New York, 1971); Paul Kleppner, *The Cross of Culture* (New York, 1970); Richard J. Jensen, *The Winning of the Midwest: Social and Political Conflict, 1888-96* (Chicago, 1971); David J. Pivar, *Purity Crusade: Sexual Morality and Social Control, 1868-1900* (Westport, Conn., 1973); John Demos, "The American Family in Past Time," *American Scholar* 43 (1974): 442-445. John C. Burnham's work has been especially valuable to me as guidance as well as inspiration: "The New Psychology: From Narcissism to Social Control," in the 1968 Braeman volume; "New Perspectives on the Prohibition 'Experiment' of the 1920's," *Journal of Social History* 2 (1968): 51-68; "The Progressive Era Revolution in American Attitudes toward Sex," *Journal of American History* 8 (1973): 885-908; furthermore, my work has been measurably enriched by Professor Burnham's personal interest. I have also learned from Gilman Ostrander's "The Prohibition Movement in the Far West" and from Paul A. Carter's "The Noble Experiment Re-Visited," both papers read at the meeting of the Western History Association in 1972. Robert E. Burke has favored me with his encouragement, sympathy, and direction, and with his own current research. All these historians are shaping new perspectives, and though it may be that none of them will agree with the explanations I am attempting here, I could not have attempted them without riding on their shoulders. Surely none of the historians here is in any responsible for confusions which I may have associated with any of their interpretations.

The books and articles cited above have abundant bibliographies, and I am listing now only those works of which I have made the most obvious use.

State Studies

James Benson Sellers, *The Prohibition Movement in*

Alabama, 1702-1943 (Chapel Hill, N.C., 1943); Daniel Jay Whitener, *Prohibition in North Carolina, 1715-1945* (Chapel Hill, N.C., 1946); Gilman M. Ostrander, *The Prohibition Movement in California, 1848-1933* (Berkeley, 1957); Paul E. Isaac, *Prohibition and Politics: Turbulent Decades in Tennessee, 1885-1920* (Knoxville, 1965); Norman H. Clark, *The Dry Years: Prohibition and Social Chance in Washington* (Seattle, 1965); C. C. Pearson and J. Edwin Hendricks, *Liquor and Anti-Liquor in Virginia, 1619-1919* (Durham, N.C., 1967); and Jimmie Lewis Franklin, *Born Sober: Prohibition in Oklahoma, 1907-1959* (Norman, Okla., 1971). I have not been reluctant to plagiarize a few passages from the study of Washington state when I have thought them to be particularly appropriate. If it appears that my interpretations lean heavily upon the history of that one state, the appearance itself may be evidence for a reasonable criticism. Actually my interpretations lean heavily upon the various state studies, which are regrettably few and of which my own is merely one.

Saloons and the Liquor Traffic

The Liquor Problem: A Summary of Investigations Conducted by the Committee of Fifty, 1893-1903 (Boston, 1905); Jack London, *John Barleycorn* (New York, 1913); E. H. Cherrington, ed., *Standard Encyclopedia of the Alcohol Problem* (6 vols., Westerville, Ohio, 1925); John Allen Krout, *The Origins of Prohibition* (New York, 1925); George Ade, *The Old-Time Saloon: Not Wet–Not Dry, Just History* (New York, 1931); Jim Marshall, *Swinging Doors* (Seattle, 1949); Herbert Asbury, *A Methodist Saint* (New York, 1929), *Carry Nation* (New York, 1929), *The Barbary Coast* (New York, 1933), and *The Great Illusion: An Informal History of Prohibition* (New York, 1950); Sinclair, *Prohibition*; Paton Yoder, *Taverns and Travelers: Inns of the Early Midwest* (Bloomington, Ind., 1969); Stephen B. Oates, "Roaring Oklahoma," in Oates, ed., *Portrait of America* (Boston, 1973); Carrie Chapman Catt and Nettie Rogers Shuler, *Woman Suffrage and Politics: The Inner Story of the Suffrage Movement* (New York, 1923); Eleanor Flexner, *Century of Struggle: The Woman's Rights Movement in the United States* (Cambridge, Mass., 1959).

Family History, Bourgeois Values, Social Purity, and Family Protection

Ariès, *Centuries of Childhood*; Ostrander, *Rights of Man and American Civilization*; Lukacs, "Bourgeois Interior"; Berthoff, *Unsettled People;* Demos, "The American Family in Past Time"; Noble, *Progressive Mind*; Flexner, *Century of Struggle*; Pivar, *Purity Crusade*; T. A. Larson, "Introduction" to Catt and Shuler, *Woman Suffrage*; Janet Zollinger Giele, "Social Change and the Feminine Role: A Comparison of Woman's Suffrage and Woman's Temperance, 1870-1920" (Ph.D. dissertation, Radcliffe College, 1961); Mary Earhart, *Frances Willard: From Prayers to Politics* (Chicago, 1944); Egal Feldman, "Prostitution, the Alien Woman, and the Progressive Imagination, 1900-1915," *American Quarterly* 19 (1967): 192-206; Norton Mezvinsky, "Scientific Temperance Instruction in the Schools," *History of Education Quarterly* 1 (1961): 48-56; Aileen S. Kraditor, *The Ideas of the Woman Suffrage Movement, 1890-1920* (New York, 1965); Kate Millett, *Sexual Politics* (New York, 1970); Roy Lubove, "The Progressives and the Prostitute," *Historian* 24 (1962): 308-330; Elizabeth Janeway, *Man's World, Woman's Place* (New York, 1971); William L. O'Neill, "Feminism as a Radical Ideology," in Alfred E. Young, ed., *Dissent: Explorations in the History of American Radicalism* (DeKalb, Ill., 1968) and, by the same author, *Divorce in the Progressive Era* (New Haven, 1967) and *Everyone Was Brave: The Rise and Fall of Feminism in America* (Chicago, 1969); Walter E. Houghton, *The Victorian Frame of Mind* (New Haven, 1957); Bernard Wishy, *The Child and the*

Republic (Philadelphia, 1968); Ruth Miller Elson, *Guardians of Tradition: School Books of the Nineteenth Century* (Lincoln, Nebr., 1968); Charles Winick and Paul M. Kinsie, *The Lively Commerce: Prostitution in the United States* (New York, 1972).

Early American Drinking and the Early American Temperance Movement

Alice Felt Tyler, *Freedom's Ferment: Phases of American Social History from the Colonial Period to the Outbreak of the Civil War* (Minneapolis, 1944; Harper Torchbook, 1962); C. S. Griffin, *The Ferment of Reform, 1830-1860* (New York, 1967); Lorman Ratner, *Pre-Civil War Reform: The Variety of Principles and Programs* (Englewood Cliffs, N.J., 1967); Lyman Beecher, *Six Sermons on Intemperance* (New York, 1843); Neal Dow, *The Reminiscences of Neal Dow: Recollections of Eighty Years* (Portland, Maine, 1898); D. Leigh Colvin, *Prohibition in the United States* (New York, 1926); Bernard A. Weisberger, *They Gathered at the River: The Story of the Great Revivalists and Their Impact upon Religion in America* (Boston, 1958); Clifford S. Griffin, *Their Brothers' Keepers: Moral Stewardship in the United States, 1800-1865* (New Brunswick, N.J., 1960); Frank L. Byrne, *Prophet of Prohibition: Neal Dow and His Crusade* (Madison, Wis., 1961); J. C. Furnas, *The Life and Times of the Late Demon Rum* (New York, 1965); Roy P. Basler, ed., *The Collected Works of Abraham Lincoln* (New Brunswick, N.J., 1953).

Temperance in Europe

Andrew A. Stromberg, *A History of Sweden* (New York, 1931); Cherrington, *Encyclopedia*; Sigfried Hansson, *Den Svenska Fackforeningröelsen* (Stockholm, 1938); O. Fritiof Ander, *The Building of Modern Sweden* (Rock Island, Ill., 1958); Henning Friis, ed., *Scandinavia–Between East and*

West (Ithaca, N.Y., 1950); J. A. Lauwerys, ed., *Scandinavian Democracy: Development of Democratic Thought and Institutions in Denmark, Norway, and Sweden* (Copenhagen, 1958); John H. Wuorinen, *The Prohibition Experiment in Finland* (New York, 1931); Annals of the American Academy of Political and Social Science, Vol. 163: *Prohibition: A National Experiment*; the Association against the Prohibition Amendment, *Finland's Prohibition* (Washington, D.C., 1930), and *Norway's Noble Experiment* (Washington, D.C., 1931); Robert Graves and Alan Hodge, *The Long Week-End: A Social History of Great Britain, 1918-1939* (New York, 1963).

Prohibition and the 1920s

Charles Merz, *The Dry Decade* (New York, 1931; Americana Library edition, Seattle, 1969) is still the best study and still the place to begin; then D. Leigh Colvin, *Prohibition;* E. J. Wheeler, *Prohibition: The Principle, the Policy and the Party* (New York, 1889); Justin Stewart, *Wayne Wheeler, Dry Boss* (New York, 1928); Peter H. Odegard, *Pressure Politics: The Story of the Anti-Saloon League* (New York, 1928); Jensen, *Winning of the Midwest*; Abigail Scott Duniway, *Path Breaking: An Autobiographical History of the Equal Suffrage Movement in Pacific Coast States* (Portland, Oreg., 1914); Clarence Darrow, *The Story of My Life* (New York, 1936); Claudius O. Johnson, *Borah of Idaho* (New York, 1936); Marian C. McKenna, *Borah* (Ann Arbor, 1961); Walter Lippmann, *Men of Destiny* (New York, 1928); Otis Pease, *The Responsibilities of American Advertising* (New Haven, 1958); Donald Kinzer, *An Episode in Anti-Catholicism: The American Protective Association* (Seattle, 1964); Kai T. Erikson, *Wayward Puritans* (New York, 1966); David Burner, *The Politics of Provincialism* (New York, 1968); Harris Gaylord Warren, *Herbert Hoover and the Great Depression* (New York, 1970); Gene Smith, *The Shattered Dream* (New York, 1970); Alfred E. Smith, *Campaign*

Addresses of Governor Alfred E. Smith (Washington, D.C., 1929); Virginius Dabney, *Dry Messiah: The Life of Bishop Cannon* (New York, 1949); Paul Carter, "WASP America's Pyrrhic Victory: Folklore of the Campaign of 1928," *Wisconsin Magazine of History* 46 (1963): 263-272; Herbert Hoover, *The Memoirs of Herbert Hoover: The Great Depression, 1929-1941* (New York, 1952); Frank Freidel, *Franklin D. Roosevelt: The Triumph* (Boston, 1956); Richard Hofstadter, *Age of Reform* (New York, 1960; Robert C. Bannister, Jr., *Ray Stannard Baker: The Mind and Thought of a Progressive* (New Haven, 1966); Albert D. Kirwan, *Revolt of the Rednecks: Mississippi Politics, 1876-1925* (Lexington, 1951); E. H. Cherrington, *Evolution of Prohibition in the United States of America* (Westerville, Ohio, 1920); Norman H. Clark, *Mill Town* (Seattle, 1970); Joseph P. Lash, *Eleanor and Franklin* (New York, 1971); Frederick R. Barkley, *Sons of the Wild Jackass* (Boston, 1932); William G. McAdoo, *The Challenge* (New York, 1928); Herman Feldman, *Prohibition, Its Economic and Industrial Aspects* (New York, 1930); Irving Fisher, *The "Noble Experiment"* (New York, 1930); Earl L. Douglas, *Prohibition and Common Sense* (New York, 1931); Blain A. Brownell, "A Symbol of Modernity: Attitudes toward the Automobile in Southern Cities in the 1920s," *American Quarterly* 24 (1972): 29-44; John H. Lyle, *The Dry and Lawless Years* (Englewood Cliffs, N.J., 1960); Burnham, "New Perspectives"; Mark H. Haller, "Urban Crime and Criminal Justice: The Chicago Case," *Journal of American History* 57 (1970): 619-635; John Kobler, *Capone: The Life and World of Al Capone* (New York, 1971) and *Ardent Spirits: The Rise and Fall of Prohibition* (New York, 1973).

Repeal

Fletcher Dobyns, *The Amazing Story of Repeal* (Chicago, 1940); Grace C. Root, *Women and Repeal* (New York, 1934); Frederick Lewis Allen, *The Lords of Creation* (New

York, 1935) and *The Big Change: America Transforms
Itself, 1900-1950* (New York, 1952); William J. Perlman,
ed., *The Movies on Trial* (New York, 1936); Richard Grif-
fith and Arthur Mayer, *The Movies* (New York, 1957);
Henry James Forman, *Our Movie Made Children* (New
York, 1935); John K. Winkler, *William Randolph Hearst*
(New York, 1955); W. A. Swanberg, *Citizen Hearst* (New
York, 1961); Hearst Temperance Contest Committee,
Temperance–Or Prohibition? (New York, 1929); Ernest
Gordon, *The Wrecking of the Eighteenth Amendment*
(Francestown, N.H., 1943); Dayton E. Heckman, "Prohibi-
tion Passes: The Story of the Association against the Pro-
hibition Amendment" (Ph.D. dissertation, Ohio State Uni-
versity, 1939); Alistair Cooke, ed., *The Vintage Mencken*
(New York, 1955); Edgar Kemler, *The Irreverent Mr.
Mencken* (Boston, 1948) and *The Deflation of American
Ideals* (New York, 1941).

Distilling, Drinking, Opiates and Drug Control

Berton Roueché, *The Neutral Spirit: A Portrait of Alcohol*
(Boston, 1960), also published as *Alcohol: Its History,
Folklore, and Its Effect on the Human Body* (New York,
1962), is a superb study of the etymology of alcohol, of
the history of distilling, of drinking habits, and of medical
research on alcohol as it was understood in 1960. More
recent research is covered in the *First Special Report to
the United States Congress on Alcohol and Health* (Washington, D.C., 1971) by the National Institute on Alcohol
Abuse and Alcoholism of the United States Department of
Health, Education, and Welfare. I have also used Jack H.
Mendelson, "Experimentally Induced Chronic Intoxication
and Withdrawal in Alcoholics," *Quarterly Journal of
Studies of Alcohol* (May 1964); Irvin Child, Margaret K.
Bacon, and Herbert Barry, III, "A Cross-Cultural Study
of Drinking," *Quarterly Journal of Studies of Alcohol* (Ap-
ril 1965); Virginia E. Davis and Michael J. Walsh, "Al-

cohol, Amines, and Alkaloids: A Possible Basis for Alcohol Addiction," *Science* 167 (1970), 1005-1006; Perry V. Halushka and Philip C. Hoffman, "Alcohol Addiction and Tetrahydropapareroline," *Science* 169 (1970): 1104-1106; Thomas Szasz, "The Second Sin," *Harper's* (March 1973); Leon Wurmser, "Drug Abuse: Nemesis of Psychiatry," *The American Scholar* (Summer 1972); Upton Sinclair, *The Cup of Fury* (New York, 1956); Nancy Oestreich Lurie, "The World's Oldest On-Going Protest Demonstration: North American Indian Drinking Patterns," *Pacific Historical Review* 40 (1971): 311-332; Calvin Trillin, "U.S. Journal: Gallup, New Mexico," *New Yorker* (September 25, 1971); Oakley S. Ray, *Drugs, Society, and Human Behavior* (St. Louis, 1972); Edward Brecher, *Licit and Illicit Drugs* (Mount Vernon, N.Y., 1972); Joseph D. McNamara, "The History of United States Anti-Opium Policy," *Federal Probation* (June 1973); David F. Musto, *The American Disease: Origins of Narcotics Control* (New Haven, 1973).

Index